Higher Creativity

Also by Willis Harman:
An Incomplete History of the Future

Also by Howard Rheingold:
*Talking Tech: A Conversational Guide
to Science and Technology*

Higher Creativity

Liberating the Unconscious
for Breakthrough Insights

Willis Harman, Ph.D.
Howard Rheingold

JEREMY P. TARCHER, INC.
Los Angeles
Distributed by Houghton Mifflin Company
Boston

Library of Congress Cataloging in Publication Data

Harman, Willis W.
  Higher creativity.

  Bibliography: p. 220

  Includes index.
  1. Creative ability. 2. Subconsciousness. 3. Insight. I. Rheingold,
Howard. II. Title.
  BF411.H37   1984   153.3'5   84-16237
  ISBN 0-87477-293-1
  ISBN 0-87477-335-0 (pbk.)

Jeremy P. Tarcher, Inc.
9110 Sunset Blvd.
Los Angeles, CA 90069

Design by MIKE YAZZOLINO

Manufactured in the United States of America
D   10 9 8 7 6 5 4 3 2 1

First Edition

This book is gratefully dedicated to Henry Rolfs, whose inspiration and support made it possible, and to Zoe Rolfs, whose channelings, though not yet made public, have been a valuable source of inspiration.

Acknowledgements

The initial preparation of this manuscript was in part funded by a grant from the Institute of Noetic Sciences, of Sausalito, California.

In addition to our gratitude to the Institute of Noetic Sciences, we would like to express thanks to numerous individuals who gave generously of their assistance along the way.

Our grateful acknowledgements and heartfelt thanks to: Stephen Antonaros, Arthur Hastings, Stephen LaBerge, Judith Maas, Joan Sadler, Edwin Severinghaus, Marshall Smith, Henry Dakin, O. W. Markley, and the staff of the Institute of Noetic Sciences: Carl Flygt, Charlene Harman, Tom Hurley, Fran Lindberg, Barbara McNeill, and Brendan O'Regan. We are especially grateful to our publisher, Jeremy Tarcher, for his wise guidance, and our editor, Hank Stine, whose efforts very nearly qualify him to be listed as coauthor.

Contents

Authors' Note

Throughout this book we will use several metaphors to help render certain difficult concepts comprehensible. They are just that—metaphors. They describe the subjective experience of creativity and point toward ways of cultivating it. They do not imply a rigorously testable theory of creative inspiration. As to that, let us reserve judgement.

We more interested in encouraging others to explore the range of human experience. We are less concerned about arguments over which theory is most likely in the end to be judged scientifically valid. These metaphors are best regarded as attentional lenses or frames to help us more readily comprehend the connections between the disparate realms of psychology and theology, individual awareness and social change.

Foreword

This is a book of stories of the triumphs of imagination of solitary geniuses of the past, from which the book's authors draw lessons for the twentieth century. It is a current interpretation, couched in computer metaphors, of the role of the unconscious in mental creation. Computers do "play the sedulous ape" to human cognition and imagination, and perhaps we all are better off for it. Part of the business of science is demystification. This book is an effort to demystify one of the few remaining holdouts of mystery: creativity and the creative process. And not just garden-variety creativity, but "the higher creativity." Willis Harmon and Howard Rheingold throw down the gauntlet to the magicians of the creative in a ringing challenge early in their book, after presenting a simple model of input, processing, and output: "As incredible as it seems, that is all there is to it. All we have to do is to consciously program the unconscious with the correct input, and, like a mathematical formula, input plus processing time will equal output. . . . Of course, we're not claiming that any one individual will get a breakthrough insight every time they use the technique, or that every single person who employs it will achieve a breakthrough, but it is our belief, based on both personal experience and our investigations, that almost everyone who follows the steps we will give later will experience a dramatic increase in the number of breakthrough experiences in their lifetimes. And that's a suggestion certainly worth considering, isn't it?"

Can the authors make good their claim? Only you, the reader, can let us know. The method must be tried in good faith by people who really want to use their own creativity more fully than they have been using it. The human potential has in fact been realizing itself so extraordinarily in our own generation that this invitation and promise of access to the higher reaches of creativity, which might have seemed a seduction or a meretricious use of the computer analogy just two or three decades ago, now has a plausibility based on the achievements of the well-organized and tested "creative education" movement of the past thirty years. As the title implies, however, the authors are reaching for a new breakthrough themselves. They seek nothing short of new insights into spiritual power, through pragmatic application of techniques and theories combining mystical and meditative practices with ideas of extrasensory communication on the frontiers of human experience.

That in doing so they place themselves in the midst of controversy goes without saying. In the phrase Rollo May has made famous, it takes *courage to create*, and they have it, as we all must. Willis Harman, a Regent of the University of California and a professor at Stanford University, knows well the standards of proof in performance required by scientific knowledge claims; and he is careful to say that he is expecting such claims to be put to scientific test. Whether or not "breakthrough insights" result, at least a brave effort is being made; and if substantial gain accrues, we shall all be the better for it.

Frank Barron
Santa Cruz
August 1984

Introduction

The Cat Who Wasn't There

One evening, more than twenty years ago, I watched an apparently commonplace event take place in my neighbor's living room. A woman sat in an overstuffed chair in the center of the room. She stroked a kitten that she was holding in her lap, and talked to it, and listened to it purr. She was obviously enjoying this rapport with her feline friend. The only thing unusual about the situation was—there wasn't any kitten there! She had accepted a hynotic suggestion that there was a kitten in her lap, and to her it was completely real. All her sensory experience verified it.

It can still recall the tightness that gripped my viscera when I watched her. This odd scene, and the disturbing sensation it evoked, happened to me in the first place because I had accepted my neighbor's invitation to join a small group of amateurs who were exploring the phenomena of hypnosis. My feelings were not entirely caused by the strangeness of the experience. The main shock came with my recognition of the implication that I, too, could be fooled, that all my senses and reasoning powers and scientific sophistication might one day leave me as incapable of detecting illusion as that woman was incapable of discovering that there was no kitten in her lap.

Another aspect of the experience was even more puzzling. When I realized the depth and completeness of the woman's illusion, there came a fleeting moment during which part of me seemed to be frantically reassuring myself that I could never be fooled as that woman obviously was. And then another part of my mind seemed to speak up and say, "You already are." The kitten, and the evidence it offered of the illusions our minds can create around us, were unsettling enough. But who was the "I" that was reassuring me? And who was the "I" that exposed my self-deception? Both had seemed to come from someplace outside my conscious mind, that was somehow normally hidden from or inaccessable to our conscious awareness. Over the years, many different researchers have given this capacity of the human brain many different names—the "unconscious" being the most well-known and widely accepted—but on a personal level, in my own thoughts, ever since that day, I have called it "the hidden mind."

This seemingly trivial incident had profound implications for me, implications I did not fully understand for years to come. It was, it turned out, only one of a number of stepping-stones that have appeared over three decades of my life, leading me along a path that I would never have imagined for myself, and which led to my coauthoring this book. At the time of the "invisible kitten" incident, I had already been deviating from the normal path of an engineering professor for a half dozen years.

DIVERGENT PATHS

My formal educational background was in physics and electrical engineering. I worked at engineering only a few years, becoming greatly attracted by the prospect of a teaching career. I taught electronic engineering, systems analysis, and statistical communication theory, at Stanford and elsewhere, and published textbooks in all three subjects. Up to the age of 36, my career path, like my social life, was neat and well-ordered, with no significant deviation from my scientific specialties or outside routine academic boundaries. Certainly there was no hint of my eventual involvement with interests as far afield as futurism and consciousness research.

Then in 1954, just before my 36th birthday, a series of events began to occur—events that deeply and irrevocably changed my assumptions about the world, assumptions I had never before found the slightest reason to question. My well-ordered life, resting on a firm foundation of rational scientific knowledge of what is real and what is not, began to come apart.

I had partly been tricked, and partly tricked myself, into attending a two-week seminar on assorted moral, ethical, and spiritual issues. I say "tricked" because it turned out to be far different from the orderly academic discussions I had anticipated. Since I possessed no formal religious background, I had felt that exploring these kinds of topics would be a good way to fill in a gap in my education. But surprisingly for that period, the seminar turned out to be much more experiential than theoretical. Instead of lectures, panels, and the presentation of papers, there were group sessions that emphasized wholly unfamiliar, and often uncomfortable ideas like listening to our inner selves, learning to express feelings we'd long had trouble expressing, sharing moving experiences with others, and so on. I was totally upended when, at the final meeting, as I opened my mouth to explain what I thought I had learned, I broke into uncontrollable sobbing! The feelings that welled up inside me felt like a mixture of gratitude and relief; certainly, they were not tears of pain or sadness. At the time, I would have been quite at a loss to explain what all the tears, the gratitude, the relief were about. Looking back, it was obviously a first breaking through of mental barriers to feeling and being I had never known were there, and the beginning of a coming to myself in a sense I was not to fully understand until years later.

One of the disturbing moments of the seminar had been when I realized that the discussion leader, a dignified and scholarly professor of business and law, was convinced of the reality of various psychic phenomena that I "knew" reputable scientists had debunked. For the next few months I spent all the time I could in the Stanford library, reading avidly about topics I had barely heard of before—psychotherapy, mysticism, even parapsychology. It was a great shock to my ideals of scientific objectivity and neutrality to realize that there was far more research in this area, and of far better quality, than any of my science courses had ever led me to suspect.

I looked into various psychotherapies and assorted spiritual disciplines. I felt sure that all of these areas that related to "hidden" aspects of the mind must somehow fit together with the aims of education. Motivated by my own curiosity and a newfound desire to broaden the educational experience of my engineering students, I started a graduate seminar on "The Human Potentiality" (a fresh phrase in 1956, but somewhat timeworn by the 1980s).

It is a search pattern that doesn't seem too unusual today, but thirty years ago it was like trying to find a trail through a vast, uncharted territory—one that almost all of my colleagues were convinced didn't even exist. It was during this period that I had the experience with the "kitten that wasn't there." Then I began to have other experiences that simply didn't fit in with my previous understanding of reality.

One of the first of these experiences, and one that still arouses emotions as strong as the ones evoked by my memory of the invisible kitten, was what is often called an "out-of-body experience." This was not just a disturbing discrepancy in my traditional world view. I had never experienced anything remotely like it in my life, and in an instant it overturned assumptions about myself so basic I didn't even know I had made them.

I was quietly slouched on a sofa, spending a relaxed evening with a few friends. The incident started, I recall, with an ordinary lull in the conversation. Suddenly, without any warning whatsoever, I found myself looking down upon my own body from a height of fifteen feet or more. I could see my body clearly, reclining on the sofa with its eyes closed. I could also see what was behind the sofa, and what was in the next room—areas quite inaccessible to my physical sight from the couch, even if my eyes had been open. (It wasn't until later that it occurred to me I must have been looking "through" a quite solid roof and ceiling to get that kind of perspective.)

My first reaction, a quite reasonable response, was to be very startled. Experiences like that simply aren't supposed to happen! But right on the heels of that reaction was another reaction, a thought that came like a voice that was my own but also strangely different from my usual "rational" self. "I have always known this," this "other self" said, "I have simply forgotten until now."

Although I cannot to this very day give a totally satisfactory explanation for how and what I knew, what I felt I had always known was that I am not my body. The "I" that was looking down on my body through the roof felt a friendly detachment from that body which in other circumstances I feel quite attached to. After a brief time I felt my center of consciousness snap back into my body, and I opened my eyes on a world that has never seemed quite as unquestionably solid since.

Then, one day in the early 1960s I talked with a woman who had a few days previously experienced a kind of transcendant reality—an experience that had shaken her to the core. Her voice still trembled as she tried to describe the indescribable to me, and I was deeply moved. Then suddenly, triggered perhaps by the emotional power of her story, there came into my mind a memory of a somewhat similar experience that had come to me four years previously. The recollection was perfectly clear, but I was certain that not once in the intervening four years had it come to mind.

Not only had I "forgotten" one of the most profound experiences of my life, but during that period I never had the slightest hint of a missing memory, was never bothered by the nagging feeling of something forgotten. There was no clue or sign of a mislaid memory until the triggering incident suddenly brought it to light. Apparently the occurrence had been so totally at odds with anything else in my experience at the time that my personal belief system simply had no place for it, and I repressed the memory. Again, the realization was as profoundly disturbing as the original experience was moving. If I could hide something as important as that from myself, and hide it so completely—in what other ways was I unconsciously deceiving myself? I wondered whether most of us had such experiences from time to time, but tend to "forget" them because they are at such odds with our conceptions of the possible that we find them disturbing in one fashion or another.

If we all unconsciously erase or hide certain memories that are unacceptable to some of our basic beliefs, the question is: How much and how often do we deceive ourselves by this sort of selective remembering? Is *this* why our experience almost always tends to confirm our picture of reality—even though people in different cultures find that their experience confirms a significantly different picture of reality?

My interest in this question was intensified by a series of incidents in the late 1960s and mid-1970s. In the first I attended a brief workshop aimed at increasing the personal effectiveness of business executives. The key idea was to recognize the extent to which unconscious beliefs (such as "I am inadequate," or "I am unable to perform the job expected of me") limit effectiveness, and to then "reprogram" the unconscious mind through a technique called "positive affirmations."

Basically, the technique involves implanting new, more flexible, unconscious beliefs in place of old limiting beliefs, through repeated periods of vividly imagining them to be already true. (An example of such an affirmation is, "I like myself unconditionally.") Despite my initial skepticism, I was persuaded by the instructor's arguments and the experiences related by the other businessmen (who I knew to be sober, upright, traditionally "successful" members of the community), that the process worked. However, when it came to applying it in my own life, I kept "forgetting" to do the exercises.

A good many years later, I undertook, at the urging of a close friend, the study of something called *A Course in Miracles*. It, too, was based on this principle of reprogramming the unconscious through the use of affirmations. After I had been "working" with it for about six months, opening the books daily, I realized one day that I could not recall ever once having finished a single page of the text. I would be distracted by other thoughts. I would get uncontrollably drowsy. I would suddenly feel hungry and go to the refrigerator. Every time I opened the text, something would come up that interfered with my resolve to master the material.

It was a shock to recognize that once again, in a most clearcut way, I was exhibiting resistance to a set of exercises that some part of my mind knew was likely to bring change.

I mention all these seemingly trivial incidents because they were so significant to me, and contributed valuable clues when I later tried to understand the importance of unconscious beliefs and our defenses against changing them. Only' after recognizing this fantastic capacity for deception in ourselves are we able to see that we do it collectively as well as individually. Much of what we "know is true," perhaps even "scientifically true," is a false collective belief made difficult to check because everyone around us shares the same belief— and so their minds confirm the same view of reality. (Suppose you were paranoid in a society where everyone acted according to paranoid beliefs: How could you tell if you were crazy?)

These were not the sort of thoughts and questions that typically occupy the attention of conservative American engineering professors. By the mid-1960s I was beginning to raise issues that were too broad or hard to grasp with the tools I had been trained to use. The neat, orderly equations that could describe electrical circuits and communication systems were hardly applicable to invisible kittens and unconscious beliefs. The burning social issues of that period were beginning to make it seem that concerns that affected human lives directly were far more important than strictly technical and abstract questions.

CONVERGENT PATHS

As a result of the personal growth I had undergone I started to see ways of using my professional skills and bringing them to bear on these issues. I began attempting to apply the methods of systems analysis to issues of social policy—a largely untried and somewhat daring field at that time. Meanwhile, I also became involved with research on creative problem-solving, and with the formative stages of the Association for Humanistic Psychology. These seemingly diverse interests finally converged in the opportunity to join Stanford Research Institute in 1966, to undertake some research on the long-term future of our society.

I formed and led a team to assist the U.S. Office of Education in efforts to apply the newly emerging discipline of futures research to guiding the nation's policies in education and educational research. This was, in fact, the first non-technological futures forecasting of this sort sponsored by the U.S. government. By the time we finished our first two-year project, I had grown convinced of the importance of the changes then beginning to take place in the prevailing values and beliefs of American society.

At around this time, I received an invitation to attend a conference on "voluntary control of inner states," sponsored by the Menninger Foundation. The paper I wrote, entitled "The New Copernican Revolution," dealt with the emergence of a neglected area of science, namely the study of human "inner," or subjective, experience, as an important aspect of the external events of the near future. An unknown editor of the symposium papers added under the title his comment that "man may be undertaking a systematic exploration of the vast, imperfectly known universe of his own being, a step as epochal as his construction of a science of the galaxies."

It was becoming apparent that millions, probably tens of millions of people in the United States were seeking and having life-changing experiences that moved them to seek to understand more about their own minds. A growing number of scientists in a variety of fields—psychology, psychotherapy, anthropology, comparative religion, parapsychology—were beginning to look, in their own ways, at the puzzle of conscious and unconscious mental processes. The peculiarity of the scientific world view in neglecting this important realm of human experience was becoming noted with increasing frequency.

In a study at SRI for the Charles F. Kettering Foundation, *Changing Images of Man*, we further explored how the most fundamental premises of industrial society were undergoing a significant shift. As we said in that report: "Images of humankind which are dominant in a culture are of fundamental importance because they underlie the ways in which the society shapes its institutions, educates its young, and goes about whatever it perceives its business to be. Changes in these images are of particular concern at the present time because our industrial society may be on the threshold of a transformation as profound as that which came to Europe when the Medieval

Age gave way to the rise of science and the Industrial Revolution."

William James, one of the few American scientists to have insisted that a science of subjective experience is both possible and indispensible, had used (in *Varieties of Religious Experience*) the term "noetic quality" to describe how "mystical states seem to be . . . states of insight into depths of truth unplumbed by discursive intellect . . . They carry with them a curious sense of authority for aftertime." Mitchell adopted the adjective "noetic" to describe the science of human consciousness he envisioned.

I met Apollo 14 astronaut Edgar Mitchell in the early 1970s, when he was in the process of leaving NASA and setting up the Institute of Noetic Sciences. Mitchell had experienced a profoundly moving state of altered consciousness during his return trip from the moon. (Speaking of how the limits of credibility can change with the times, ask yourself what is the hardest part of that sentence to believe—that a man should have a profound and valid state of altered consciousness, or that it should happen to him on the way back from the moon?)

The deep sense of cosmic order that Mitchell felt, and the self-evident ability of the human mind to know itself far beyond the dimensions of ordinary experience, so impressed him that by the time the space capsule splashed down he had made a decision he hadn't known he was going to make. The real next frontier of human exploration, Captain Mitchell was suddenly convinced, would be the human mind. He decided to devote his energy and time to fostering development of the much neglected science of human consciousness.

Mitchell's founding of the Institute of Noetic Sciences was well-timed. During its first decade, the climate of opinion regarding the scientific exploration of human consciousness steadily improved. Non-ordinary experiences and extraordinary capabilities are now being studied in the most prestigious universities and research institutions. Eminent scientists— even Nobel laureates—now discuss the possible necessity of considering aspects of reality that are not directly measurable (in a physical sense) but must nonetheless must be postulated in order to make sense of observed phenomena in physics and biology. There are many signs of increasing humility among scientists, and there is much less insistence that positivistic, reductionistic explanations tell all there is to know.

One of the Institute's chief activities in behalf of the new study of consciousness was to bring together forward-looking funding sources and leading edge researchers whose topics were either too bold or unfashionable for more traditional funding institutions. Much of this research was carried out in such prestigious institutions as the Harvard Medical School, the School of Engineering and Applied Science at Princeton University, the Menninger Foundation, and Stanford Research Institute.

Over a decade, we watched as research related to the capabilities of the hidden mind that was considered quite radical when we first supported it—in areas such as biofeedback training, guided imagery in healing, and autosuggestive approaches to stress-reduction—gained increasing acceptance by psychotherapeutic, health-care, research, and educational communities. These leading edge researchers, it seemed to me, were all validating in different ways the theory that whatever "mind" may be, the "hidden mind" is potentially far more capable than we were taught to believe—particularly in its intuitive and creative aspects.

Another hypothesis suggested by the range of research I had closely observed over those ten years, and which resonated very strongly with my own personal experiences with anomalous phenomena, was that we humans limit ourselves to a far greater extent than anyone can comfortably believe. If we have such enormous potential, the obvious question is why don't very many people manifest it? The answer seemed to be—we stand in our own way. This conclusion emerged, not from any one experiment or research field, but rather from the bringing together of knowledge from diverse fields and research areas.

The work of this new Institute was parallel to interests that had by then become compelling in my own life and work, and when in 1977 I was invited to join the Institute of Noetic Sciences as President, I accepted. After twenty years of stumbling upon, seeking to explain, and slowly understanding the importance of this area of knowledge, the opportunity to work with the great pioneers of consciousness research was irresistible. On the other hand, I wanted to maintain my involvement with futures research, and so I retained a part-time position with SRI as well.

The Convergence: Consciousness with the Future

Throughout the 1970s, the various sciences of human consciousness began to converge, it seemed to me, with many of the same issues I was growing concerned about in regard to the contemporary crisis global civilization. It became more and more clear to me that as a deeper understanding of our mind increasingly intersects with a developing awareness of the most important choices confronting modern society, this intersection might quickly become the most crucial area of knowledge in our time.

For over a quarter of a century I had been tracking, personally and to an increasing extent professionally, two fascinating puzzles—the nature of human consciousness and the transformation of societies. As the missing pieces of both puzzles fell into place, an unexpected relationship between them emerged. My growing conviction, which I certainly hadn't anticipated when I started, was that these two apparently unrelated topics were in fact different aspects of the *same* puzzle. Our relative ignorance of our own minds, and our current confusion about meanings and values, are best understood in terms of our history. And in a deeper understanding of our own consciousness lie important clues to resolving the global dilemmas that so beset our time.

The quest for deeper understanding of our own minds has been one of humankind's oldest pursuits; yet we are able to think about this question today in ways that would not have been possible even twenty years ago. The question of societal change and evolution is of perennial interest, but it has become especially timely because of the indications I had seen that our society is passing through the early stages of a transformation as fundamental as any in history. Both my own work and that of the Institute of Noetic Sciences began to focus on this convergence.

"CHANNELING" CREATIVE INSIGHT

In the early part of the seventh century of the Christian calendar, a poor camel-driver in an obscure corner of the world saw an angel in a dream; by the eighth century, the armies of those who believed the revelation of Mohammed's dream had conquered an arc of territory stretching from the south of Spain to the northwest part of India. In the late nineteenth century a teenage Jewish physics student in Zurich imagined himself to be riding along a lightbeam, looking back at himself in a mirror; the resulting train of thought led to the formula $E=mc^2$, the theoretical basis for the nuclear bomb.

There is no way to deny it. At certain times in history, certain people seem to have extraordinary experiences which literally make history and change the world—to insights so far-reaching and profound that they revolutionize science, the arts, and society itself. G. N. M. Tyrrell, an early British investigator of inspiration, expressed it well in *The Personality of Man:*

> It is a highly significant, though generally neglected, fact that those creations of the human mind which have borne preeminently the stamp of originality and greatness, have not come from within the region of consciousness. They have come from beyond consciousness, knocking at its door for admittance: they have flowed into it, sometimes slowly as if by seepage, but often with a burst of overwhelming power.

This "breakthrough experience" has long been honored, if not explicitly, then in covert terminology. A wide variety of terms have been used to refer to its diverse manifestations—terms such as creativity, inspiration, poetic imagination, intuition, mediumship, and revelation.

No single term has seemed to satisfactorily cover, without undesirable or limiting connotations, the wide range of forms in which this kind of breakthrough phenomenon has appeared. During the past twenty years or so there has emerged in semipopular usage the rather neutral term "channeling," implying that the image or information is coming via some unspecified channel from some unspecified source outside conscious awareness.

Almost everyone has had some experience of a channeling of creative insight, a breakthrough of deeper intuition, a moment of knowledge recognizable as something beyond the usual reach of the cognitive mind. Some people find such experiences to be commonplace. The insight can relate to daily life or to one's professional problems (i.e., the arts, science, business, etc.) or to social or spiritual matters.

Yet, vital and important as these experiences are, both research and common discourse have in recent times at least treated them with relative neglect. Largely in the past decade or so has there been signs of what psychologist R. R. Holt called "the return of the ostracized." (Some of the reasons for this past ostracism will be explored later in this book.)

The point where human consciousness and societal transformation seems to meet in history is in this personal breakthrough to untapped potentials. Few of us doubt that Western society is going through a period of critical change—probably a very difficult period. Each of us faces daily the effects of that change, in the form of dilemmas that perplex, daunt, and sometimes threaten to crush us. Yet within us we might well have a capacity to break through to the kind of insight and resources that can resolve even our greatest difficulties. *Especially* our greatest difficulties—including the most sobering threat of all, that of self-annihilation.

Western industrial society is faced with challenges that may well imperil civilization as we know it. The old solutions and procedures for dealing with political and social problems no longer appear to work. Hope seems to lie in beginning to seek new creative solutions, new approaches and breakthroughs for the global dilemmas we now face. Any understanding we can achieve regarding the kinds of breakthroughs to creativity that have led to past social and political advances, have high promise for helping us in our present travail.

It was with these kinds of growing convictions that I joined with writer-researcher Howard Rheingold to write this book. In two years of reading, observing, and interviewing, our ideas of the extent of these hidden capabilities have been stretched still further. Our sense of the importance of this emerging pattern to the future of the world grew as well, until it has become—for me, at least—an all-consuming passion.

Some of the premises we see emerging from current scientific studies and reported experiences in this area of human capabilities may strike you at first as shocking and even preposterous. We have no expectation of "proving" these premises, or of convincing anybody by logical argument. We wish only to report with integrity what we think we have found, and to confess honestly to considerable psychic discomfort along the way as we repeatedly discovered the need to reexamine our own premises and perceptions.

Willis W. Harman
Stanford, California
August 1984

The Spectrum of Creativity
From the Mundane to the Miraculous

*The action of the child inventing a new game with his playmates;
Einstein formulating a theory of relativity; the housewife devising a
new sauce for the meat; a young author writing his first novel; all of
these are, in terms of our definition, creative, and there is no attempt
to set them in some order of more or less creative.*

CARL R. ROGERS, *On Becoming a Person*

THE SPECTRUM OF CREATIVITY

One of the great discoveries of physics was that the ordered
array of different colors one sees in a rainbow or when white
light is refracted through a prism constitutes but a narrow portion of a vast, continuous electromagnetic spectrum.

A similarly momentous discovery has been emerging
over the last century or so with regard to the human mind.
Through the ages there had been instances of "genius" or "inspiration" in which superior capabilities of the mind became
manifest. Gradually, through the scholarship of such men as
Sigmund Freud, F. W. H. Myers, and Carl Jung, it became apparent that these recognized instances of creativity are, in a
sense, the "visible spectrum" of a far vaster range of manifestations of the creative unconscious mind. This greater spectrum
of creative imagination ranges from mundane acts of habit and
memory to miraculous instances of revelation and prophecy.
In connecting the mundane and the divine lies an immense
spectrum of creativity, the source of pragmatic as well as spiri-

1

tual inspiration. Thus the most ordinary and the most extraordinary manifestations of our minds are not entirely unrelated phenomena, but rather the extreme ends of a continuum of creative consciousness.

Between the most ordinary creative manifestations of the "hidden mind" and the "higher" unseen spectrum lies the middle ground, the recognized "visible" part of the creative rainbow. Among the names we give to some of the more familiar creative hues are *intuition, inspiration, imagination, insight, vision, talent, foresight.*

But just as outside the luminous spectrum with its multiple hues there are much broader regions of electromagnetic radiation that have wavelengths longer than those of red and shorter than those of violet light not visible to ordinary vision, so there are what might be called creative "ultraviolets" (such as extraordinary insights and inspirations in the religions, arts and sciences) and intuitive "infrareds" (such as hunches and "gut feel"). This analogy suggests that these ranges could be charted and used—just as science has handled the unseen wavelengths of the electromagnetic spectrum. In fact, more is known about the means of opening the channel, of harnessing the creative rainbow, than one would suspect from orthodox writings on education and psychology. Furthermore, as we shall see later on, these spectra are more accessible to us than we have been led to believe.

At the "low" end of this spectrum the phenomena are so much an accepted part of everyday life that most of us never stop to think about the mysterious power behind some of our most ordinary mental activities. For example, you are asleep, and although an assortment of familiar city noises occur during the night, you continue to sleep peacefully. Then you are jolted awake by one quiet sound that doesn't fit—perhaps it is the squeaking hinge of a door that normally remains shut. You sit up in bed, feeling slightly alarmed, but you aren't entirely sure why you are alarmed until the door squeaks again and your conscious sense of hearing tunes in to it. You get up, close the door, and return to bed. Within seconds, you fall asleep.

A perfectly mundane occurrence. The mystery begins when you start to wonder why that particular sound happened to register in your consciousness while the much louder sound of the bus that passes under your window every half hour never wakes you. What is the "other part of your mind" that watches over you and remains conscious of the environment even when ordinary consciousness is extinguished in sleep?

Consider another example. You are trying to recall someone's name. It just won't come, but you have a teasing feeling that you actually do know it, somewhere deep inside. In desperation, you think about the alphabet, or run down all the names you know that begin with "B"—or is it "P"? The harder you strain with the rational, conscious, analytic parts of your mind, the more elusive the name becomes.

Finally, having tried everything, you give up. You "file a request" with that other part of your mind—what we sometimes call the unconscious, or creative or intuitive, part—and go on about your other business. Later, while you are talking about something totally unrelated, or just as you step aboard a bus, or as you doze before a fire, up pops the name! Consciously, you have no idea of how your mind searched through all your memories, recognizing and bringing to the surface the name you were trying to remember.

Now consider another kind of experience, one that might at first appear to be in a wholly different dimension from the squeaky door or the forgotten name. There is a certain state of heightened awareness, an experience of intense "breakthrough" insight, that, although it is a less common occurrence, happens to us all at one time or another. It is a state in which the floodgates of thought seem suddenly thrown open and profound ideas and images, often solutions to our deepest problems—questions about life, our work, or our relation to the universe around us—are revealed in an instant.

It might last a few seconds or it might go on for hours or weeks. It hits while you are swinging at a pitch, singing a hymn, applying a brush stroke, watching your child play. The setting can be a cathedral or a meadow. It might result from a very meaningful ceremony, or it might simply strike you out of the blue as you look at the sunlight on a leaf in a quiet forest or as you stare at a traffic light while you wait to cross a busy street.

Our language offers a choice of words to describe such moments of unusual awareness—words like *premonition, inspiration, intuition,* and *illumination*—each of which implies something different about the nature of the experience. We treat these extraordinary moments with varying degrees of credibility, depending on what we believe to be possible— which in turn depends on what our society taught us *ought* to be possible (or at least what it *thinks* ought to be possible).

We can see the aftereffects of these experiences all around us in the form of the scientific and mechanical marvels that contribute so much to our well-being. We can share the experience of such a moment, preserved for history, by listening to a great musical recording or reading a great book. We can find mute testimony to the power of these moments, displayed for all the world to see, by walking through any museum.

Those members of our society designated by such terms as *artist, inventor, genius, visionary,* and so forth—the great creative thinkers and orginators—have almost invariably experienced this kind of "breakthrough" state in the course of producing their most valuable scientific theories, their most acclaimed works, their most revolutionary social or religious insights.

In these cases, the hidden part of the mind didn't lead to a squeaky door hinge or a long-forgotten name but to a new idea powerful enough to enrich humankind or alter the course of history.

Might the sound of the squeaky hinge that wakes you in the middle of the night and the melody that floods into the mind of the composer be more closely related than we have heretofore thought?

Were the breakthrough experiences of Descartes or Mozart the result of some inborn capacity—or did they somehow *learn* to break through?

Are these kinds of talents and abilities rare and innate, possessed only by the few lucky enough to have been "gifted" with them? And if so, are they the result of chance mutation or inherited genes?

Or are they, instead, innate capacities we all possess and lack only the knowledge or training necessary to make proper use of them—capacities others have learned to use before and which we can learn to use ourselves?

As we shall see when we turn to the accounts of the people who have undergone these experiences, some seem to have stumbled into these extraordinary moments accidentally, with no conscious intention of seeking them, while others seem to have learned to consciously "invoke the muse" by following certain steps that triggered the breakthrough.

A great many of these individuals have perceived the experience as so extraordinary, they have made record of and left for posterity a description of breakthrough moments—in diaries, letters, journals, autobiographies. From their accounts, a pattern begins to take shape, one that other explorers of the creative faculty—the mathematician Poincaré working in the late 1800s, and the early-twentieth century psychologist Graham Wallas foremost among them—have noted before. This pattern is even more striking today than it was then, for it is emerging again, only this time from apparently unrelated contemporary research on consciousness.

There seems to be something in all these accounts, despite their sharp individual differences, that speak of a *capacity* for creative breakthrough—a capacity that might be independent of talent, or field of endeavor, or life circumstances.

THE BREAKTHROUGH PHENOMENON

Common to these anecdotal reports are a range of what might be called breakthrough states or breakthrough experiences.

Surprisingly, in the case histories of scientists, we found that not only many specific scientific discoveries but the very foundations of science itself were built on breakthrough experiences, later backed up by empirical investigation. It is ironic that science, the institution that has most strongly branded these kinds of experiences as daydreams, delusions, or hallucinations, appears to have been born in just such a state—in a fever dream, in a flash to an individual who could not solve the problem with the conscious portion of the mind.

The physical power of science and technology is the primary example of how Western industrial culture has used the rational mind to accomplish astounding feats. But we gain a new perspective or the irrational, however, when we learn how many of the greatest scientific insights, discoveries, and revolutionary inventions appeared first to their creators in the form of fantasies, dreams, trances, lightning-flash insights, and other nonordinary states of consiousness.

These creative leaps have occurred again and again in many scientific fields, under many different circumstances. But biologists, chemists, physicists, mathematicians, attempting to extend the boundaries of human knowledge, all report very similar experiences in which the hidden mind broke through with an answer the conscious, rational mind had been struggling, unsuccessfully, to find for weeks or months.

The longer story of evolution and revolution in science is made of specific events in the minds of historical characters. We are taught the laws, equations, and formulas that emerged from these people's insights. Yet history books focus mainly on the products of those mental events, while they typically overlook the inner history of the special state of consciousness that led to creation of those products.

Not only scientists, but poets, painters, and composers as well seem to tell variations of a similar, basic experience. But generations of historians have ignored what might be some of the most important events in history.

As we carried out our research for this book, we found that there is indeed a "secret history of inspiration," although in fairness, it is more ignored than hidden. Western society, and science in particular, has generally dismissed, denied, or ignored the importance of these extraordinary states of mind, leaving genius for the geniuses to worry about. But anyone can read the source materials and discern the truth. An afternoon in even a small public library will furnish a wealth of data for anyone interested in this fascinating field. Just pick your genius, a field of genius, then read biographies and autobiographies—you'll find the telltale passage.

GENIUS

There is something in our very name for these boundary cross-ers that sets them apart from the rest of us but that also con-ceals our deeper beliefs about the source of their capabilities. We call them geniuses, and for the most part leave it at that. Although we relish the enjoyment or insights their paintings or compositions afford us, we don't give much thought to the mental state of these exceptional individuals when they had their stroke of genius.

The most important clue to the puzzle of human creative potential might be staring us all in the face. Our language itself is the encoding mechanism par excellence for preserving cer-tain kinds of meaning in the face of changing cultural values. The newer word *genius*, for example, contains a significant resonance with the much older term *genie*.

A genie is a magic spirit, sometimes benevolent, now considered to be mythical, who is able to grant miraculous favors to mortals on special occasions. In a sense that has lived on in our language for generations, people have believed that certain specially talented individuals must possess the aid of a genie.

This interpretation of the word would seem to place ge-nius beyond the grasp of ordinary folk, even the most talented. Not all of us, after all, have the opportunity to meet a genie.

Is another interpretation possible? Again, our language offers clues. *Intuition* can be interpreted as "knowing from within"; *inspire* literally means "inner breath." A group of re-lated words, including *knowledge, gnosis,* and *ignore,* hint at an active but subtle contrast between knowing something and ignoring it: one pays attention to something in order to know about it—the opposite of ignoring it.

Another word—*insight*—is also significant example of the "etymological unconscious" that seems to acknowledge the linkage between attention and understanding. By cultivat-ing insight, in the sense of looking at what is in our minds, can we gain insights, in the sense of new and useful understand-ings?

Perhaps what we call genius has something to do with a

learned state of conciousness, a way of attending to the stream of mental experience. Perhaps many more of us could hear inner melodies, find guidance and inspiration, achieve breakthrough insight—if we would only pay more attention to the fleeting, images, and the quiet intuitions presented to us by the creative mind.

Creativity researcher John Curtis Gowan, in *The Journal of Creative Behavior*, draws our attention to the fact that: "When Michelangelo did the Sistine Chapel he painted both the major and minor prophets. They can be told apart because, though there are cherubim at the ears of all, only the major prophets are *listening*. Here, exactly stated, is the difference between genius and talent."[1]

Gowan's statement seen in this light also implies that scientists and artists are not the only ones who seem to have learned the secret of inner listening. The founders and prophets of the world's great religions also appear, when the accounts are compared, to have obtained their inspiration from the same source. The insights they gained into spiritual, metaphysical, and cosmological matters have affected and transformed the world in no less earthshaking a way than have the insights of artists and scientists.

The role of this inner listening in our cultural history is largely ignored or dismissed—and modern science has found strangely little to say about this consummately significant phenomenon.

THE UNCONSCIOUS IDEA PROCESSOR

Michelangelo's image of the prophets and the words of other visionaries in the arts and sciences suggest an obvious question: If the people who experience the breakthrough state are all listening, what are they listening to? Whatever that "other part of the mind" happens to be, is there a way we can all learn how to tune in and listen to it, too?

As various persons in diverse walks of life have undergone their own breakthrough experiences and come upon their own inner discoveries, they have all wrestled with the problem of how to describe their personal key to unlocking these kinds of insights. "Inner listening" is the term they seem to use most often, and in many of these experiences the communication even seems to come in the form of an audible voice—the capacity to "hear" the speech of the "other self." Inner listening might be the capacity that lies dormant with everybody, waiting to be awakened.

Other metaphors express the sense of tapping into a "flowing" source of creative imagination—an "underground river" or "wellspring of inspiration." Others have spoken of "opening the mind's gate." Still others have emphasized the sense of inner illumination, or insight, speaking of a "lightning flash" of intuition. One of the most popular metaphors in recent years has been that of the "channel," either from a "creative unconscious" within the psyche or from some external source, divine or otherwise.

A more contemporary metaphor, drawn from modern computer terminology, likens the unconscious mind to an idea-and-image processor. As with a computer, part of the operation is automatic, taking place somewhere out of sight of the "screen" of our surface awareness. And as with the computer, this processor can be reprogrammed and debugged to help serve us better, allowing us to solve different and more difficult problems than we have ever tackled before. Some of these reprogramming methods, which come from the disciplines of the world's spiritual traditions as well as from modern psychology and psychotherapy, are discussed in chapter four in terms of a "tool kit for personal breakthrough."

There is nothing particularly new about the idea that the unconscious mind plays a central role in human creativity. But now, for the first time in history, access to the bridge between the compartments of the self is becoming available for everyone who wants to find it. Recent scientific discoveries about the nature of the unconscious—and some not-so-recent knowledge that has begun to surface—point to an understanding of how we can all learn to use our unconscious idea processor more effectively.

THE UNCONSCIOUS:
GOLD MINE OR RUBBISH HEAP?

Few theories in the psychological sciences are now so well established as the discovery, or more accurately, the rediscovery, that only a small part of our total mental activity takes place in the conscious part of the mind, while a vast portion takes place somewhere in our unconscious. This portion involves continual processing, night and day, of ideas, images, and sensations.

Some of this out-of-consciousness activity is, so to speak, in the "deep unconscious," and we become aware of it only through inference. Some of it, though, is partially accessible to conscious awareness under certain conditions, facilitated by attention to feelings, emotions, and visual imagery, or through dreaming, meditation, biofeedback training, and so forth.

Most of us have not been made aware that there exist effective ways to make contact with our unconscious components, methods that both remove blocks and reveal potentials —and do not require mediation by an expensive professional, nor a lifetime of meditation in some unusual and uncomfortable body position. Even those who do not question the existence of that other part of the mind and the efficacy of techniques for contacting it typically live and think without taking seriously the implications of these findings.

There seems to be something almost "unconscious" about the way nearly everybody ignores the existence of their unconscious. To most persons the word *unconscious,* when used as a noun, connotes a region where we have buried out of sight all manner of rejected and denied memories and urges. Our culture has not encouraged us to think of the creative side of the unconscious, and this bias is mirrored by a similar bias in scientific thought.

One of the earliest and most crucial conflicts in the history of research into human consciousness was between two concepts of the unconscious that we may, at the risk of oversimplifying, identify with Sigmund Freud and his far less famous contemporary Frederick W. H. Myers.

Freud's theories of the unconscious were based on his

years of observation of the process of psychoanalysis. The people who furnished the material for his theories were either neurotic or psychotic. Consequently, the Freudian concept was strongly influenced by its origins in the study of psychopathology. This view emphasized the negative role of the unconscious—its role in *inhibiting* the full flowering of the individual's potential. To Freud, the unconscious was full of horrible memories and repressed thoughts hidden away from conscious awareness by a kind of internal censor.[2]

Myers, on the other hand, had been a classical scholar at Cambridge. His concept emphasized the role of the unconscious as the source of intuition and creativity. As Myers put it, the unconscious might more profitably be regarded as "a gold mine as well as rubbish heap." To Myers, the source of those cultural treasures most valued by our civilization—art, religion, invention—were also to be found there.[3]

Myers' 1903 book *Human Personality and Its Survival of Bodily Death* laid out a daring map of a vast terrain, at that time little explored by science. It included such areas as the study of unconscious processes, sleep and dreams, hypnosis, creativity and inspiration, psychic phenomena, and evidences of survival of the personality after physical death. William James, the father of psychology in the United States, had high regard for Myers' work and was "disposed to think that Frederic Myers will always be remembered in psychology as the pioneer who staked out a vast tract of mental wilderness and planted the flag of genuine science upon it." But history had it otherwise.

The concept of the unconscious as a unsavory part of human nature, often a source of sickness and terror, was more in tune with nineteenth-century ideas of human frailties and limitations. Vienna was victorious over Cambridge. The "rubbish heap" concept of the other side of consciousness won the battle for scientific and popular opinion, at least temporarily. Hence, the main reason to study creativity, for the majority of orthodox researchers during much of the past century, was to learn about its relationship to psychosis and neurosis.

Eventually, some of the subdivisions plotted by Myers were admitted to scientific respectability—unconscious processes, hypnosis, dream and sleep research, for instance. Other subdivisions have been regarded as taboo topics even very recently. The proposition of continued existence after death implied by Myers' title was also more than a little embarrassing for psychologists of the time, who were struggling to gain scientific legitimacy for their field of endeavor.

It seems likely that in the long run, both schools will turn out to have been correct, because each was describing a different aspect of the same phenomenon. It often happens in the early history of a science that different investigators will get hold of different aspects of the same problem and argue fruitlessly over who has the "right" approach. Is the rubbish heap the better metaphor for the unconscious, or is the gold mine closer to the truth? It may be that the question itself is the problem, rather than lack of an answer.

For example, throughout the nineteenth century and into the early part of the twentieth century, physicists were fiercely debating the meaning of certain experiments and theories concerning the nature of light. One school had equations and arguments to prove that light is essentially a particle—a definite object with a specific spatial location. Another school of physicists, apparently in direct conflict with their particle-minded colleagues, had the equations and arguments to prove that light is essentially a wavelike phenomenon that is not localized in space but spread out over an indefinite area like waves in a pond.

The peculiar thing about this debate was that both sides could produce sound mathematics and could point out experiments and observations that the other side couldn't explain, but neither side was able to come up with a way to disprove the opposing point of view. When the Danish physicist Niels Bohr solved this problem by developing the principle of complementarity, it was one of the early recognitions that reality is too rich to be adequately represented by any one model or even one paradigm.[4]

Complementarity in physics means that light cannot be fully explained by either wave or particle theory alone. Light, in fact, is simultaneously a wave and a particle and possesses characteristics of both; the particle model does not contradict, but complements the wave theory.

This famous scientific conflict and its unexpected resolution happened well over half a century ago. It has only been much more recently that scientists in the field of consciousness research have started to become comfortable with the proposition that the complementary views of both Freud and Myers both bring unique contributions to the fuller understanding of the mysteries of our minds.

Thus, the hidden mind seems to have many aspects. Moreover, the relationship between these different aspects contains the key to higher psychospiritual development.

While one aspect of this "hidden mind" does appear to judge certain memories or data to be threatening or unpleasant and hides that information away from the conscious mind, another aspect of the self, some sort of deep intuition, seems to know the way to wholesome growth and development and gently guides the individual in this direction. Unless the various fragments of one's being can be induced to align themselves toward the same end (producing a state of integration, or a "person of integrity"), this fragmentary nature can indeed become a breeding ground for the kind of inner conflicts that came to life on Freud's famous couch. But, when they are brought together and aligned, the ground has been prepared in the best way possible for deep personal breakthroughs to take place.

THE CREATIVITY HARVEST

If there is one lesson to be learned from the most world-shaking events of the last fifty years, it is that new scientific knowledge discovered by one or two people can quickly become the concern of everybody on the planet. Half a century ago, a small group of physicists inquired into the secrets of the atomic nucleus, with grave consequences for all of us. Two centuries before that, a new way of thinking called the scientific method helped build the world we live in today.

It appears that we are in the middle of yet another such transformation of our thinking. This time, though, the subject is not the shape of the Earth, or the energy at the heart of atoms, but what might be the most awesome puzzle of all—the source of human creative power. Because this emergent field of knowledge is intimately related to our ideas about our own limits and abilities, the changes in our personal lives and in our entire society are likely to be scientifically valid methods for cultivating breakthrough experiences.

The current change is happening at a much faster rate than previous systemwide transformations. It took tens of thousands of years for hunters and gatherers to stop roaming and start farming. The Industrial Revolution took half a dozen generations to totally reconfigure ten millenia of agricultural civilization. The latest such change will probably become evident to everyone in less than a generation.

Investigators from many different fields—psychiatrists, neuroscientists, psychologists, sociologists, anthropologists, computer scientists, educators, even quantum physicists—are putting together a new picture of human capabilities, motivations, and inhibitions. The outlines of this picture are still hazy; grand unifying theories are lacking, and experimental findings in many areas are fragmentary. But the fragments are fitting together more and more often, and even the preliminary research indicates we must make radical changes in our present beliefs about the limits of human creative capacity.

Those who contributed to this convergence of knowledge were scientists and mystics, therapists and yogis, shamans and historians, as well as some of the greatest creative minds of history—but those who will reap the benefits are likely to be the majority of ordinary people who are not full-time scientists, mystics, or inspired artists. The ultimate beneficiaries of the creativity harvest will be businessmen, accountants, homemakers, schoolchildren.

Our intention here is only to point out certain findings and suggest certain experiments and show the reader how much today's infant sciences of consciousness have to contribute to the solution of the kinds of problems we face in our lives today. When we all learn the tricks of the creativity trade that were formerly reserved for geniuses, the masterpiece of our collective endeavors and breakthroughs could be not a painting or a theorem, but a new way of life.

One visionary who grasped the implications of creativity research stated its potential eloquently and succinctly[5]:

About 9,000 years ago, prehistoric man was suddenly catapulted into history as the result of an astonishing social discovery. Previous to this, small bands of nomadic tribes had roamed ... looking for game and gathering fruits and vegetables wild. Then someone found out that if one domesticated animals and plants, one could have a ready supply of food always at hand. ... Thus was agriculture and civilization born. ... Fortunately we are on the brink of another momentous discovery which will have even greater impact on cultural and personal escalation.

Heretofore we have harvested creativity wild. We have used as creative only those persons who stubbornly remained so despite all efforts of the family, religion, education, and politics to grind it out of them. In the prosecution of this campaign, men and women have been punished, flogged, silenced, imprisoned, tortured, ostracized, and killed. ...

If we learn to domesticate creativity—that is, to enhance rather than deny it in our culture—we can increase the number of creative persons in our midst by about fourfold. That would put the number and percent of such individuals over the "critical mass" point. When this level is reached in a culture, as it was in Periclean Athens ... and our own Federalist period, there is an escalation of creativity resulting and civilization makes a great leap forward. We can have a golden age of this type such as the world has never seen, and I am convinced that it will occur early in the twenty-first century. But we must make preparations now, and the society we save will be our own. ...

Suppose that it turns out to be true that the tools of Western science and the wisdom of the East could be applied to this goal of a worldwide "creativity harvest," that the technology of "breakthrough" is available to everyone. Consider then, what your life and the condition of the whole world would be like if it was true that:

The capacity for achieving fundamental insights isn't only for geniuses, but is at least partially a learned skill.

Profound inspiration isn't strictly reserved for artists, but can be a meaningful dimension of anybody's life.

The power of deep intuition can be an accessible source of guidance for individuals and societies.

Each of us has the capacity to become much more than we think we can be, if we choose to stop believing otherwise.

However, any new technology, whether a psychological one or a physical one, is always a two-edged sword. If we can indeed learn to harvest breakthroughs and increase our cultural creativity by tenfold or a hundredfold or a thousandfold, it would indisputably solve many of our most pressing problems, including flagging industrial productivity and inventiveness. But creativity and breakthrough insights can be harnessed to destructive as well as constructive ends, as this century's conflicts and genocides demonstrate.

And even when the intentions with which a new idea are implemented are unequivocally good, the results can often turn out to be the opposite of what was intended. Many of those inspirations which had as their avowed purpose the achievement of social good—various utopias, industrialization, Prohibition, nuclear energy, puritanical rules of morality —are recorded in history as having rather sorry outcomes.

On the other hand, breakthrough discoveries that in the long term have proved to have great social value were often originally motivated by personal interest or the ferment of war, and history indicates that some of the most beneficial creations of the past were seen by contemporaries as evil or socially destructive.

The only certain rule is that the greater the novelty, originality, and depth of the breakthrough—be it an idea, a work of art, or a scientific discovery—the more likely it is to be seen at first as false, pernicious, or just plain foolish.

But there are criteria we can apply in evaluating the products and potential products of creativity. In *On Becoming a Person*, Carl Rogers offers the following set of internal and external conditions that must be present to ensure that creative inspirations will be constructive instead of destructive.[6]

To the extent that the individual is denying to awareness (repressing) large areas of his experience, then his creative form-ings may be pathological, or socially evil, or both. To the degree that the individual is open to all aspects of his experience, and has available to his awareness all the varied sensings and per-ceivings which are going on within his organism, then the novel products of his interaction with his environment will tend to be constructive both for himself and others.

What are the conditions for constructive creativity? Rogers listed three "inner conditions" and two "outer condi-tions." The inner conditions are:

1. *Openness to Experience: Extensionality.* This is the opposite of psychological defensiveness, of rigidity and rigid boundaries in concepts, beliefs, perceptions, and hypotheses. Openness to experience implies a tolerance for ambiguity where ambiguity exists, and the ability to receive much con-flicting information without forcing closure in the form of "I agree," "I disagree," "I believe," "I don't believe," "It can't be true," "Science says. . . ."

2. *An Internal Locus of Evaluation.* The value of a cre-ative person's product is established for the individual not by the praise or criticism of others, but by oneself. This does not mean that the individual is oblivious to, or unwilling to be aware of, the judgments of others. But the final evaluation lies in the person's own organismic reaction to and appraisal of the creation. It is right when it feels satisfying and authentic.

3. *The Ability to Toy with Elements and Concepts.* The ability to play spontaneously with ideas, colors, shapes, rela-tionships—to juggle elements into impossible juxtapositions, to shape wild hypotheses, to take the given as problematic, to express the ridiculous, to translate ideas and principles from one form to another, to transform opposites into improbable but logical equivalents. From this spontaneous toying and ex-ploration there inevitably arises the hunch, the vision of life in a new and creative prospective way.

These are the internal conditions we must foster within ourselves if we want our creative urge and breakthrough in-sights to spring from constructive impulses and be put to con-structive purposes.

But, as many sages have noted over the centuries, we do

not live in a void. For all our good intentions, we put out to some degree what we take in. If we find ourselves in a destructive environment, we are bound to absorb a certain amount of it, and it becomes difficult to keep this taint from the output of our creative processes.

So to foster constructive creativity, there are external as well as internal conditions we must seek to ensure. Rogers describes these as:

1. *Psychological safety.* This may be established by having an environment in which the person is accepted as being of unconditional worth; external evaluation is absent (no one is being critical of them), and there is empathic understanding from those around the person.

2. *Psychological freedom.* Creativity is fostered when the individual is permitted complete freedom of symbolic expression. That is the freedom to think, to feel, to be, whatever is most true for oneself. This should not be confused with permissiveness, which is soft and indulgent; it is permission to be free, which is also persmission to be responsible. It is permission to be afraid, to be wrong, to feel confused.

The catch is that such circumstances are not only a matter of the immediate physical surroundings, or even one's social circle or business acquaintances. They arealso a matter of our cultural and political surroundings. To the same degree that a person who fosters such conditions promotes the constructive aspects of personal breakthroughs, does a culture that fosters those conditions promote the beneficial aspects of breakthroughs within it.

And to exactly the degree that the culture fosters and promotes the reverse conditions, it potentiates the negative, dangerous, and destructive aspects of its creative resources— which takes us from consciousness and creativity back to social and political considerations, demonstrating once again, as we observed in the Introduction, how closely interrelated they are.

②

Lightning Bolts and Illuminations

The Hidden History of Creativity

> *Side by side with the subconscious (or unconscious) and conscious levels in human personality, a third stratum—the supraconscious—is gaining increasing recognition. It is not the subconscious or unconscious, but the supraconscious energies that are beginning to be considered as the real source of all great human creations, discoveries and inventions in all fields of culture—science, philosophy, law, ethics, fine arts, technology, politics and economics. . . . Such phenomena as extrasensory perception and psychokinesis; as the supraconscious religious experience of the great mystics; as precognition; as the so-called "calculating boys" or "arithmetical prodigies"; as the state of samadhi of the Yoga, or satori of the Zen Buddhists; as cognitive and creative intuition are neither subconscious nor unconscious, but supraconscious, and, as such, are not reducible to the lower forms of vital and mental energy.*
>
> PITIRIM A. SOROKIN, *Psychic Source Book*

Along with the orthodox history of scientific-technological cultural progress we learn about in school, there is another, less well-known account, a hidden history that is not so much suppressed as repressed. The evidence itself is not hidden. Of course, it is easier to find books about Cartesian philosophy or molecular biology or the construction of sewing machines than it is to find books about Descartes' dreams, or Kekule's snake

19

or Elias Howe's nightmare. But the information is there for anyone who takes the time to seek it out.

In their autobiographies and memoranda, many artists and creative geniuses single out one or more insights as being somehow different from their "normal working day" moments of inspiration. In our culture, we pay attention to the products and artifacts that result from these creative breakthroughs but have ignored the often impassioned pleas of geniuses to look more carefully at those special moments in their own lives when they were more than usually aware.

Of course, the general population of a century or two in the past, or even a decade or two ago, had a negative mental picture of what such extraordinary mental events might be like and thought they resulted from—either witchcraft or hallucination—and had an almost universal distaste for the proposition that they themselves might choose to undergo such an ordeal. They were willing to believe in the creations they valued most in their lives, from the scientific basis of their household appliances to the words of their scriptures, but ignored the words of the people who created those artifacts.

Part of what this book is meant to convey is a fuller explanation of why the people who have these "breakthrough" experiences considered a study of the state so valuable. Some of the paradoxical attitude our culture adopts toward these experiences is revealed by the fact that our most conservative institutions and repositories of what we claim to value most— the institutions of science and the various organized religions —are almost always based on the words of people who have experienced these states, and who hundreds of millions of people take very seriously. Yet society as a whole tends to look askance at such experiences—even treating them as grounds for the diagnosis of mental illness.

Some of the people who have this experience do sound partially crazy—going into trancelike reveries, hearing voices no one else hears, jumping up frantically to record dreams and hallucinations. Young Mozart's companions learned that he was likely to halt their games at any moment, admonishing his playmates to be silent while he scribbled out the melodies that rushed into his mind; and the great mathematician Ramanujan kept a note pad next to his bed to write down the formulas that he claimed were revealed to him in dreams by the goddess of his native village.

Our interest here, however, is what sets geniuses apart from lesser minds, not what their neighbors thought of their behavior. Through focusing on the difference between the way they thought about the world and the way the rest of us perceive reality, we could learn something about the nature of genius itself.

By looking closely at what people have said about these moments, some guiding principles can be discerned by which it is possible to integrate more scientific findings relating to consciousness and creativity and derive an overall pattern toward which anyone can apply to achieve or increase the incidence of their personal breakthroughs. In the end, we want to discover the importance—to our civilization as well as to our daily lives—of these special states of awareness.

Whoever examines personal accounts of great creative breakthroughs is sure to find what we and previous investigators have discovered—that certain elements are present in every one of these accounts and form a pattern that anyone can apply to achieve their personal breakthroughs.

One of the earliest of the paradigms for the creative process suggested by these characteristics was made by British writer Graham Wallas in his 1926 book *The Art of Thought*. For three-quarters of a century, anyone who has sought to understand the nature of the creative process has sooner or later come across Wallas' paradigm.

Wallas proposed that the creative process consists of four components: preparation, incubation, illumination, and verification. A distinguished contemporary creativity researcher, John Curtis Gowan, discussed the Wallas paradigm in his examination of creative insight:[1]

By incubation, he meant any technique of relaxation of the conscious cognition (left-hemisphere function), such as, but not confined to, dreams, daydreams, fantasy, hypnosis, meditation, diversion, play, etc., which allow subliminal processes (right-hemisphere functions) to operate. He saw preparation (academic discipline), as the necessary, and incubation (relaxation) as the sufficient condition for creative insights to emerge.

Wallas formulated his paradigm long before the age of the computer, but his idea had obvious similarities to our more contemporary metaphor of an unconscious image-and-idea processor. If Wallas had lived in the computer age, he might have formulated his model more like this: input mode (preparation), processing mode (incubation), output mode (illumination), verification mode (verification).

In a recent *Los Angeles Times* article, Kenneth Atchity, editor of *Dreamworks*, discusses the relevance of such a metaphor:[2]

> The computer analogy is not far-fetched. Humans designed computers and it's not surprising that mechanisms might reflect something of the creator's mind better even than the designer himself might have predicted. Those who know the intimacy of working with a computer will ... explore its ramifications and test its validity against their own experience.

Thinking about the brain in computerlike terms makes some people uncomfortable because they consider it dehumanizing. On the other hand, they see nothing dehumanizing about thinking of the body in terms of muscle, leverage and nerve when it comes to discovering ways to develop and utilize its maximum capacities for sport or music or the performing arts. Nor do they consider it dehumanizing to develop and utilize the maximal capacities of their intellectual powers in work and play or to expect this of their children in school.

No one seems to have any difficulty in thinking of the computer in brainlike terms, but we often overlook the real significance of this analogy. The capacities computers possess are designed to replicate and multiply capacities which the brain already possesses. If we did not inherently have the ability to add, store, retrieve, and evaluate data, to project possibilities and determine options—we would have no way of knowing such capacities existed to build into computers. Since these capacities are as natural a part of our biological and psychological heritage as muscles or intelligence, there is no reason we should feel hesitant to use them.

In addition to a data-storage program, the brain has a problem-solving program. We often employ it at our conscious behest, without being consciously aware that that is what we are doing. Otherwise we could not add "two plus two" and get "four." Arriving at the answers to simple arithmetic problems doesn't require any real thought, but occurs spontaneously as that "program" is accessed by some intermediate part of the mind, outside our awareness. We no longer have to stop every time and consciously rework the math, or more fundamentally, relearn how to solve problems—as we undoubtedly did at one point, at an age so young we no longer recall the time or that this is, in fact, a separate process.

This problem-solving capacity of the mind is, in a sense, what we have been referring to as the unconscious idea processor. But as we get into some of the higher spectra in the creative rainbow, we may ultimately find the need to discard this terminology, along with a number of other conceptions, preconceptions, beliefs, definitions, ideals, and outlooks.

As incredible as it seems, that is all there is to it. All we have to do is to consciously program the unconscious with the correct input, and, like a mathematical formula, input plus processing time will equal output.

Of course, we are not claiming that any one individual will get a breakthrough insight every time they use the technique, or that every single person who employs it will achieve a breakthrough, but it is our belief, based on both personal experience and our investigations, that almost everyone who follows the steps we will give later will experience a dramatic increase in the number of breakthrough experiences in their lifetimes. And that's a suggestion certainly worth considering, isn't it?

Most people are accustomed to thinking of people like Brahms and Beethoven as "naturally inspired." Yet they both took pains to point out that certain inspirations, more valued than the others, seemed to come from someplace other than what they normally thought of as their self.

Poets have always been particularly aware of the elusiveness of inspiration and have often noted how the muse can come, unbidden, and virtually dictate entire lines, passages, or works.

George Eliot told J. W. Cross that in all of what she considered her best writings, something that was "not herself" took possession of her, and that she felt her own personality to be "merely the instrument through which this spirit, as it were, was acting."And George Sand in a letter to another writer, wrote:[3] "The Wind plays my old harp as it lists. . . . It is *the other* who sings as he likes, well or ill, and when I try to think about it, I am afraid and tell myself that I am nothing, nothing at all."

PREPARATION, OR THE "INPUT" MODE

Your unconscious idea processor is waiting at your beck and call. All you have to do is assign it a problem, instruct it, and it will immediately go to work on a problem for you.

It does this for you most of the time anyway, whenever we have a problem that the conscious is to solve immediately. But the more clearly, completely, and intently you formulate a question and direct it to the unconscious, the more quickly and effectively the unconscious can come up with an answer to it.

Clearly, because the more precisely you can state any problem, the more swiftly and accurately your unconscious idea processor can churn out the solution. This is probably most apparent in mathematics, business, and the sciences, where rigor of definition is required, than in, say, the arts or where purely personal and familial insights and intuitions are involved—but the same principle holds true.

Completely, because the more fully and thoroughly you program a computer the more sophisticated and precise its answer will be. This applies to everything from the kinds of landscapes a painter might have seen in his or her life and the kinds of problems a mathematician has already learned to solve to focused concentration and assimilation of material about the job at hand.

Intently, because the strength of the intent with which we program our unconscious affects the priority our idea processor assigns to a problem. The more important we make a question seem to the processor, the higher a priority it sets on arriving at a solution, preempting programs of lesser importance, assigning larger segments of the mind's capacities to it, and so forth.

This is where many books go wrong. They assume that input consists purely of informational data, because that is the kind of data a computer is limited to. But the human computer is infinitely more sophisticated than the kind that utilize microchips, and it can not only accept, but requires, more complex forms of input to do its job properly—and can produce more complex forms of solutions in return.

By intensively examining a problem, visualizing and creating scenarios of possible solutions, learning even the most tangential facts about it, and deeply intending and desiring to solve it, the overall knowledge available to the memory, unconscious as well as conscious, of the creative person is brought into play. The program that this deeper knowledge carries into action comes from preparation and intention directed at the problem of the moment.

Speaking of the kind of intense emotional concentration on a subject that can often be a prelude to deep illumination, the composers Puccini and Strauss seem to echo each other and countless others who have also achieved the breakthrough state.

According to Strauss:[4]

I can tell you from my own experience that an ardent desire and fixed purpose combined with intense inner resolve brings results. Determined concentrated thought is a tremendous force. . . . I am convinced that this is a law, and it holds good in any line of endeavor.

Puccini told one biographer:[5]

The conscious purposeful appropriation of one's own soulforces is the supreme secret. . . . I first grasp the full power of the Ego within me. Then I feel the *burning* desire and *intense resolve* to create something worthwhile. This desire, this longing, implies in itself the knowledge that I can reach my goal. Then I make a fervent demand. . . . This perfect faith opens the way for vibration to pass from the dynamo which the soulcenter is, into my consciousness, and the inspired ideas are born.

INCUBATION, OR THE "PROCESSING" MODE

At a certain stage in every creation, preparation ceases, and the ingredients have to be left to "cook" in order to allow the subconscious to operate on the problem. Just as every computer has to switch its mode of operation when all the relevant instructions and data have been fed into it, a similar shift in states of consciousness seems to be necessary before our hidden mind can go into operation and produce a solution to the problems we set it.

In his book *Landscapes of the Night: How and Why We Dream*, Christopher Evans suggests one of the reasons this incubation period might be required, and some of the ways the brain processes the questions with which we program it:[6]

> Waking brings such a mass of incoming data to the brain that it stands to reason a sorting period is required.... Suppose the short-term system could hold information circulating, so to speak, in an immediate access store, but that the system was unable to keep this information indefinitely "on hold.".... Sleep is one period when the brain comes off-line, cutting itself off from the sensory input, and restricting psychomotor input.... With sensory input reduced, some part of the brain would not get to work on the sensory data pool, sorting out the material ... filing the data ... the great software files of the brain open and available for revision.... In sleep, man with his own tremendously advanced computer—his brain—might be performing an operation similar to and as vital as the modern computer.

Going into the processing mode, then, can involve anything from turning the problem over to the unconscious and forgetting it (which at least stops "input" on that question and frees more of the computer's time to work on the rest) various methods of going "off-line," from relaxation, to daydreaming, to meditation, to sleep.

ILLUMINATION, OR THE "OUTPUT" MODE

As a result of the consciously initiated processes of preparation and incubation, a mysterious process produces the solution to our problem in a flash, from out of nowhere, in the form of a religious illumination, a literary image, a scientific understanding, the theme of a concerto, a business innovation, and so forth. The particular state of heightened awareness and expanded knowledge that accompanies the output of a solution, an image, an idea, or a theme, is the one we have called "the breakthrough state." In the creative realm, every problem is unique and every output is unique. The results and nature of these illuminations seem to vary so widely in their form, their impact on the world, that this stage appears to cover a sub-spectrum within the greater spectrum.

For instance, the phrase "like a flash of lightning" occurs again and again in these firsthand descriptions. There is no doubt that this is an observation repeatedly confirmed by independent and reliable sources, a clue to the *state* in which deep insights occur.

Many creators have spoken of a state of being in which ideas and inspirations seem to flow into them in a stream, or bubble up from a source. Many of these men and women are widely separated by time, nation, and field of interest, but the words in which they describe this state are surprisingly similar. That this is more than just a metaphor is apparent. Perhaps the moment of flow indicates a moment when we have total access to the unconscious idea processor, and it begins to read out solutions without stopping. Perhaps in this state, if we could but attain it, we could ask questions and have them answered as fast as we could formulate them.

And others, still, have spoken of a feeling that their greatest inspirations come from somewhere "not myself"—from outside themselves or from some other force or being altogether.

VERIFICATION

The verification mode is the stage when phantasms are distinguished from inspirations, and legions of delusions are sifted to reveal the insights buried among them. Now that the illumination has occurred and the output has been communicated, the computations of the unconscious idea processor are compared to reality—the urgings of the inner voice are held up to the rules of reason: chemical formulas glimpsed in a dream are tested in the crucible of the laboratory; the inspired theme that rushed in like an invisible river is written into a musical score for the world to judge; the mathematical equation that came in a flash is checked and double-checked.

PREPARATION: CASE EXAMPLES

The stories of mathematician Poincaré, physics teacher Mendeleev, inventor Elias Howe, and composer Richard Wagner all demonstrate different aspects of the intense preparations that can be required to program our unconscious processor for a breakthrough insight.

Henri Poincaré was a first-rate mathematician of the late nineteenth century; fortunately for our present investigation, he was also an acute observer of his own creative process and a respected historian of scientific thought. His account of the extraordinary roots of his mathematical creations sheds light not only on one mathematician's breakthroughs, but also on the comments of others who have had the same experience.

Using himself as an example, Poincaré painted a picture of the kind of intensely concentrated conscious work that preceeds a revelation—the kind of stubborn hammering away at a problem that can be fruitless, frustrating, even desparate, but is later seen as a necessary preparation for the incubated solution:[7]

> For fifteen days I strove to prove that there could not be any functions like those I have since called Fuchsian functions. I was then very ignorant; every day I seated myself at my work table, stayed on an hour or two, tried a great number of combinations and reached no results. One evening, contrary to my custom, I drank black coffee and could not sleep. Ideas rose in crowds; I felt them collide until pairs interlocked, so to speak, making a stable combination. By the next morning I had established the existence of a class of Fuchsian functions. . . . I had only to write out the results, which took but a few hours.
>
> Just at this time I left Caen, where I was then living, to go on a geologic excursion. . . . The changes of travel made me forget my mathematical work. Having reached Coutances, we entered an omnibus to go some place or other. At the moment when I put my foot on the step the idea came to me, without

anything in my former thoughts seeming to have paved the way for it, that the transformations I had used to define the Fuchsian functions were identical with those of non-Euclidean geometry. I did not verify the idea; I should not have had the time, as, upon taking my seat in the omnibus, I went on with a conversation already commenced, but I felt a perfect certainty. On my return to Caen, for conscience' sake I verified the result at my leisure.

How mundane, how casual can seem the moment of illumination. An idea of great complexity and theoretical importance occurs while stepping onto a bus—and with such self-evident conviction that the mathematician confidently resumed his conversation and waited to verify the revelation later, at his leisure. He even noted that sense of what we have called "noetic" rightness that accompanied certain illuminations. "I have especially noticed this fact," he wrote, "in regard to ideas coming to me in the morning or evening in bed while in a semi-hypnagogic state."

Poincaré had concentrated, had worked and had given up working (preparation plus incubation), then suddenly and unexpectedly the solution occurred to him, which he verified later (illumination). He didn't suspect that even this sequence, now apparently complete, was in fact the first stage of a larger cycle yet to come:[8]

Then I turned my attention to the study of some arithmetical questions apparently without much success and without a suspicion of any connection with my preceding researches. Disgusted with my failure, I went to spend a few days at the seaside, and thought of something else. One morning, walking on the bluff, the idea came to me, with just the same characteristics of brevity, suddenness and immediate certainty, that the arithmetic transformations of indeterminate ternary quadratic forms were identical with those of non-Euclidean geometry.

Returned to Caen, I meditated on this result and deduced the consequences. The examples of quadratic forms showed me that they were Fuchsian groups other than those corresponding to the hypergeometric series; I saw that . . . there existed Fuchsian functions other than . . . those I then knew. Naturally I set myself to form all these functions. I made a systematic attack upon them and carried all the outworks, one after another. There was one however that still held out, whose fall would involve that of the whole place. But all my efforts only served at first the better to show me the difficulty, which indeed was something. All this work was perfectly conscious.

Thereupon I left for Mont-Valerian, where I was to go through my military service; so I was very differently occupied. One day, going along the street, the solution of the difficulty which had stopped me suddenly appeared to me. I did not try to go deep into it immediately, and only after my service did I again take up the question. I had all the elements and had only to arrange them and put them together. So I wrote out my final memoir at a single stroke and without difficulty.

Poincaré underwent a process that took years to complete, during which his progressive understanding of the mathematical mysteries that obsessed him through long conscious labor were unexpectedly revealed to him in several moments of breakthrough insight.

In the long hours of conscious work, the goals seemed doubtful, the problems loomed large. In the instants of realization, problems fell away without difficulty and he merely had to look at a solution that was presented unbidden and with quiet clarity, to his mind's eye, a solution whose essential "rightness" seemed so strong that doubt was diminished and he often put off the verification procedure for hours or days.

Noting that this experience compelled him to turn his attention to other examples of sudden illumination in mathematics, Poincaré used his own experience as raw data for a detailed analysis of mathematical creativity. Although this little essay was first published in 1908, it remains one of the most insightful documents in the literature of the creative process. Poincaré's first conclusion was that the "appearance of sudden illumination," was "a manifest sign of long, unconscious work."[9]

The case of Dmitri Mendeleev provides another example of how intense concentration can program the unconscious for breakthrough:[10]

In 1869, D. I. Mendeleev went to bed exhausted after struggling to conceptualize a way to categorize the elements based upon their atomic weights. He later reported, "I saw in a dream a table where all the elements fell into place as required. Awakening, I immediately wrote it down on a piece of paper. Only in one place did a correction later seem necessary."

There is a certain cultural potency to the idea that something useful could come, either symbolically or directly, from a dream. There can be little question about the utility of the sewing machine. The history books mention that Elias Howe worked intensely for several years on a scheme to invent a lockstitch sewing machine and eventually succeeded. What they do not mention is the fact that his years of labor did not bear fruit until a nightmare suggested the solution in symbolic form.

The version of Howe's dream quoted here is from the 1924 edition of *A Popular History of American Invention, Vol. II.*, by W. B. Kaempffert:[11]

> Howe made the needles of his early failure with a hole in the middle of the shank. His brain was busy with the invention day and night and even when he slept. One night he dreamed ... that he was captured by a tribe of savages who took him prisoner before their king.
>
> "Elias Howe," roared the monarch, "I command you on pain of death to finish this machine at once."
>
> Cold sweat poured down his brow, his hands shook with fear, his knees quaked. Try as he would, the inventor could not get the missing figure in the problem over which he had worked so long. All this was so real to him that he cried aloud. In the vision he saw himself surrounded by dark-skinned and painted warriors, who formed a hollow square about him and led him to a place of execution. Suddenly he noticed that near the heads of the spears which his guards carried, there were eye-shaped holes! He had solved the secret! What he needed was a needle with an eye near the point! He awoke from his dream, sprang out of bed, and at once made a whittled model of the eye-pointed needle, with which he brought his experiments to a successful close.

The origin of *Das Rheingold*, the opening of composer Richard Wagner's epic Ring Cycle, offers an artistic example on the kind of emotional preparation great inspiration can sometimes demand.

At the age of 40, Wagner suffered a deep spell of what would today be called a midlife crisis. His artistic career was unsatisfactory, his marriage dull, his finances disastrous. His inspiration seemed to be failing him. Desperate, searching for themes, the composer started to travel, seeking perhaps to find an external place where his power to create internal worlds might return to him. But travel only exhausted him.

Later, in a letter, Wagner described how at Spezia, in northern Italy, in September, 1853, when all that he held most dear seemed lost, when he finally gave up the relentless drive to consciously invoke his muse and let the problem go off-line, he heard, in a dream, a musical theme—one that was to alter his life and influence the history of music:[12]

> After a night spent in fever and sleeplessness I forced myself to take a long walk through the country. It looked dreary and desolate. Upon my return I lay down on a hard couch. Sleep would not come, but I sank into a kind of somnolence, in which I suddenly felt as though I were sinking in swiftly flowing water. The rushing noise formed itself into a musical sound, the chord of E flat major, whence developed melodic passages of increasing motion. I awoke in sudden terror, recognizing that the orchestral prelude to *Das Rheingold*, which must have been long lain latent within me, had at last been revealed to me. I decided to return to Zurich at once and begin the composition of my great poem.

INCUBATION: CASE EXAMPLES

When the mind of the creative person is prepared by experience, education, and concentration; when the problem or the creation is addressed, visualized, struggled with, studied; when all relevant data is fed to the unconscious idea processor, and the request is made, the program is submitted, it seems as if the best thing to do is to *let it all go*. The state of consciousness and the mode of knowing about the world associated with the kind of work done in the preparation stage is precisely what must change so that the mind can go off-line and incubation can occur.

In this respect it is probably not surprising that so many great ideas seem to arrive during reveries or trances, when the mind is already halfway transported from the bright white light of consciousness to the less visible frequencies of the unconscious.

In the latter part of the eighteenth century, Wolfgang Amadeus Mozart wrote this revealing passage in a letter to a friend:[13]

> When I am, as it were, completely myself, entirely alone, and of good cheer—say, travelling in a carriage, or walking after a good meal, or during the night when I cannot sleep; it is on such occasions that my ideas flow best and most abundantly. *Whence* and *how* they come, I know not; nor can I force them. Those pleasures that please me I retain in memory, and am accustomed, as I have been told, to hum them to myself. If I continue in this way, it soon occurs to me how I may turn this or that morsel to account, so as to make a good dish of it, that is to say, agreeably to the rules of counterpoint, to the peculiarities of the various instruments, etc.
>
> All this fires my soul, and provided I am not disturbed, my subject enlarges itself, becomes methodized and defined, and the whole, though it be long, stands almost complete and finished in my mind, so that I can survey it, like a fine picture or a beautiful statue, at a glance. Nor do I hear in my imagination the parts successively, but I hear them, as it were, all at once. What a delight this is I cannot tell! All this inventing, this producing, takes place in a pleasing lively dream. Still the actual hearing of the *tout ensemble* is after all the best. What has been thus produced I do not easily forget, and this is perhaps the best gift I have my divine Maker to thank for.

We shall hear these words echoed in passages from the writings of great scientists, artists, and inventors. In many of them, the creative people appealed to some external source. Often the creative person personifies this source, as a divinity or some kind of internal "Daemon," or even a workshop full of "brownies."

Rudyard Kipling, agreed the key to gaining access to this inner helper was "not to think consciously," but to "drift":[14]

> Let us now consider the Personal Daemon. . . . Most men, and some most unlikely, keep him under an alias which varies with

their literary or scientific attainments. Mine came to me early when I sat bewildered among other notions, and said: "Take this and no other." I obeyed, and was rewarded. . . .

After that I learned to lean upon him and recognize the sign of his approach. If ever I held back, Ananias fashion, any-thing of myself (even though I had to throw it out afterwards) I paid for it by missing what I then knew the tale lacked. . . .

My Daemon was with me in the Jungle books, *Kim*, and both Puck books, and good care I took to walk delicately, lest he should withdraw. I know that he did not, because when those books were finished they said so themselves with, almost, the water-hammer click of a tap turned off. . . . *Note here.* When your Daemon is in charge, do not try to think consciously. Drift, wait, and obey. . . .

Kipling's effort to disengage his conscious mind at a cer-tain point, and "drift" in a reverie, is an example of perhaps the mildest kind of shift, to the processing or incubator mode. Wordsworth, on the other hand, apparently experienced many of his greatest inspirations while in a more trancelike state of consciousness than Kipling's reverie:[15]

Wordsworth told Bonamy Price that the line in his ode begin-ning: "Fallings from us, vanishings," which has since puzzled so many readers, refers to those trancelike states to which he was at one time subject. During these moments the world around him seemed unreal and the poet had occasionally to use his strength against an object, such as a gatepost, to reassure himself. And when the power would not come, the conscious mind was helpless. . . .

Although popular wisdom associates trances with seers and yogis and hypnotists, we all experience several varieties of trance state every morning and night. The threshold awareness that often comes upon awakening—called the *hypnopompic* state by contemporary psychologists—is one of these periods. The twilight state that happens right before the conscious mind drifts off to sleep—called the *hypnagogic* state—is an-other.

The British novelist William Thackeray made excellent use of the hypnopompic state, although most would think that the measures he took to ensure he would begin his creative activities in the right part of the cycle were rather drastic—his servant had orders to awaken him in the morning by flinging á wet towel in his face![16]

Henry Wadsworth Longellow, hardly the most bohemian of American writers, apparently found some of the most important verses for his masterpieces while his waking consciousness was in the hypnagogic state:[17]

> Last evening . . . I sat till twelve o'clock by my fire, smoking, when suddenly it came into my mind to write the "Ballad of the Schooner Hesperus," which I accordingly did. Then I went to bed, but could not sleep. New thoughts were running in my mind, and I got up to add them to the ballad. I felt pleased with the ballad. It hardly cost me any effort. It did not come into my mind by lines, but by stanzas.

Of course, one of the classic ways of triggering a kind of "consciousness shift" in the hope of achieving creative inspiration is through chemical means of realigning, stimulating, or quieting the consciousness. (Clearly, the brain goes "off-line" in terms of its normal consciousness.) Poincaré noted the numerous cups of coffee that kept him awake but half-dozing while the ideas "rose up" and collided. In this regard, the most celebrated dream in literature was not, properly speaking, a dream at all. By his own admission, Samuel Taylor Coleridge's vision of Xanadu took place in an opium-induced reverie. In his *Literary Reminiscences*, referring to himself as "the author," calling laudanum "an anodyne," Coleridge wrote:[18]

> In the summer of the year 1797 the author, then in ill health, had returned to a lonely farmhouse between Porlock and Linton, on the Exmoor confines of Somerset and Devonshire. In consequence of a slight indisposition, an anodyne had been prescribed, from the effects on which he fell asleep in his chair at the moment that he was reading the following sentence, or words of the same substance, in "Purchas's Pilgrimage': "Here the Khan Kubla commanded a palace to be built, and a stately garden thereunto. And thus ten miles of fertile ground were enclosed with a wall." The author continued for about three hours in a profound sleep, at least of the external senses, during which time he had the most vivid confidence, that he could not have composed less than from two to three hundred lines; if

that indeed can be called composition in which all the images
rose up before him as things, with a parallel production of the
correspondent expressions, without any sensation or consciousness of effort. On awakening he appeared to himself to have a
distinct recollection of the whole, and taking his pen, ink, and
paper, instantly and eagerly wrote down the lines that are here
preserved. At this moment he was unfortunately called out by a
person on business from Porlock, and detained by him above an
hour, and on his return to his room, found, to his no small
surprise and mortification, that though he still retained some
vague and dim recollection of the general purport of the vision,
yet, with the exception of some eight or ten scattered lines and
images, all the rest had passed away like the images on the
surface of a stream into which a stone has been cast, but, alas!
without the restoration of the latter!

Do so many inspirations come in dreams because that is
when the consciousness is off-line, and the unconscious is in
control and can speak to us directly at last, unfettered by the
constraints of waking awareness?

Niels Bohr, a physicist, dreamed of a planetary system as
a model for atoms as well as celestial bodies led to the "Bohr
model" of atomic structure and a Nobel prize.[19] And insulin to
the list of life-saving discoveries that came from the dream-
state, for that is where Sir Frederick Grant Banting found his
.aboratory procedure for the mass production of insulin.[20]

The composer Giuseppe Tartini, who is credited with the
invention of the modern violin bow, had an extraordinary nocturnal revelation when he was twenty-one, as a result of which
he composed his best-known work, The Devil's Sonata. Tartini
dreamed that the devil had become his slave; in the dream,
Tartini handed his violin to the devil to see what he could do
with it. Tartini's biographers quote his description of what
happened:[21]

But how great was my astonishment when I heard him play
with consummate skill a sonata of such exquisite beauty as sur-
passed the boldest flights of my imagination. I felt enraptured,
transported, enchanted; my breath was taken away, and I
awoke. Seizing my violin I tried to retain the sounds I had
heard. But it was in vain. The piece I then composed, The

Devil's Sonata, was the best I ever wrote, but how far below the one I had heard in my dream!

Tartini was certainly not the only artist to declare that his greatest inspiration came from a dream. But Robert Louis Stevenson occupies a special category in the psychic history of art—for his outright commercial exploitation of his extraordinary dream capacities, and his frank description of his waking ego's relationship to the "other part" of his psyche.

As a child, Stevenson suffered from vivid nightmares, which continued to plague him into his early adult life. In a conscious effort to ward off these night terrors and redirect the course of his turbulent inner life, Stevenson put himself to sleep by concocting stories for distraction and his personal pleasure. His dreams took on a less nightmarish but no less vivid cast as a result of these efforts, and he began to write them down and to sell them.

In his memoirs, Stevenson quite candidly revealed his reliance on an experienced cadre of dream helpers he called his "brownies," and explained how he came to use and finally to exploit them. Stevenson had a bit to say about them in a little-known essay entitled "A Chapter on Dreams":[22]

The more I think of it, the more I am moved to press upon the world my question: Who are the Little People? They are near connections of the dreamer's beyond doubt; they share in his financial worries and have an eye to the bank-book; they share plainly in his training; they have plainly learned like him to build the scheme of a considerable story and to arrange emotion in progressive order; only I think they have more talent; and one thing is beyond doubt, they can tell him a story piece by piece, like a serial, and keep him all the while in ignorance of where they aim. Who are they, then? And who is the dreamer?

Well, as regards the dreamer. I can answer that, for he is no less a person than myself . . . and for the Little People, what shall I say they are but just my Brownies, God bless them! who do one-half my work while I am fast asleep, and in all human likelihood, do the rest for me as well, when I am wide awake and fondly suppose I do it for myself. That part which is done while I am sleeping is the Brownies' part beyond contention; but that which is done when I am up and about is by no means necessarily mine, since all goes to show the Brownies have a hand in it even then. I am an excellent advisor, much like Moliere's servant. I pull back and I cut down; and I dress the whole in the best words and sentences that I can find and make; I hold the pen, too; and I do the sitting at the table, which is about the worst of it; and when all is done, I make up the manuscript and pay for the registration; so that, on the whole, I have some claim to share, though not so largely as they do, in the profits of our common enterprise.

. I can but give an instance or so of what part is done sleeping and what part awake, and leave the reader to share what laurels there are, at his own nod, between myself and my collaborators; and to do this I will first take a book that a number of persons have been polite enough to read, "The Strange Case of Dr. Jekyll and Mr. Hyde." I had long been trying to write a story on this subject, to find a body, a vehicle, for that strong sense of man's double being which must at times come in upon and overwhelm the mind of every thinking creature. I had even written one, "The Travelling Companion," which was returned by an editor on the pleas that it was a work of genius and indecent, and which I burned the other day on the ground that it was not a work of genius, and that "Jekyll" had supplanted it. Then came one of those financial fluctuations to which (with an elegant modesty) I have hitherto referred in the third person. For two days I went about racking my brains for a plot of any sort; and on the second night I dreamed the scene at the window, and a scene afterward split in two, in which Hyde, pursued for some crime, took the powder and underwent the change in the presence of his pursuers. All the rest was made awake, and consciously, although I think I can trace in much of it the manner of my Brownies.

Beethoven took a similar interest in the inspiration that seemed to spring forth from his dreams:[23]

On my way to Vienna yesterday, sleep overtook me in my carriage. . . . While thus slumbering I dreamt that I had gone on a far journey, to no less a place then Syria, on to Judea and back, and then all the way to Arabia, when at length I arrived at Jerusalem. The Holy City gave rise to thoughts of the Holy Books. . . . Now during my dream-journey, the following canon came into my head. . . .

But scarcely did I awake when away flew the canon, and

I could not recall any part of it. On returning here however, the next day, in the same carriage . . . I resumed my dream journey, being on this occasion wide awake, when lo and behold! in accordance with the laws of association of ideas, the same canon flashed across me; so being now awake I held it as fast as Menelaus did Proteus, only permitting it to be changed into three parts. . . .

The 1936 Nobel Prize in Physiology and Medicine was awarded to a physiologist by the name of Otto Loewi. Loewi discovered and demonstrated that the nerve impulses, the characteristic activity of the basic component of all nervous systems, is both a chemical and an electrical event.

While he was just starting out his career, a hunch occured to Loewi during a conversation with a colleague—a wild idea that the nerve impulse might have a chemical as well as an electrical aspect. But he couldn't think of an experiment to test his hypothesis. It was just a fleeting thought, one of hundreds of tentative stabs at problem-solving that any good scientist goes through every day.

Seventeen years later, the idea emerged again, in the form of an experimental procedure that came to him in a dream. According to Loewi's account:[24]

The night before Easter Sunday of that year (1920) I awoke, turned on the light, and jotted down a few notes on a tiny slip of thin paper. Then I fell asleep again. It occurred to me at six o'clock in the morning that during the night I had written down something important, but I was unable to decipher the scrawl. The next night, at three o'clock, the idea returned. It was the design of an experiment to determine whether or not the hypothesis of chemical transmission that I had uttered seventeen years ago was correct. I got up immediately, went to the laboratory, and performed a simple experiment on a frog's heart according to the nocturnal design. . . . Its results became the foundation of the theory of chemical transmission of the nervous impulse.

The initial appearance of the idea as a hunch, the long latency period, its reappearance as a dream, seems to follow the pattern of many other such discoveries. The fact that Loewi's waking mind was not aware of the contents of the dream he had tried to capture on the shred of paper—but did know it was very significant—furnishes a glimpse at the way the multiple components of one person's mind often converse with each other.

If you close your eyes for a moment and invoke the image of your own home, you will see many objects that are the products of synthetic chemistry. The drapes, the floor covering, most of your clothing, the dyes in the food and some of the food itself, everything made of plastic—virtually the entire material superstructure of the ideal consumer household—are the products of laboratory chemistry.

It would be a gross simplification to point to a single breakthrough or thinker as the foundation of the great collective enterprise of such a vast branch of science. But few chemists or historians of science would dispute that the dream-inspired structural theory of August Kekule von Stradonitz, known as Kekule, was one of the critical foundations of organic chemistry. Kekule's vision of molecular structure has been called "the most brilliant piece of prediction in the whole history of science."

In the mid-nineteenth century, the most perplexing challenge in the new science of chemistry was the problem of analyzing the molecular structure of chemical compounds. The new atomic theories gave chemists a way to envision models of the molecular building blocks of the compounds known in nature, but the way in which these building blocks were fitted together to make those compounds was a great puzzle. Not only the development of the theory, but the possibility of ever applying chemical theory to creating new substances, was blocked by the problem of structure.

Because of their abundance and apparent importance, compounds containing the element carbon were of special interest—in fact, the broad definition of organic chemistry is "the chemistry of compounds containing carbon." One of the critical puzzles was the structure of benzene. Chemists felt certain that if they could only figure out how the carbon atoms were arranged in this compound, they could begin deciphering the structure of many others.

Kekule, a Flemish professor living in London, spent a

number of years experimenting and thinking about possible ways molecules might connect to one another. As with similar instances in Einstein's and Poincaré's lives, the first of two key visions came to Kekule while he was riding aboard a streetcar. He related the story in a famous lecture he gave to a society of chemists toward the end of his career:[25]

> One fine summer evening, I was returning by the last omnibus, "outside" as usual, through the deserted streets of the metropolis, which are at other times so full of life. I fell into a reverie, and lo! the atoms were gambolling before my eyes. Whenever, hitherto, these diminutive beings had appeared to me, they had always been in motion; but up to that time, I had never been able to discern the nature of their motion. Now, however, I saw how, frequently, two smaller atoms united to form a pair; how a larger one embraced two smaller ones; how still larger ones kept hold of three or even four of the smaller; whilst the whole kept whirling in a giddy dance. I saw how the larger ones formed a chain. . . . I spent part of the night putting on paper at least sketches of these dream forms.

This image, or quasi-hallucination, of dancing atoms in the form of "diminutive beings," continued to haunt the chemist, but did not immediately lead to his famous insight. The moment of greatest illumination, in which the image engendered a new kind of understanding of the role of carbon atoms in molecular structure, came years later, in the form of a dream:[26]

> I turned my chair to the fire and dozed. Again the atoms were gambolling before my eyes. This time the smaller groups kept modestly in the background. My mental eye, rendered more acute by repeated visions of this kind, could now distinguish larger structures, of manifold conformation; long rows, sometimes more closely fitted together; all twining and twisting in snakelike motion. But look! What was that? One of the snakes had seized hold of its own tail, and the form whirled mockingly before my eyes. As if by the flash of lightning I awoke. . . . Let us learn to dream, gentlemen.

The chemists in Kekule's audience assuredly got the point: benzene is a "cyclic" or "ring" structure, and the carbon chain at the molecular core of the compound does indeed form a chain that swallows its own tail.

Kekule's dream marks a significant contribution to the study of creativity as well as the field of chemistry, for it is perhaps the single most often cited example of unconscious functioning in scientific discovery. But it is one thing when well-educated, traditionally trained mathematicians or artists happen to have extraordinary intuitive insights, even if the creative breakthroughs came as dreams or reveries. After all, their unconscious processor had access to the data. Yet what is one to make of an uneducated, lower-middle-class lad from a small village in India, whose exposure to mathematics was minimal at best, but who leaped directly to the forefront of mathematics, guided by a series of dreams in which the goddess of his village directly imparted mathematical wisdom?

Incredible as it may sound, such a man did exist—Srinivas Ramanujan. Significantly, his story is corroborated, not in the literature of psychic investigators, or by the research of psychologists, but in the pages of *Scientific American* and in the memoirs of eminent, thoroughly orthodox mathematicians.

Here is an area where mathematical insights offer a particularly good instrument for validating the more incredible ranges of the human creative spectrum. It is one thing to claim access to unusual informational channels, as the mystics and psychics do, but it is another, and quite a bit more impressive, to produce accurate solutions to well-known and previously unsolved problems in higher mathematics. Perhaps because the established mathematicians of Oxford and Cambridge knew a brilliant theory when they saw one, they also were quick to recognize the extraordinary intuitive character of Ramanujan's solutions to age-old mathematical problems.

Ramanujan, born in 1887 to a high-caste but poor family, exhibited his extraordinary mathematical skills very early during his rudimentary education. When he was fifteen, someone gave him an out-of-date textbook on mathematics, which he read and from which he constructed his private, massive body of mathematical knowledge. According to his own accounts, soon after the goddess Namagiri presented him with formulas in his dreams.

In 1909, having failed several times to secure scholar-
ships to government colleges—owing to his ignorance of non-
mathematical subjects—Ramanujan was given a recommenda-
tion to a certain "lover of mathematics" by the name of
Ramachandra Rao. James Newman, in the *Scientific American*,
quoted Rao's description of his first meeting with Ramanujan:[27]

> A short, uncouth figure, stout, unshaved, not overclean, with
> one conspicuous feature—shining eyes—walked in with a
> frayed notebook under his arm. He was miserably poor. He had
> run away from Kumakonam to get leisure in Madras to pursue
> his studies. He never craved any distinction. He wanted leisure;
> in other words, that simple food should be provided for him
> without exertion on his part and that he should be allowed to
> dream on.
>   He opened his book and began to explain some of his
> discoveries. I saw quite at once that there was something out of
> the way; but my knowledge did not permit me to judge whether
> he talked sense or nonsense. Suspending judgment, I asked him
> to come over again, and he did. And then he had gauged my
> ignorance and showed me some of the simpler results. These
> transcended existing books and I had no doubt that he was a
> remarkable man. . . .

Rao secured a job for the young mathematician, who published his first article at the age of twenty-three, in 1911. The
astonishing forward leaps of this unknown's thought eventually brought him to the attention of G. H. Hardy, a famous
mathematician of Cambridge. Along with his letter of introduction to Hardy, Ramanujan enclosed a few of his findings, of
which Hardy said:[28]

> A single look at them is enough to show that they could only be
> written down by a mathematician of the highest class. They
> must be true, because, if they were not true, no one would have
> had the imagination to invent them. Finally . . . the writer must
> be completely honest, because great mathematicians are com-
> moner than thieves or humbugs of such incredible skill. . . .

Hardy secured a scholarship, but Ramanujan's mother

refused to give her consent. Again, according to Newman's account, Hardy wrote of this episode:[29]

> This consent was at last got very easily in an unexpected manner. For one morning his mother announced that she had had a dream on the previous night, in which she saw her son seated in a big hall amidst a group of Europeans, and that the goddess Namagiri had commanded her not to stand in the way of her son fulfilling his life's purpose.

Ramanujan died in India in 1919, at the age of 33. Of his arrival and impact on the history of mathematical thought, Newman says:

> In areas that interested him, Ramanujan arrived in England abreast, and often ahead of, contemporary mathematical knowledge. Thus in a long, mighty sweep he had succeeded in re-creating in his field, through his own unaided powers, a rich half-century of European mathematics. One may doubt that so prodigious a feat had ever before been accomplished in the history of thought.

To those familiar with Wallas' paradigm, there is one especially interesting aspect of Ramanujan's powers, no matter what one is to make of his dream-revelations—the fact that he often took many hours, even months, to laboriously verify and prove what he often received in an instant, and that sometimes his original insight turned out to be wrong!

Where do these stories leave our beliefs about the boundaries and limits of the "hidden mind"? Even granting the unconscious idea processor the capacity to take as little information as is in an elementary school book on mathematics and eventually produce something as complex and elegant as Ramanujan's equations—even then the situation raises more questions than it answers. Ignoring any metaphysical explanations, or the "mind-is-the-whole-universe" explanation, the powers suggested here for the unconscious are staggering. Certainly, in this case at least, these powers are beyond the limits of most people's belief system and violate altogether our collective cultural beliefs about these limits. How can one program oneself to know more than one already knows? And if the hidden mind allowed to go off-line can do this—what *can't* it do?

ILLUMINATION: CASE EXAMPLES

The moment of illumination almost always comes as a suprise, without warning. It cannot be predicted or forced; it must arrive of its own accord when the unconscious has finally finished processing all the data. Then it simply springs into our consciousness and fills our attention.

Percy Blythe Shelley, the last of the great romantic poets, declared that:[30]

> Poetry is not like reasoning, a power to be exerted according to the determination of the will. A man cannot say: "I will write poetry." The greatest poet even cannot say it. It is not as though this material came passively floating towards them.

According to Keats, the description of Apollo in the third book of his epic poem, *Hyperion*, came to him "by chance or magic—to be, as it were, something given to me." Keats added that he had "not been aware of the beauty of some thought or expression until after I had composed and written it down." It then struck him with "astonishment" and seemed "rather the production of another person" than his own.[31]

The great Russian composer, Tchaikowsky, described this aspect of his breakthrough expriences vividly in one personal account:[32]

> Generally speaking, the germ of a future composition comes suddenly and unexpectedly.... It takes root with extraordinary force and rapidity, shoots up through the earth, puts forth branches and leaves, and finally blossoms. I cannot define the creative process in any way than by this simile.... I forget everything and behave like a mad man; everything within me starts pulsing and quivering; hardly have I begun the sketch, ere one thought follows another. In the midst of this magic process, it frequently happens that some external interruption awakes me from my somnambulistic state.... Dreadful indeed are such interruptions.... They break the thread of inspiration....

The sensation of ideas seeming to flow in an almost endless stream is the most commonly reported aspect of the break-through experience. Brahms told one biographer that when the inspirations for his most famous compositions came to him:[33]

> Straightaway the ideas flow in upon me, directly from God, and not only do I see distinct themes in my mind's eye, but they are clothed in the right forms, harmonies, and orchestration. Measure by measure the finished product is revealed to me when I am in those rare, inspired moods.

The German poet Goethe described the writing of his novel, *Werther*, in very similar terms, when he told one friend: "I wrote the book almost unconsciously, like a somnabulist, and was amazed when I realized what I had done." And the English poet William Blake said of his work, *Milton*, that "I have written this poem from immediate dictation, twelve or sometimes twenty or thirty lines at a time, without premeditation, and even against my will."[34]

In seventeenth-, eighteenth-, and nineteenth-century accounts, those interviewed inevitably spoke of this sensation as coming, in terms of the belief system of the period, from God or some divine source. For instance, Richard Strauss, the waltz king, said:[35]

> While the ideas were flowing in upon me—the entire musical, measure by measure, it seemed to me that I was dictated to by two wholly different Omnipotent Entities.... I was definitely conscious of being aided by more than an earthly Power, and it was responsive to my determined suggestions....

Puccini described the inspiration for his greatest opera in similar terms:[36]

> The music of this opera *(Madam Butterfly)* was dictated to me by God; I was merely instrumental in putting it on paper and communicating it to the public....

And Brahms remarked that:[37]

> When I feel the urge I begin by appealing directly to my Maker.... I immediately feel vibrations which thrill my whole being.... In this exalted state I see clearly what is obscure in my ordinary moods; then I feel capable of drawing inspiration from

above as Beethoven did. . . . Those vibrations assume the form
of distinct mental images.

Other accounts have put the same experience in terms of
more contemporary metaphors like the conscious and unconscious.

Brahms, for instance, noted that:[38]

I have to be in a semitrance condition to get such results—a
condition when the conscious mind is in temporary abeyance,
and the subconscious mind is in control. . . .

The English poet Shelley declared that "One after another the greatest writers, poets, and artists confirm the fact
that their work comes to them from beyond the threshold of
consciousness."[39]

Still others have described the moment of illumination as
striking them like a flash of lightning from out of the blue. A
century before Ramanujan, another mathematical prodigy was
born to poor parents, but this lad was born in Germany. Like
Ramanujan, Johann Friedrich Karl Gauss exhibited his remarkable talents very early in life: at the age of three, he interrupted
his father to tell him that the complicated sum he was writing
was incorrectly calculated. After teaching the lad no more than
the alphabet, his father watched him go off to teach himself to
read several different languages!

Like Descartes a century before him, Gauss mastered classical education while still a teenager. His biographers noted
that Gauss decided to specialize in mathematics the afternoon
he discovered how to construct a seventeen-sided polygon using only a compass and ruler—the solution came to him "in a
flash," as did his career decision.

Throughout his life, he claimed to be plagued by such a
constant and rich stream of ideas that he only had a small
fraction of time available in his life to pursue them. By the age
of twenty-one he was deeply involved in the most momentous
discovery in number theory since the time of Pythagoras—the
theory of complex numbers.

Stories abound of Gauss' ability to perform complex calculations seemingly instantaneously. There are significant differences in the kinds of creativity involved in lightning calcu-

lation and the equally instant apprehension of a new theory or
mathematical field. Gauss was known as a perfectionist who
would never dare to publicly announce an idea until he had
rigorously proved it. In a letter to a French scientific journal in
1886, referring to an arithmetic theorem, the proof of which he
had unsuccessfully pursued for years, Gauss wrote:[40]

> Finally, two days ago, I succeeded, not on account of my pain-
> ful efforts, but by the grace of God. Like a sudden flash of light-
> ning, the riddle happened to be solved. I myself cannot say
> what was the conducting thread which connected what I previ-
> ously knew with what made my success possible.

In light of others' reports, Gauss' use of the image of a
lightning bolt to describe this very special kind of insight is
also intriguing. Why does the lightning-bolt image seem to
crop up again and again in the reports of inspired individuals
and in the mythologies of nearly every culture?

Might we learn something about the psychological significance of this intuitive lightning by looking at the mytholog-
ical significance of the image?

Zeus' thunderbolts and the lightning on Sinai are the
most well-known lightning-image myths in the Western world.
In the opinion of one eminent student of myth, Joseph Campbell, the lightning bolt and the larger myth cycle of which it is
a part is a code for the process of unlocking the creative life
force:[41]

> The effect of the successful adventure of the hero is the unlock-
> ing and release again of the flow of life into the body of the
> world. The miracle of this flow may be represented in physical
> terms as a circulation of food substance, dynamically as a
> streaming of energy, or spiritually as a manifestation of grace.
> Such varieties of image alternate easily, representing three de-
> grees of condensation of the life force. An abundant harvest is
> the sign of God's grace; God's grace is the food of the soul; the
> lightning bolt is the harbinger of fertilizing rain, and at the same
> time the manifestation of the released energy of God. Grace,
> food substance, energy: these pour into the living world, and
> wherever they fail, life decomposes into death.

Or, as Puccini put it:[42]

The great secret of all creative geniuses is that they possess the power to appropriate the beauty, the wealth, the grandeur, and the sublimity within their own souls, which are a part of Omnipotence, and to communicate those riches to others.

VERIFICATION: CASE EXAMPLES

Not every breakthrough insight turns out to be valid or verifiable of course, although many do. In Ramanujan's case, later double-checking of his results often revealed that the instant intuitions were not necessarily true. The more normal consciousness involved with the verifying mode seemed to work more slowly, even for an extraordinarily rapid thinker like Ramanujan—but the verification mode was far more reliable in terms of producing valid results. His intellectual flexibility, the ease with which he altered his carefully built hypothetical structures, was another characteristic noted by those who worked with him.

The question of verification in something as subjective as music or literature appears to be very difficult, but objective evidence of a kind does exist. For Robert Louis Stevenson, the verification mode occurred when he contributed his own editing talents to polish the work presented to him by his "brownies." For composers, the melodies they heard in their inspired moments had to be transcribed and scored.

In an important sense, the participation of those who experience the art forms is a kind of verification. How could such intangible artifacts as symphonies or cantatas be so well-known and loved unless we all participate in the composer's world when we listen? The mystery of music, although "subjective" in the positivistic sense, can also be shared by independent observers across centuries. For how else does a series of invisible pressure fluctuations against our eardrums become an immortal aria?

RESEARCH ON THE PSYCHOLOGY OF CREATIVITY

What has scientific research revealed about the nature, limits, and origins of creativity? In some ways, less than we might hope. However, if we are willing to speculate, extrapolate, and correlate diverse research findings from several different fields, some startling ideas emerge.

Very little work was done on what Fredrick Myers termed "inspiration" until after World War II, when scientific inventiveness became an issue of wide concern. Since then, a good deal of research has been carried out on the nature, incidence, and cultivation of creativity. Again, it makes a difference what you call things: the word "inspiration" implies one thing, "innovation" another, and "creativity," another still.

The common-usage meaning of the word *creativity* implies novelty and innovation. Psychological experiments in the fields of motivation and learning have disclosed the power of novelty as an inducement to action. There appears to be an essential tension between the seeking of equilibrium (homeostasis, maintenance of stable conditions, security, and so forth) and the seeking of new possibilities of experience. Studies of highly creative people have brought out this tension typically in terms of such dualities as intellect and intuition, conventional and unconventional, conscious and unconscious, mental health and mental disorder, and complexity versus simplicity. According to creativity researcher Frank Barron:[43]

> The creative individual not only respects the irrational in himself, but courts the most promising source of novelty in his own thought.... The creative person is both more primitive and more cultured, more destructive and more constructive, crazier and saner, than the average person.

The ways scientists formulate and approach their research questions are much affected by explicit or implicit models of how the creative process takes place and what inherent limits are assumed. For example, if one assumes that the new product of the creative process is a consequence of hitherto isolated or disparate or incommensurate elements coming together, it seems reasonable enough to ask questions relating to a "mechanism" of creativity: What kinds of computer-programlike activities in the brain might account for the coming together of different elements and for the "signal" to be sent to consciousness that something new has been formed? These questions can be fruitful within the limits of that "mechanism" model but might not be appropriate ways to investigate less obviously mechanistic aspects of creativity.

A useful distinction has been made between "convergent" thinking, the analytical reasoning measured by intelligence tests that tends to use rationality to move toward a single goal, and "divergent" thinking, a richness of ideas and originality of thinking characterized by movement away from set patterns and goals. While both convergent and divergent thinking are involved in creative activity, it is the divergent thinking that especially characterizes that which is most widely recognized as creative.

Psychologist Roger N. Shepard contrasted the imagery-oriented and logical modes of human thought by comparing them to the differences between analog and digital processes in computers, and claimed: "I submit that there are both logical and analogical processes of thought, and that processes of the latter type, though often neglected in psychological research, may be comparable in importance to the former."[44]

A more contemporary account of the creative process, by Albert Rothenberg, summarized several of the most significant theories regarding the creative process:[45]

Mednick proposed that creative thinking was based on the combination of elements that were remotely associated with one another. As he put it, "The more mutually remote the elements of the new combination, the more creative the process or solution." The mechanisms he described for producing such combinations were the associational ones of serendipity (accidental contiguity of elements), similarity, and mediation....

Arthur Koestler's theory of bisociation refers not only to thought process but very broadly to any biological, psychological, or social phenomenon. Bisociation consists of the coming together of two self-consistent but habitually incompatible frames of reference. Koestler considers creation to be a matter of a single act rather than a process, and his theory, like Mednick's, is based on the principle of association of elements or entire frames of reference....

Lateral thinking, a term introduced by De Bono, refers to the capacity to shift the context of thought from ordinary or "vertical" progressions. This type of thinking is somewhat similar to tolerance for ambiguity in its shifting away from fixed, predefined concepts and it is also quite similar to the productive-thinking mechanism, the "breaking of old gestalts" or the shifting out of habitual formulations, ways of seeing, or contexts, proposed some time ago by Wertheimer. . . .

Even these definitions do not explicitly recognize the hallmark of creativity as we are using the term here, namely the central role of the unconscious mind.

THE LEARNING PROCESS: IMAGES AND ENHANCED INSIGHT

Two of the central questions that all this research fails to address are: Is creativity a learnable skill? And can anyone learn to perform those extraordinary feats we traditionally think of as limited to a few talented individuals? Questions such as these have triggered at least one research revolution, in the kind of laboratory work that has the highest scientific credibility. Those messages from the past, from Brahms and Einstein and Poincaré, were not lost on pioneer researchers in biofeedback and sleep research, for these contemporary investigators were after the same prey as their predecessors—the link between states of consciousness and the source of creativity.

Of course, the present culturally dominant view is that creativity is a talent, not a skill; however, until biofeedback came along, it was believed that nobody could learn to control their heart rate, brain waves, or blood pressure.

Elmer and Alyce Green of the Menninger Foundation, who have been studying the psychophysiology of consciousness and especially of creativity for nearly thirty years. They zeroed in on the reports of Poincaré and others and started to look at brain-wave correlations with hypnagogic or hypnapompic "twilight states" of consciousness. One important clue was the evidence from other investigators, in Japan and India, that certain adept meditators exhibited a slowing of the dominant alpha frequency (eight to twelve cycles per second) to a dominance of theta frequency (six to eight cycles per second). It was already known that the hypnagogic state, before the brain waves slow to delta (around four cycles per second), is the time when unusual creativity imagery tends to appear spontaneously. Somewhere in the theta realm, between sleeping and waking, they theorized, might be a psychophysiological gateway to creativity.

In reporting the findings of their earliest explorations of creativity training, the Greens' focused on the "reverie" reported by so many:[46]

> The "reverie" that accompanies the semiconscious production of theta waves and low-frequency alpha seems to be associated with and make possible, under certain conditions, the detection of hypnagogiclike imagery, the *sine qua non* of creativity for many outstanding people. In order to remain conscious and alert during theta production without long autogenic or yogalike training, it seems that it will be necessary for most people to make use of instrumental aids such as those, for example, which we are developing and testing.

If, as suspected, creative or imagistic modes of thought are somehow related to the brain state associated with theta rhythm, what light does it shed on the question of whether creativity is a trainable skill? According to the Greens:[47]

> It may be asked at this point, "What reason is there to believe, that just because low-frequency alpha and theta waves have been found to be associated in some people with reverie and hypnagogiclike imagery, the reverse will be true; that *training* a subject to achieve or produce theta waves or low-frequency alpha, a purely physiological accomplishment, will bring about a state of reverie in which hypnagogiclike images and other phenomena will appear?"...
>
> In answer to the preceding question it can be said that we do not attempt to train people in the production of low-frequency alpha and theta rhythms, but rather to train them in the voluntary control of certain existential states whose central-nervous-system correlates are revealed by the presence of low-frequency alpha and theta rhythms in the EEG record.... Brain waves, as such, are not known to have any sensory representation whatsoever by means of which they can be detected. What *are* detected and manipulated in some unknown way are foci of attention, thought processes, and subjective feelings. The *voluntary*-controls program in our laboratory is one of thought, emotion, and attention control. Brain-wave control, temperature changes, and striate muscle reduction in our work are thought

of primarily as physiological correlates of psychological processes. . . .

In less technical terms, the Greens' answer affirms that by using biofeedback, it is possible to train people to shift from the normal state of waking consciousness to what we have called the incubation and illumination states.

If it is true that we can learn to achieve the breakthroughs we need for help in our own problems—as the great composers, poets, and inventors appear to have done—how is this learning mediated? What ordinary skills do we possess that might, without the aid of biofeedback, be turned to the invocation of extraordinary insights?

The relationship between the ability to concentrate on visual images and the ability to invoke creative states is one of the latest frontiers in cognitive psychology and some forms of psychotherapy. The case of the inventor Nikola Tesla seems to substantiate the existence of such a relationship.

"Nikola Tesla" is hardly a household name. Yet if it weren't for Tesla's discoveries and inventions, the typical industrial-era household would scarcely be what it is today. If you were to remove all traces of Tesla's major contributions from your home, you would have to eliminate the electrical power grid that your wall socket taps into to feed your appliances. You would also have to eliminate many of the appliances, starting with your television and radio, as well as fluorescent and neon lighting.

Other items, not exactly of the household variety, but essential to scientific research, would also disappear: the molecular bombardment lamp that led to the electron microscope and atomic particle accelerators, research on cosmic rays and artificial radioactivity, and high-frequency electrical currents used in medicine and industry, radio-controlled vehicles, and weaponry.

Although Tesla died more than forty years ago, many of his discoveries—long thought too "fantastic" to be practical—are only now beginning to generate serious laboratory research: wireless power transmission, solar and oceanic power generators, the use of the earth itself as a transmission medium and source of energy, robotics, and (particularly germane to' our investigation) the use of trained visualization capacities in stimulating the inventing process.

Every schoolchild knows that Thomas Edison invented the light bulb, but it is a less-advertised fact that Edison was stubbornly committed to a direct-current power distribution system that would have required generating stations every few miles along the power grid. Tesla's invention of the first practical alternating-current dynamo and power transmission system made the electric age possible and made billions of dollars for manufacturers and financiers. His patented inventions made radio a practical idea, although Marconi is the inventor we all remember today. Although Tesla's early electrical research was funded by $1 million given to him by George Westinghouse, Tesla died broke and bitter.

While the story of this bizarre genius is fascinating in its own right, Tesla's value to this book is specifically due to the extraordinarily detailed and self-documented flashes of insight and deliberately cultivated visualization techniques that he used.

Tesla's unusual powers of visualization first showed up in his early years in the form of an affliction. The young Tesla was tormented by terrifying memories of such clarity that it was if he was witnessing two realities—the world around him, and, simultaneously, the detailed re-creation of a world from his past. For example, he might be sitting in a classroom or walking down a street when the scene of a funeral he had attended years earlier would jump up, unbidden, in his field of vision. This new vision, which he knew to be a memory, was perceptually no less authentic than the other, "real" scene he was also watching.

To free himself from these maddening apparitions, out of sheer defense of his sanity, Tesla set himself the task of gaining control of these episodes. Like Robert Louis Stevenson, he found that the self-administered psychotherapy he devised in order to soothe his terrifying visions could be refined into a precise tool for "dreaming up" his inventions.

At first, if an unpleasant visual memory presented itself, young Tesla tried to counter it with a memory of a more pleasing sight. But he found that he had to continually summon "fresh" images—because for some reason, after a while, the pleasant images lost their ability to stave off the less-pleasant ones. Since he was young and had seen little of the world, his store of pleasant counterimages was quickly exhausted. By the time he had run through his store of pleasant memories for the third time, they had completely lost their power to stave off the terrifying apparitions. In his own words:[48]

> Then I instinctively commenced to make excursions beyond the limits of the small world of which I had knowledge, and I saw new scenes. These were at first very blurred and indistinct, and would flit away when I tried to concentrate my attention upon them, but by and by I succeeded in fixing them; they gained in strength and distinctness and finally assumed the concreteness of real things. I soon discovered that my best comfort was attained if I simply went on in my vision farther and farther, getting new impressions all the time, and so I began to travel— of course, in my mind. Every night (and sometimes during the day), when alone, I would start on my journeys—see new places, cities, and countries—live there, meet people and make friendships and acquaintances and, however unbelievable, it is a fact that they were just as dear to me as those in actual life and not a bit less intense in their manifestations.

He continued to refine this ability until he was about seventeen, when he began seriously to think about inventing. He was delighted to discover that he was able to visualize possible inventions with great facility. He didn't need to make models or drawings or perform experiments—all he had to do was set his mind's eye to work. He began to evolve what he later considered to be a much more efficient approach to materializing inventions than the age-old process of trial and error, sketch and experiment.

Tesla took pains to note that he regarded his method to be just as "real," and very much more powerful, than any of the more analytic, less "subjective" tools of the inventor's trade. Over half a century before the invention of the computer, he discovered what modern programmers know as "modeling and simulation." He found that he was able to construct, modify, and even operate his hypothetical devices, purely by visualizing them:[49]

> It is absolutely immaterial to me whether I run my turbine in thought or test it in my shop. *I even note if it is out of balance.* There is no difference whatever, the results are the same. In this way I am able to rapidly develop and perfect a conception without touching anything. When I have gone so far as to embody in the invention every possible improvement I can think of and see no fault anywhere, I put into concrete form this final product of my brain. Invariably my device works as I conceived that it should, and the experiment comes out exactly as I planned it. In twenty years there has not been a single exception. . . .

When Tesla was a student, a fateful incident occurred one day in a classroom. A dynamo, of the sort then available, was imported and demonstrated for his class. The young inventor, who had by that time gained a high degree of mastery over his visualization powers and considered himself well-versed in electrical engineering, pointed out that a more efficient dynamo might be built on slightly different principles. His professor lectured the class on the impossibility of what young Telsa had proposed. Goaded by the challenge:[50]

> I started by first picturing in my mind a direct current machine, running and following the changing flow of the currents in the armature. Then I would imagine an alternator and investigate the processes taking place in a similar manner. Next I would visualize systems comprising motors and generators and operate them in various ways. The images I saw were to me perfectly real and tangible. All my remaining term . . . was passed in intense but fruitless efforts of this kind, and I almost came to the conclusion that the problem was unsolvable. . . .
>
> In attacking the problem again I almost regretted that the struggle was soon to end. I had so much energy to spare. When I undertook the task it was not with a resolve such as men often make. With me it was a sacred vow, a question of life and death. I knew that I would perish if I failed. Now I felt that the battle was won. Back in the deep recesses of the brain was the solution, but I could not yet give it outward expression.

Although he was anticipating a breakthrough, the solution came unexpectedly to the young inventor, when he and a friend were walking through a park, reciting poetry. Tesla, ever the careful observer of his own mental processes, even noted that the poem he was reciting just before the illumination occurred was Goethe's *Faust*. As the sun was setting, he was reminded of the passage:

> The glow retreats, done is the day of toil
> It yonder hastes, new fields of life exploring;
> Ah that no wing can lift me from the soil,
> Upon its track to follow, follow soaring! . . .
> A glorious dream! though now the glories fade.
> Alas! the wings that lift the mind no aid
> Of wings to lift the body can bequeath me."

He later wrote:[51]

As I uttered these inspiring words the idea came like a flash of lightning and in an instant the truth was revealed. I drew with a stick on the sand the diagrams shown six years later in my address before the American Institute of Electrical Engineers, and my companion understood them perfectly. The images I saw were wonderfully sharp and clear and had the solidity of metal and stone, so much so that I told him: "See my motor here; watch me reverse it." I cannot begin to describe my emotions. Pygmalion seeing his statue come to life could not have been more deeply moved. A thousand secrets of nature which I might have stumbled upon accidentally I would have given for that one which I had wrested from her against all odds and at the peril of my existence. . . . For a while I gave myself up entirely to the intense enjoyment of picturing machines and devising new forms. It was a mental state of happiness about as complete as I have ever known in life. Ideas came in an uninterrupted stream and the only difficulty I had was to hold them fast. The pieces of apparatus I conceived were to me absolutely real and tangible in every detail, even to the minutest marks and signs of wear. I delighted in imagining the motors constantly running, for in this way they presented to the mind's eye a more fascinating sight. When natural inclination develops into a passionate desire, one advances towards his goal in seven-league boots. In less than two months I evolved virtually all the types of motors and modifications of the system which are now identified with my name.

Creative solutions, generated in the out-of-conscious-awareness processes of the mind, often come into awareness in the form of images. Imagery, say contemporary cognitive psychologists, appears to be an integral part of the way our brains function.

Another significant clue to the role of imagery in creativity is Kekule's phrase "rendered more acute by repeated visions." Although others like Tesla were much more conscious of how to use, enhance, and apply this visualization skill to technical problems, Kekule was enough of a trained observer to note that some type of quasiconscious learning process was taking place over the years as his visions grew toward a coherent structural concept.

During more recent times, psychologists working in the areas of creativity, memory, and visualization have rediscovered the keys to this kind of mental training, and several disciplines and schools now exist that can assist almost anyone in gaining some degree of proficiency in learning to "see" images with the mind's eye, like Tesla and Kekule. In a similar fashion, scientists have discovered clues that allow almost anyone to gain access to a number of the phenomena or states that seem to be associated with or lead to deep creative breakthroughs.

Looking Where the Light Is

Inner Limits and Unconscious Beliefs

UNCONSCIOUS BELIEVING, CHOOSING, AND KNOWING

Why aren't there Beethovens, Gandhis, or Einsteins in everybody's family? If everyone possesses an inate capacity for breakthrough to higher kinds of creativity—what is it, exactly, that hides the key and holds most of us back from discovering how to use these talents?

Among the deep unconscious beliefs everybody holds are beliefs about human potentialities and limitations—one's own, and other people's. These limits tend to be confirmed by experience, not because they are true but because they are believed. In the familiar phenomena used in demonstrations of hypnosis, a hypnotized person told to perceive a "solid wall" where there is none can "perceive" the experience as so real that capillaries burst and the hand becomes physically bruised from "striking" the wall.

On the other hand, a different kind of suggestion may lead to the body being able to perform feats it could not otherwise do—form a rigid bridge between two chairs or lift a heavy object.

The currently acceptable models of human capacities, and people's beliefs about the limits of those capacities, as viewed by our society and "approved" by science, tend to be based on a number of implicit premises that have gone unchallenged until recently. Following are examples:

1. "Mind is a function of the physical components of the brain, and *only* a function of the brain. Scientific understanding of

human behavior ultimately can be framed in terms of physical processes in the brain."

2. "The only way people can acquire knowledge is, in the last analysis, through the physical senses."

3. "All qualitative properties are ultimately reducible to quantitative ones; in other words, color can be reduced to a relationship between wavelengths and events in the brain, hate and love and consciousness will one day be reduced to a chemical reaction of glandular secretions, etc. What we know as consciousness, or awareness of our thoughts and feelings, is really only a side effect of these physical and biochemical processes occurring in the brain."

4. "There is a clear distinction between the objective world, which is perceivable by anyone, and subjective experience, which is perceived by the individual alone in the privacy of his or her own mind."

5. "The concept of the 'free person' is a prescientific explanation for behavior. Behavior is determined by forces impinging upon individuals from the environment, in interaction with internal tensions characteristic of the human biological organism. From the standpoint of behavioral science, psychic freedom and free choice are mere illusions. 'Freedom' is behavior for which scientists have not yet found the cause."

6. The average person possesses little or no genius or talent, and their capacity for inspiration is limited intellectually to the extent of whatever IQ they were fortunate (or unfortunate) enough to be born with.

7. Belief in extraordinary psychic talents, such as ESP, out-of-body experiences, etc. are superstitious holdovers from a less sophisticated era, and do not exist at all except as hallucinations, delusion or wishful thinking.

Each of these statements seem reasonable enough and compatible with science at its best—yet the evidence that we are examining in this book will challenge all seven of these statements. Many of you may not even look upon these statements as "beliefs," but consider them to be "facts"—in the same way that several decades ago you might have argued that it was a "fact" and not a "belief" that something could not be both a wave and a particle at the same time.

History has shown, time and again, that popular opinion about human limits can change, and that human limits themselves can change drastically. In Europe, for thousands of years, there was no "fact" considered more well established than the innate inability of peasants to learn how to read. In the fifteenth century, the printing press was invented, and the literate population jumped from a miniscule elite to a significant portion of the general population. While in the time of Samuel Johnson the simple ability to perform sums in arithmetic was considered to be something of an esoteric art. Johnson's biographer, Boswell, noted how hard it was for Johnson, surely one of the most educated men of his era, to teach himself this arcane art.

Our lives and our behaviors are much more profoundly affected by the beliefs we hold unconsciously than by the beliefs we hold consciously. It is apparent that to reach the breakthrough state we must make a fundamental shift in consciously and unconsciously held beliefs we all hold about our own limitations. Moreover, it appears that there are ways in which unconscious beliefs can be deliberately reprogrammed. And *knowing* about the possibility of reshaping one's beliefs is the necessary prelude to *doing* so.

The influence of beliefs begins with perception, the main tool we have to judge external reality. Of all the stimuli that impinge on the sensory receptors of sight, hearing, touch, smell and taste, only a small portion ever reach our conscious experience awareness. Some "inner observer" or mechanism unconsciously selects which inputs should reach awareness and shunts the rest to some other part of the mind. This selection is influenced by people's expectations, particularly as they are conditioned by beliefs arising from previous experience or learning, and by what people *want or believe they need to perceive*—or need *not* to perceive.

The effect of beliefs and attitudes on visual perception even appears to extend to the pupil of the eye, which tends to dilate (and thus increase perception of light) when we are presented with something we want to see, and contract (thus decreasing visual input) when there is something before us we want not to see. Similar effects seem to hold for the other senses as well.

Our processes of interpretation—the ways we organize sensory experience and the methods we learn by which we assign meaning to what we perceive—are also influenced by beliefs. For example, in an otherwise darkened room, when an oversized playing card is displayed considerably further away than an undersized football, both are seen as normal-sized, with the playing card appearing closer and the football further away. In another well-known experiment, rapidly exposed playing cards with reversed color-suit combinations (black hearts, red spades) were often perceived as the subject would normally expect to see them (red hearts, black spades).[1]

One of the most often cited examples of seeing what we expect to see is the finding that poor children see coins as larger than do the children of wealthy parents. Hungry subjects see more food objects in vague pictures (so vague, in fact, that they are actually no more than smudges) than do well-fed subjects, etc.

One of the most powerful formers of beliefs is the surrounding culture. People who grow up in different cultures literally perceive the world in different ways. The 1898 Cambridge anthropological expedition to Torres Straits found that the natives were not fooled by optical illusions that uniformly deceived Europeans.[2] Malinowski observed that the Trobriand Islanders, who believed that all characteristics are inherited from the father, regularly failed to see resemblances of the child to the mother's side of the family.[3]

Extensive clinical and experimental research and anthropological observations have provided further support for the hypothesis that to some degree we only see what our culture tells us we can see, only know what our society tells us we can know.

The findings from studies of hypnosis are particularly startling. Through hypnotic suggestion we may see what no one else sees, or fail to see what everyone else can see clearly; we may experience limitations where there are none, or display extraordinary strength or mental facility. The implication is especially jarring when we recognize the similarity between the "state of suggestibility" characteristic of hypnosis and the power of the suggestions given by one's culture. We do not know the extent to which we are all hypnotized to perceive the particular version of reality that is communicated by our culture.

This cultural consensus changes over time, in both conscious and unconscious aspects, in a variety of ways. Some beliefs, close to the "surface," but nevertheless connected to our deeper feelings about ourselves, can be modified through the historical processes of science and education. In 1492, the educated majority "knew" that the Earth is both flat and the center of the universe. When sailors looked at the horizon back then, they saw a place where they might very well fall off the earth. A few people like Columbus suspected that this knowledge was not factual, but a matter of incorrect belief.

Even more deeply held and less consciously sensed beliefs about one's most basic identity as a human being, and sense of one's relationship to the rest of the universe, may be formed early in life and remain essentially unchanged throughout life; if they are altered, it is likely to be in the context of a life trauma of major proportions. "Enlightenment," "satori," "samadhi," "being born again," are among the many names people have given to those singular experiences powerful enough to reconfigure the deepest unconscious beliefs.

In fact, we not only believe unconsciously but we also choose unconsciously. One way we choose unconsciously is to protect ourselves by blocking from our awareness information or experience that contradicts our unconscious belief system (in what psychotherapists call "denial"—not seeing what's there) or that implies any need for change in those beliefs (what psychotherapists term "resistance"). According to this hypothesis, if we encounter knowledge that would change our personality (an essential belief system), the internal censor, operating deep in the unconscious, treats such knowledge as a threat and attempts to ignore it.

Psychologist Abraham Maslow pointed out that we are all ambivalent when it comes to knowing about ourselves; we want to know (consciously) and yet we also go to great lengths (unconsciously) to prevent ourselves from knowing. He identified this taboo against some kinds of inner knowledge as "the need to know and the fear of knowing." As Maslow has said, we fear to know the fearsome and unsavory aspects of ourselves (what Jung aptly named "the shadow"), but we fear even more to know "the godlike in ourselves."[4]

We are ambivalent about our desire to know ourselves. We will *resist* that knowledge which we most deeply desire. We think we want to see reality as it is, to see it truthfully. But the illusions we harbor are part of an unconsciously held belief system. Any attack on those illusions is perceived (unconsciously) as a threat. Thus, an effort to dispel illusion, although ultimately beneficial, may nevertheless generate resistance. We may truly desire to discover and actualize our highest capabilities. Yet to the extent that removing illusion is essential to that discovery, we will resist that which we truly desire. We may, in fact, resist it by using the msot convincing "scientific" arguments and concepts.

Part of the reason for this is that in our culture we have been systematically taught not to trust our own minds. The Darwinian theory of evolution was a product of the Victorian age, and even though our understanding of evolutionary process has become much more sophisticated since then, the idea still persists in our culture that there is only a "thin veneer of civilization" between our conscious, socialized, ego-minds and the seething subconscious memories of "nature red in tooth and claw" that lurk, barely controlled, as animal urges just beneath the surface.

Freud's concept of unconscious sexual and aggressive forces at odds with the rules of civilized life added sinister and emotionally laden connotations to the Victorian interpretation of evolution, as did tales of people who "went off the deep end" because of their foolhardy insistence on exploring the depths of their own minds. Better not to look in there, or if you must, be sure to have a psychiatrist present to watch after you, because what you find might drive you crazy. Of course, if one deeply believes that the unconscious realms are to be generally feared and distrusted, unpleasant experiences undoubtedly await one.

But surely there is something very strange if not almost insane about the idea that one can't trust one's own mind. We go to sleep every night, and part of us remembers how to breathe. Every time we take a step, we throw our leg into space and fall forward, trusting that our foot will land in just the right way to prevent us from pitching onto our face. Learning how to walk in the first place was one part learning how to master the movements and nine parts learning how to trust the self to do it.

When you think about it, many of the things we do in a normal day involve an enormous amount of trust in the capabilities of our minds. We put ourselves in control of a vehicle weighing thousands of pounds and navigate it through rush-hour traffic, all the while trusting our ability to perceive accurately and make split-second, life-or-death decisions.

This cultural predisposition toward mistrust of our unconscious minds (while relying on them at the same time) means that any serious attempt at self-revelation will arouse strong and subtle resistance. Even reading the relatively innocuous paragraphs above may arouse objections that one can recognize as resistance by the intensity of associated feeling: "People do 'go off the deep end'!" "Society would fall apart if we didn't rationally control our unconscious minds!" And so on.

THE TABOO AGAINST INNER KNOWING

Science is a method for gathering and validating knowledge, a method that has extraordinary credibility because of the technological marvels it has wrought. But science, in the sense it is used when we judge something to be "not scientific," is also an *ideology*—an *institutionalized belief system*—and like any other belief system, science tends to have its dogmas and its taboos. One of these taboos is very closely related to the kind of resistance toward knowing about ourselves that we exhibit as individuals.

The particular kind of cultural trance induced on inhabitants of the Western world in the twentieth century involves the disguised enshrinement within the institution of science of a long-standing and powerful taboo against inner knowledge of an unauthorized kind. Modern science developed in an *industrializing* society that put high value on those kinds of knowledge that would contribute to the generation of mechanical technologies. This emphasis led to a tendency to test all knowledge by its usefulness in predicting and controlling the natural world.

The question of whether this emphasis might have contributed to a hidden bias—that the scientific beliefs in *reductionism* (the idea that the best and only way to understand something is to reduce it to its parts) and *positivism* (the belief that only publicly measurable phenomena can be studied) have prevented serious study of some aspects of human consciousness that might be vital to everyone—ought not to be unaskable. Yet such questions, potentially valuable as they might be, have not been seriously pursued. In many instances, those who have attempted to do so were actively discouraged by the scientific orthodoxy.

Since we can easily observe that other cultures, past and present, have their hidden biases and blind spots—from societies that tolerate slavery or cannibalism, to those that worship cats or live in fear of eclipses—it is reasonable to assume that our culture probably has its own biases. But to anyone with years of scientific training, all through which the conviction was thoroughly drummed in that conventional science is our surest guide to truth, it can come as a shock to realize that science itself (or unreasoning belief in its unlimited power) might be seriously biased.

We have all chuckled over the story of the drunk who lost his house key in a dark alley and was caught looking for it under the corner streetlight "because the light is better here." Scientific research has been looking largely "where the light is better"—where the knowledge can be measured and quantified, where hypotheses can be tested with neatly controlled, repeatable experiments, where deterministic models and reductionistic explanations seem to fit comfortably. As it happens, many useful things have been learned under the light of science—but that doesn't mean that the world outside that circle of light may not offer much of value, once it is illuminated by an expanded concept of scientific inquiry.

The validity of science as a way of predicting and controlling many aspects of the universe is not to be denied. However, as we shall see later on, some of the most eminent scientists have begun to question whether other kinds of knowledge less amenable to the prediction-and-control criterion might be critically important at this time in history.

One of the more puzzling aspects of the history of science has been its relative neglect of the topic of human consciousness—especially the role of extraordinary states of consciousness in which creative breakthroughs often occur. It is surely not because the topic was unimportant; the study is quite evidently of central importance to any understanding of human consciousness, motivation, and well-being. But it has been an awkward subject to deal with.

Because of this extraordinary power to foster consensus, this "new method of thought," as some European reformers referred to it when it was first constructed, seemed to transcend all other ideologies. The positivistic bias became an unspoken code of conduct for researchers, indicating through the shared attitudes of a community what is "scientific" and what is "not scientific." In this sense, "scientific" became a euphemism for "proper."

Despite the universal consensus about scientific knowledge of the external world, no such agreement has been reached about how to go about publicly validating knowledge of private experience, in particular, the experience of the deep intuition. Indeed, there is no obvious agreement about the content of such knowledge, or its use to individuals or societies, if the knowledge happens to be outside the image of human nature and capacities that is maintained within industrial cultures. Strangely, this lack of agreement among scientists differs sharply from the apparent recent convergence of views held by various spiritual traditions around the world, regarding the same subject.

The historical circumstance was such that positivism gained its power before psychology and anthropology were developed, and before the influence of unconscious beliefs was scientifically validated. The implications that recent anthropological and psychological findings about beliefs and belief systems contain, regarding the very nature of the scientific enterprise, were not immediately and enthusiastically recognized, even in a community committed to objectivity and the discovery of truth, for much the same reasons that individuals resist self-knowledge that threatens their delusions.

The problem in dealing with such matters of the mind and the soul in such a system is the difficulty in looking objectively at any minds or souls other than one's own. These difficulties include the problem of how to treat self-reports of subjective experience; the problem of the relative non-replicability of consciousness-related phenomena; the problem of observer influence; the problem of data reliability with sentient subjects who are capable of conscious and unconscious choice deception; the problem of individual uniqueness; the question of the place of purpose and meaning; and the question of the appropriate basis for public validation of that knowledge. The first scientists quite justifiably started by looking at those aspects of nature that all observers could easily agree upon.

Even before the solidification of the scientific method in the eighteenth century and its marriage to industrial technology in the nineteenth century, a worldwide consensus developed on how the positivistic kind of knowledge should be openly sought and validated. Thus, in the physical and biolog ical sciences a coherent body of scientific knowledge developed, with near global agreement about its contents. Because of this agreement, we need not speak of an American biology or a German mathematics, a socialist physics or a capitalist astronomy.

When science was young, important psychological and cultural factors were combined in keeping the mysteries of human consciousness outside its boundaries. Part of it was rooted in a desire to keep the scientific mode of inquiry clearly distinct from the religious dogmatism of the past. During its emergence in 17th century Europe, science encountered fierce religious opposition, and the authority of the church was preeminent. As a result, an almost territorial consensus developed, whereby science would concern itself with the body and the physical world, and the church would concern itself with the soul and the psyche.

But at the heart of the scientific hesitation to encompass "subjective" or "metaphysical" knowledge can be found not a methodological difficulty or a scientific theory or a body of experimental findings, but a philosophical attitude known as *positivism*, first articulated over a century ago. This assumption places valid knowledge about reality exclusively in the realm of direct, externally oriented, ("positive") sensory experience. This unspoken, by now partly unconscious belief at the center of the scientific system holds that *only* this kind of experience is verifiable, and hence is the only proper base for valid ("scientific") knowledge.

The scientific method is of course not in any sense "wrong." Its present form is simply not very suitable for probing some of the secrets of the human mind, despite our widespread belief that the relentless progress of science is marching toward solving all the mysteries of human nature. The problem for those who have tried to study some of these mysteries has been the unspoken, but widely implicit *denial* of the usefulness of looking outside the illuminated circle of measurable, repeatable, predictable, controllable data.

Since our readers, like ourselves, were raised within a society that deeply cherishes the scientific tradition, many of you will undoubtedly experience difficulty in accepting the suggestion that science as it exists today might be perpetuating a limiting and damaging cultural bias. We are not insisting that the bias be seen. Rather, we are raising the question: "How do we know the bias is *not* present?" As the famous neurophysiologist Warren McCulloch was known to say: "Don't bite my finger. Look where I'm pointing."

Since the scientific method depends on logic, on the mathematical accumulation of facts, and because this is how we have been taught to judge the reality of an assertion, you would expect that the origin of the scientific method itself would be the result of just such a rigorous compilation of cool, dry, reason.

But strangely, there is a good case to be made for the proposition that the scientific method was, to a significant degree, the result not of logic, but of a fever dream, an experience of exactly the sort that our cultural and scientific bias has taught us to shun. One of our reasons for recounting this dream is to raise the question of what it might imply if this is true.

THE MAN WHO DREAMED UP SCIENCE

It is rare indeed for historians to pinpoint a great cultural turning point to a specific date and locale, and rarer still for them to agree about the meaning of philosophical discoveries. But modern historians concur that over three and a half centuries ago, in a day of thinking and a night of dreaming, a twenty-three-year-old soldier-philosopher succeeded in reforming the entire structure of Western knowledge by setting down the foundations of a new philosophy, science, mathematics—and a new way of thinking about the world.

In 1619, in a form revealed by his visions and shaped by his labors, René Descartes set down four rules for applying his new method for finding truth:

1. Never to accept anything for true which I do not clearly know to be such.

2. Divide each of the difficulties under examination into as many parts as possible.

3. Begin with the simplest and easiest and then work step by step to the more complex.

4. Make enumerations so complete and reviews so general that I might be assured that nothing is omitted.

These rules and the entire *Discourse on Method* constituted a one-man watershed in the history of thought. Together with the thoughts and writings of other men in other countries at about the same time—Copernicus, Galileo, Francis Bacon among them—Descartes created the foundation of modern rationalism. The impact of Descartes' work on the world of his time was summarized by Jane Muir in *Of Men and Numbers* (Dodd Mead, 1966, p.47):

Truth lay just around the corner like a veiled statue waiting for men to uncover it. The causes and effects of everything from comets to heart palpitations could be made known, and, in Descartes' words, men would soon be "the lords and possessors of nature."

This was the epic scale on which Descartes dreamed. He had discovered a wonderful new method for discerning the truth—a method totally different from the ones men had been using. It was to apply the method of mathematics to every area of life. By using logic, step by step, all the secrets of nature could be laid bare. And with knowledge would come control.

Today, three hundred years later, when men can cause rain to fall, plants to grow, or fatal diseases to disappear, the idea of mastering nature or of understanding the universe— from the molecule to the moon—does not seem so new and wonderful. But three hundred years ago, the idea that man might actually control nature was either unimaginable or sacreligious or both. It was arrogating God's power. Yet Descartes, with a handful of other men—Francis Bacon being the most famous—dared to think along this truly original line. And slowly, bit by bit, man *has* made himself lord and possessor of nature.

Descartes was one of those rare cases where an entire civilization adopted a new way of seeing the world at the instigation of one person. Others added important refinements to his "method"—but the very idea of applying a single, agreed-upon method to the quest for truth was revolutionary. Others took up the task of reforming the knowledge system of the day, turning attention away from logics and theologies and toward direct observations of nature. The grand unification of the sciences he predicted was fulfilled beyond the original seer's wildest dreams—and as we shall see, he went in for some wild dreams.

The success of this method, especially when it was turned to the ends Francis Bacon urged—the control of nature, the "wresting of her secrets" through the disciplined use of human minds—became the ideological framework for science, and led to the marvelously effective technology used to build the world that grew up around science. Taken together, the method, the reformation, the unification, and the practical goal constitute what has been called "the Cartesian worldview." In many ways, the actions of the people who adopted this world-view constructed the world we live in today.

Now that the problems of Western industrial society have become more evident, and the unpleasant, possibly fatal side-effects of controlling nature by an uncontrolled science are becoming more widely known, the old concept of "man conquering nature" has come under fire from some critics. A few have gone to the extreme of denouncing scientific, analytic, "Cartesian" thought as the primary cause of global problems. An inward but by no means falsely modest person, Descartes himself would have been most amused to learn that people would be debating the impact of his ideas three and a half centuries in the future.

René Descartes was born to a noble French family in 1596, and at the age of ten commenced his studies of what was then the totality of Western knowledge—logic, ethics, metaphysics, literature, history, science, and mathematics. Since there had been few experimental scientists to speak about since the fall of Rome, a great deal of this education had to do with memorizing what the Greeks and Romans had to say. Descartes wasn't entirely convinced that this was all there was to learn about the world. In fact, at the age of eighteen, he declared that the whole educational scheme was a farce, since the only certainty he had attained in eight years of schooling was a knowledge of his own ignorance, and of the limitations of the known systems of gathering and validating knowledge.

At that time, if a young French gentleman didn't study the classics, he studied law, so Descartes studied law for two years in Poitiers. As soon as he attained his degree, he declared law to be as intellectually bankrupt as the rest of Western knowledge, and set off for Paris, where he met notable success—as a gambler.

Anyone who twice rejects the fruits of years of education, declaring them inadequate to satisfy his need for knowledge, is a person who thinks highly of his own intellectual abilities. Eventually, it dawned on Descartes that if nobody else was going to think about making a little progress beyond what Aristotle knew about things, it would have to be him.

Renouncing his decadent social life as abruptly as he had

renounced his earlier schooling, Descartes retired, at the age of twenty, to explore the limits of knowledge on his own. He literally disappeared from sight, leaving no forwarding address. His methodology, from the beginning, was unorthodox, and would have outraged many modern proponents of the scientific method: It had long been his habit to linger half the day in bed, thinking—an indulgence he continued through much of his life. Indeed, it has been said that Descartes later invented analytic geometry while watching a fly crawl on the ceiling.

After two years of this reclusive regimen, an old friend succeeded in tracking down the reclining gentleman-philosopher, and persuaded him to return to normal society, albeit briefly. The other young aristocrats of his circle were hardly likely to appreciate the progress he felt he was making in his thought-project. There was an amazing lack of system to what his teachers had tried to pass off as knowledge, he had been thinking. There were many explorations of the unknown recorded in the books he read, and many little bits of knowledge scattered sparsely through those books. But there was no method for gathering and making sense of it all.

As was the custom for young gentlemen of his age and class, Descartes volunteered for the army of the Prince of Nassau (confessing to a friend that he was hardly aware of what side he was expected to fight on, and who he was expected to fight) and was eventually ordered to Germany, where the Thirty Years' War was underway. Although his external circumstances had changed abruptly, his intellectual journey continued to carry him further into unknown territory.

At that point in his life, Descartes was making monumental breakthroughs in mathematics, and steady progress but no real breakthroughs in his search for a new method of finding knowledge. Military service, apparently, was no cause for suspending his intellectual endeavors. Quartered in the town of Ulm for the winter, awaiting the resumption of hostilities in the Spring, Descartes moved toward his moment of noetic thunder.

The night of November 10, 1619, found Descartes in an overheated room, virtually feverish with "enthusiasm" about the intellectual adventure upon which he had embarked. Descartes wrote much of his journal in Latin (and it is worth remarking that the meaning of en theos—the root of enthusiasm—is "God within"). That night he dreamed three dreams, sleep images of such staggering import that he took care to write out detailed descriptions.

To the modern reader, the contents of the dreams may appear to be relatively mundane, but Descartes was convinced that these enigmatic images held the key to his quest for a new kind of knowledge.

In the first dream episode, he experienced strong winds blowing him away from a church building toward a group of people who didn't appear to be affected by the gale. After this image, Descartes awoke and prayed for protection against the bad effects of the dream. Falling asleep again, he was then filled with terror by a burst of noise like a bolt of lightning, and dreaming that he was awake, saw a shower of sparks fill his room. In the third and final dream of the series, Descartes saw himself holding a dictionary and some papers, one of which contained a poem beginning with the words "What path shall I follow in life?" An unknown man handed him a fragment of verse—the words "Est et Non" caught the dreamer's mind's eye.

At the end of the third dream came an even more extraordinary state of consciousness—a dream within a dream. Descartes dreamed he awoke to the fact that the shower of sparks in his room was in reality a dream, and then he dreamed that he interpreted the previous dream!

In the dreamed interpretation, Descartes explained to himself that the dictionary represented the future unity of science—"all the various sciences grouped together"; the sheaf of poems symbolized the linkage of philosophy and wisdom; "Est et Non" signified "Truth and Falsity in human attainment and in secular sciences."

In his journals, Descartes revealed that he took the overall meaning of the dreams to be that he was the person destined to reform knowledge and unify the sciences, that the search for truth should be his career, and that his thoughts of the previous months—about knowledge and methods and a unifying system—were to become the foundation of a new method for finding the truth.

Rene Descartes' diary entry for that day has since become famous. It confidently proclaimed that he had constructed a universally applicable tool for finding truth, and had answered his dissatisfaction with the previous history of Western thought by building the foundations of "an admirable science" which could proceed beyond the boundaries of existing methods of inquiry.

"I begin to understand the foundations of a wonderful discovery . . . all the sciences are interconnected as by a chain; no one of them can be completely grasped without taking in the whole encyclopedia at once," he wrote, turning from his dream directly to the beginning of the work that has come to us as *The Discourse on Method*, but which was originally titled: "Project of a Universal Science Destined to Raise Our Nature to Its Highest Degree of Perfection."

If that brilliant young aristocrat had not dreamed those three curious dreams of November 10, 1619, the course of science and Western civilization would have been significantly different. But on that winter evening in Germany, during a lull between battles in a particularly vicious war, the inner and outer spheres of knowledge met for a moment in the mind of a particular human being. A surprisingly large portion of the world we inhabit at this moment stems from that moment.

The dream of Descartes is an important episode in the secret history of inspiration, for it represents a milestone in the institutionalization of the taboo against inner knowing—and, ironically, also represents a prime example of the potential power of the same inner knowledge. Although the ideas that manifested in that moment appear to have been apprehended in an altered state of consciousness, and involved non-rational means of "knowing," a direct consequence of the revelation was the growth of rational, reductionist, positivist science—the same institution that later questioned the validity of "subjective knowledge."

There has been no argument, even from the most conservative historians, about the fact that Descartes' dreams did occur on the same day as his epochal journal entries. His own account attributes the inspiration for his "admirable science" to these dreams. In fact, Descartes stated that the dream was the most decisive event in his life, and proclaimed his intention to make a pilgrimage from Venice to Lorette as an act of thanksgiving for this supernatural guidance.

Upon reflection, it is odd that the dream-origins of modern thought are but a footnote to history. While Descartes' more useful ideas were adopted wholeheartedly, the reaction to their source was savagely negative. Descartes himself noted the deep importance of his dream images as well as his calculations and logical operations as tools for constructing the method. But few of his contemporaries would accept the anomaly of the dream-knowledge.

When Baillet's *Life of M. Descartes* was first published, August Comte (the originator of the philosophy of positivism) referred to that fateful night as a "cerebral episode." Christian Huygens, a towering scientific figure of the day, at the urging of the equally monumental Gottfried Leibniz, wrote: "The passage in which he relates how his brain was overstimulated and in a fit state for visions, and his vow to Our Lady of Lorette, shows great weakness. . . ." Baillet himself tried to reduce the embarrassing illumination to a case of nervous exhaustion: "He tired himself to such an extent that his brain became overheated and he fell into a kind of rapture which so worked upon his already exhausted spirit that it became predisposed to the reception of dreams and visions."

Suffice it to note that Descartes engaged in a long, intense period of preparatory thought before his night of revelation, that the insights came in a series of images, one of which was the image of a bolt of lightning, and the message not only addressed broad, abstract topics like the search for truth, but directly addressed the question of what the dreamer should do with his life.

One reason we have dwelt on this tale is to draw attention to the non-rational moments at the very foundations of science. But the fact that the new method of thought Descartes dreamed up evolved into a belief system known as contemporary science is also important to our discussion. Science is not a static edifice, built out of facts piled up like so many bricks, but is in fact a *way of looking at the world*, a perspective that *changes* from time to time. This fact was not a popular thought in science until very recently.

The psychological aspects of the process of science only became a subject of critical inquiry after Thomas Kuhn's 1962 publication of *The Structure of Scientific Revolutions*. In that book, Kuhn challenged the then-dominant view that scientific progress is a simple cumulative process. He did this by introducing the notion of "paradigm." In the sense that Kuhn meant it, paradigms are the systems of common assumptions that scientists (and others) share about the meaning of problems they consider. To a scientist, or a citizen of a society, a "dominant paradigm" might not even be consciously articulated, but it is nonetheless a basic way of perceiving, thinking, valuing, and doing, associated with a particular vision of reality.

A dominant paradigm is seldom if ever stated explicitly; it exists as an unquestioned, tacit understanding that is transmitted through the culture and to succeeding generations through direct experience (rather than being "taught"). A paradigm cannot be defined precisely in a few well-chosen sentences. In fact, it is not something to be expressed verbally at all. It is what the anthropologist hopes to understand after he or she has lived in a foreign culture for a long time—what the natives in a society perceive with their eyes and value with their feelings. A dominant paradigm encompasses more than an ideology or a world view but less than a total culture.

Other social scientists and historians such as Lewis Mumford, Arnold Toynbee, and Fred Polak, whose ideas will be discussed in other chapters, have pointed out the ways in which civilization-wide paradigms sometimes undergo rapid, violent transformations. The breakdown of the indusrial-era paradigm and its replacement by another would be accompanied by drastic changes in our society's operative values and institutions. More profoundly, it would involve a change in the basic perception of reality.

We recall our definition of the social paradigm as "the basic way of perceiving, thinking, valuing, and doing, associated with a particular vision of reality." It is change in that vision of reality that is the hallmark of the historically rare fundamental transformations of civilizations.

We have noted a close relationship between three kinds of paradigm-shifts that appear to be in the process of occurring: First, there is a change of paradigm in the sciences involved with the study of human nature, a shift to a way of seeing the world that no longer excludes those profound experiences that are difficult to quantify but which seem to be the source of our most deeply held values. Second is the paradigm shift within individuals—the breakthrough experience—that often precedes and accompanies the attainment of higher knowledge and capabilities. Last is the most important transformation, the system-wide transformation of our society, which we think is closely related to the other two varieties of paradigm-shift.

(4)

Opening the Mind's Gate

A Tool Kit for Personal Breakthrough

PERSONAL BREAKTHROUGH AND SOCIAL TRANSFORMATION

Once we push the gate of the mind slightly ajar and let the light stream in, the meaning of life becomes silently revealed to us. The gate may be open, for one minute or for one hour, but in that period we discover the secret and neither weary time nor bitter woe can tear that priceless knowledge away from us. . . .

Those of us who have taken this peep through the door of our own being, are dumbfounded. We draw back, surprised, at the inscrutable possibilities of the Overself. Man as a spiritual being possesses a capacity for wisdom which is infinite, a resource of happiness which is startling. . . .

PAUL BRUNTON, *The Secret Path*

Stories of inspirations and breakthroughs are fascinating in their own right, while the sheer weight of evidence (only a fraction of which has been cited here) demonstrates that over and over again fortunate individuals have indeed found the gateway leading to the vast creative resources of the breakthrough state.

Earlier chapters have suggested reasons why most people are not ordinarily aware of their potential—the social taboo against inner knowledge, the individual need to know and the fear of knowing, the bias in our scientific and social systems against examining those possibilities, and so forth.

But the building or assembling of a tool kit for personal breakthrough is possible. From relaxation and imagery to dreamwork, inner dialogue, and affirmation, a broad assortment of learning tools and reprogramming techniques are available for our use. These tools have been known to the Western world, although largely ignored, for centuries. The increasing scientific validation of many of these techniques, and the growing interest in them of the public, have helped to make resources accessible to those who want to undertake the inner journey.

Although in some cases they predate Wallas' paradigm by thousands of years, the tools we are about to discuss seem almost to have been designed with it in mind, suggesting that a sophisticated level of creativity research existed at times so remote that the idea challenges the limits of our belief systems. Even casual examination of the literature—from the yoga sutras of Patanjali to the mystical texts of esoteric Christianity, Judaism, Buddhism, and Islam—makes it clear that the tool kit is not exclusively an invention of the modern age.

The first tool in our kit, guided imagination or *imagery*, is a way of understanding and employing the language of the unconscious mind so that we can both reprogram it for more effective living and can better understand its "output" when the moment of illumination comes.

The second, and closely related tool, *affirmation*, is a way of reprogramming the unconscious idea-and-image processor through mental and vocal repetition of the ideas or images which we want our minds to accept as "input."

The third tool, *alert relaxation*, is designed to induce what has been called in medical science the relaxation response. This facilitates the "incubation mode"—through taking the mind "off-line" and quieting down surface thoughts that might disturb the workings of the deep unconscious—and helps promote the "output" mode.

The fourth tool, *dreamwork*, takes us directly into the heart of the idea processor, the deep unconscious, and shows us how to mine and bring back the nuggets of wisdom we find there.

Oddly enough, these tools are as simple as they are effective. None of them requires any great effort or special discipline or long and arduous practice. It is almost as though our unconscious is trying to make access as easy for us as possible while our normal difficulty in reaching it only results from psychological resistance and the limitations of our collective beliefs.

Used alone or in combination, these tools have been the key or prelude to achieving breakthrough for countless numbers of people across the centuries. There is no reason they cannot be yours.

EDUCATING THE MIND'S EYE: VISUALIZATION AND IMAGERY

The abilities that we have in the way of memory and imagination, of symbolism and emblem, are all conditioned by the sense of sight. It is sight which dominates this kind of sequence, how we think of things that appear in the mind. And I come back to saying "visual," "vision," and "visionary,"; "image," "imagery," "imagination." ... We cannot separate the special importance of the visual apparatus of man from his unique ability to imagine, to make plans, and to do all the other things which are generally included in the catchall phrase "free will." What we really mean by free will, of course, is the visualizing of alternatives and making a choice between them. In my view ... the central problem of human consciousness depends on the ability to imagine.

JACOB BRONOWSKI, "The Mind As an Instrument for Understanding,"
The Origins of Knowledge and Imagination

Imagery offers us a direct clue to the nature of the creative process. It is no coincidence that our culture equates creativity with imagination. The ability to imagine, to conjure up images or visions of things different than our ordinary reality, has always been recognized as the hallmark of the innovative mind. And if we learn how better to imagine or see images, we have taken the major step toward becoming more creative.

The image is also a way of knowing about the world that is older and more global than language and verbal symbolism. The oldest cave paintings are thought to date from the very period when *Homo sapiens* began to emerge as a distinct species. Examination of the fossil record indicates that long before the anatomical apparatus for spoken language evolved, the organs of vision were already highly developed, and visual communication was an important tool of the evolving human species.

Gestures and postures conveyed such messages as peaceful intent, transactions and trade, hunger, personal desires, and so forth. Perhaps because it was our first and oldest way of describing the world to ourselves and others, there is still great power in the image.

Because vision is the dominant means of perception in our species, and because a relatively large portion of the brain seems to be devoted to this sense, cognitive scientists are very interested in the way vision appears to influence the way the brain structures perceptions—even when those perceptions come from within the psyche instead of the outside world. Just as the "eye of the flesh" appears to structure perceptions inferentially, it seems that the "mind's eye" also imposes a kind of structure on the information generated from within the brain.

When Bronowski wrote that the eye "interprets the world by a process of inference," he was referring to the findings regarding the way our visual system makes decisions about what we are seeing—decisions that we normally think of as the province of our conscious choice.[1] Back when our ancestors were swinging from limb to limb in the primeval forest, vital decisions about what to avoid and what to grab next had to be made very quickly—too quickly for the eye to absorb an object's distinguishing characteristics and relay a decision back to the hands and body in time to take the correct action. Survival demanded the evolution of a brain mechanism for instantly identifying the most common objects—branches, limbs, leaves, trunk, other monkeys—from their grosser characteristics.

For example, it may not be surprising to learn that the sensory detectors in the eye are arranged in such a way that edges and boundaries (by which we can distinguish limb from sky or a background of leaves) are detected automatically, without extensive mediation by the higher faculties of the nervous system. This tendency of the eye to detect boundaries is the reason why certain optical illusions can fool almost everybody.

The important point about these aspects of vision, for our purposes, is that our attention and other characteristics of our consciousness are structured, largely unconsciously, by our visual apparatus. This is not to say that all visual processing, or even most of it, occurs before visual stimuli are transmitted to the brain.

But just as the eye makes inferences about objects and what they are merely from shape or outline, so the brain, without ever bothering to examine the "distinguishing characteristics" very closely to see if they match or not, tends to perceive ideas, concepts, and feelings as being related if their general shapes and outlines seem to be similar.

Since the mind also operates by the process of inference, the mere creation of a mental image, similar to the real object, will cause it to react as if faced by the actuality. As Dr. Roger N. Shepard wrote in a recent issue of the *American Psychologist*:[2] "Mental imagery is remarkably able to substitute for actual perception: Subjects make the same judgments about objects in their absence as in their presence. . . ."

His experiments and those of his colleagues show that the image of an imagined object has mental effects that are in some ways very similar to the image of an object that is actually perceived. This phenomenon might furnish at least part of the explanation for the effectiveness of active imagery and affirmation, because if one is able to imagine something to be true, part of the mind appears to accept that imagined outcome as reality.

Imagery is the language of the unconscious, and the power of the unconscious is most directly evoked by the deliberate practice of imagery and visualization skills.

This communication channel works both ways: If images are the messengers dispatched from the deeper mind to carry inspirations to surface awareness, then images are also the form in which messages can be transmitted from the conscious mind to deeper parts of the unconscious. Imagery, it seems, is the "language" of our unconscious idea processor.

The power of imagery in carrying messages results in its being one of the most effective tools in the tool kit for personal breakthrough.

Jung was not the only early psychotherapist to look beyond pathology and consider the kind of growth that could continue after "health" has been achieved. By 1911, the Italian psychoanalyst Roberto Assagioli was already working under the hypothesis that the inner resources and the guidance necessary to achieve wholeness were naturally present in the pscyhe. *Psychosynthesis* is the name Assagioli gave his system for contacting and assisting the natural inner processes from which guidance can be found.

Psychosynthesis is still alive and well as an international psychotherapeutic movement, and it still is basically defined as a means of cooperating with the natural tendency people have to harmonize their various aspects at ever-higher levels of personal development. Psychosynthesis combines such techniques as guided imagery, waking dialogue, meditation, artwork, journal-keeping, movement, and other methods in order to contact the transpersonal aspects of the greater self.

Psychosynthesis makes particularly effective use of mental imagery as a tool for using the imagination, under the direction of the intellect and the will, to explore unconscious aspects of the personality. The connection between conscious, rational faculties, and deeper, unconscious, aspects is deliberately maintained in order to teach the skill of "shifting gears" between these states. In this way, the gap between the different parts of consciousness can be bridged.

In the journal *Synthesis*, Martha Crampton, the Director of the Canadian Institute of Psychosynthesis, recently described a simple technique for using imagery to create dialogue with the unconscious:[3]

> Mental imagery techniques can play a valuable, integrative role by bridging the conscious and unconscious as well as the rational and effective dimensions of our personality.
>
> There is a broad range of techniques available. Some are best used with an experienced person who can serve as a guide, while others can be employed effectively with or without such

help. Among the latter, one technique with many varied applications is the method known as "answers from the unconscious." This method is generally used to acquire information, obtain guidance and gain better understanding of our inner processes. The basic idea is to *formulate a question*, addressing it to one's unconscious, and *allowing the answer to emerge in the form of a mental image*. Such an answer will emerge spontaneously, in most cases with surprising facility. It is important not to reject images that may seem irrelevant. Usually, given sufficient attention, their significance will become clear. And if a sequence of unrelated images emerges, often the very first one turns out to be the most meaningful.

For those who find it easy to see images in their mind's eye, such a technique may offer a direct and immediate answer to the question of where to find guidance through one's inner explorations. For those for whom visualization is not something that comes readily, the following exercise, repeated over a period of time, will strengthen the mind's ability to see images—to literally imagine and to strengthen their imagination.

The scenario presented below is an example of the kind of imagery that is helpful in the early stages of visualization training. The purpose of this particular image-journey is to open the mind's gate to the flow of images, and to start awakening the skill of summoning helpful images. It is meant to be a guide and model, not a strict prescription. As you become accomplished in visualizing, and as you learn more from some of the sources cited here, you will undoubtedly want to experiment with your own forms of "insight engineering." Perhaps your own inner messengers will suggest ways to change and expand these imagery calisthenics.

At first you should have a friend read this sequence to you, or you should record it yourself on a tape recorder. It often helps to play your favorite, most soothing (instrumental, not vocal) music very quietly in the background. Later, when you have committed the chain of images to memory, you can dispense with external aids and simply journey from image to image on the basis of your memory. To begin, simply relax and close your eyes; then:

Imagine yourself reclining on a bed of soft, fragrant moss,

on a gentle slope beneath a large tree, on a hillside overlooking the ocean. The sky is clear. The ocean is calm. The air is skin temperature. With each breath, your lungs fill with fresh, clean, air that is at the same time soothing and revitalizing. Don't count or change your breaths, but pay attention to them as they become deeper and more relaxed. Although your "eye of flesh" is closed to the external world, your mind's eye is awake and alert. With each breath, you feel lighter, and the interior landscape comes into sharper focus.

You take a particularly deep breath and discover that you are floating effortlessly above the ground. You float around the tree and see what was behind you, opposite the seascape. Gently rolling green hills stretch out to the blue horizon. In the distance, a single snowcapped mountain peak beckons.

As you start to gently float toward the distant peak, you notice a path across the foothills, aimed directly at the mountain. As you move faster, the mountain grows nearer. You can discern the rocky crags and cliffs as you float closer. All your senses seem to sharpen, and a feeling of well-being and pleasant anticipation grows within you as the mountain looms ahead. What new discoveries does it hold for you?

As you move faster and faster, the mountain grows still nearer. You are still perfectly relaxed, still floating, but now you are ascending higher and higher with every breath. There is no physical or mental effort involved in your ascent, but you notice that the path and the plain and the tree are far, far, below and behind you as the foothills rise into the base of the mountain and the path climbs up the mountain toward the peak.

At the top of the mountain, the green countryside rolls and the shining sea ripples into the distance. The sky is deep blue above you. You look over the top of the peak and discover that you are atop an extinct volcano. In the crater is the clearest lake you have ever seen. So clear is the lake, in fact, that you don't notice it until you notice the small, wooded island in the center of the crystalline waters.

You descend to the island, skimming a few feet above the ground. On the island, beneath a small, old bonsailike tree, a clear, cool spring bubbles forth from the roots and cascades down to the lake. You lie on the ground and peer into the roots at the very source, and when your eyes adjust to the darkness, you see something in the depths. What is it? Remember whatever you see. Study it. And then let it go.

Drink from the spring, move away from the tree, float away from the island, up over the lip of the crater, down the other side of the mountain, and at the crest of a foothill, pause for a moment to look at a small valley you've never seen before. What do you see? Go down into it. Who and what do you meet? Do they have anything to say to you, show you, give you? Be sure to thank them for their gifts, and prepare to return to your "other" world.

When you are ready to return, imagine yourself back at the tree on the hillside overlooking the sea. Imagine that the sun is slowly setting. When darkness begins to fall, take a deep breath and open your eyes. Try to fix the impressions from your journey in your external consciousness, then immediately write or draw your impressions and images.

The images that may appear on this first journey are often clues to your most important feelings, solutions to current problems, or helpers on your journey to full visualization skills. But sometimes, the meaning of images only become clear later, when other images can furnish a context.

Don't be discouraged if nothing spectacular happens at the beginning. Simply repeat the exercise daily, until you are comfortable with it and the images grow vivid. After all, it is worth a little practice and effort to learn the language of the unconscious so that when it speaks you can understand and communicate with it. It is actually easier than it may seem, since all you really have to do is to "imagine" a breakthrough.

AFFIRMATION: PROGRAMMING AND REPROGRAMMING THE UNCONSCIOUS IDEA PROCESSOR

Recently, psychology and medicine have rediscovered another profound law of the psyche that the ancients knew and developed into a highly effective mental technology.

Similar techniques are used in a number of seminars available to business executives and others. Whether they go by the name "creative problem solving," "executive development," "how to be successful," "active imagery," or the most common name, "affirmation," the process is simple. The person is taught to imagine success, in whatever form may be meaningful to that person, and hence to help bring about that success. Most of the seminar is devoted to persuading the person to believe in the process enough to give it a try.

Unconsciously held beliefs can be deliberately changed. The process, however, is very different from the ways in which consciously held beliefs are altered. The latter process is familiar enough—we call it education.

Reprogramming the unconscious depends upon the basic characteristic of this part of the mind which we have already noted namely that it responds to what is vividly imagined in essentially the same way that it responds to what actually happens.

"This is not so difficult nor so mystical as it may first appear," Maxwell Maltz points out in *Psychocybernetics*. You and I do it every day of our lives. What, for example, is worry about possible unfavorable future results, accompanied by feelings of anxiety, inadequacy, or perhaps humiliation? For all practical purposes we experience the very same emotions in advance that would be appropriate if we had already failed. We picture failure to ourselves, not vaguely, or in personal terms—but vividly and in great detail. We repeat the failure images over and over again to ourselves." The result? A tendency to fail.[4]

On the other hand, the lucky or successful person has learned a simple secret, Maltz adds. "Call up, capture, evoke the *feeling of success*. When you feel successful and self-confident, you will act successfully. . . . Define your goal or end result. Picture it to yourself clearly and vividly. Then simply capture the *feeling* you would experience if the desirable goal were already an accomplished fact. . . . Then your internal machinery is geared for success: to guide you in making the correct muscular motions and adjustments; to supply you with creative ideas, and to do whatever else is necessary in order to make the goal an accomplished fact."

Athletic coaches make use of affirmation techniques regularly. To practice for the pole vault, for example, an athlete may relax on a couch and vividly imagine going over the bar, time after time, successfully, higher than the athlete has ever vaulted before. This removes negative beliefs regarding our physical limitations and prepares the athlete for successful performance on the field. Some tennis coaches, such as Tim Gallwey, teach "the inner game of tennis," a letting go to the unconscious mind "which already knows how to play tennis."[5]

The uses of this kind of affirmative imagery in healing is an ancient tradition, and it should be noted that today's medical doctors still use the intertwined serpents of Aescalapius, the dream-healing god, as their emblem. Shamans and folk healers around the world consider the use of images a key factor in awakening their patients' self-healing powers. Recently, however, two pioneers in the field of medical therapeutic imagery, Dennis T. Jaffe, of UCLA's Center for Health Enhancement, Education and Research, and David E. Bresler, professor of anesthesiology and director of Pain Control, UCLA Hospital and Clinics, presented both theory and data demonstrating the efficacy of active imagery techniques, or affirmation, in medicine. They compared the technique to the mysterious phenomenon known as the placebo effect, in which substances with no therapeutic value, such as flour and sugar, have been shown to have measurable physiological benefits for patients who were told that they were taking "real medicine":[6]

> This account also illustrates another important therapeutic use of imagery, namely, the use of positive future images to activate positive physical changes. Imagining a positive future outcome is an important technique for countering the initial negative images, beliefs and expectations a patient may have. In essence, it transforms a negative placebo effect into a positive one. . . .
>
> By imagining the end point a person seeks—full health, some specific career or life goal—without willing it or forcing oneself to desire it, the mind is carried in that direction. This is especially important when a person may be imagining or ex-

pecting a negative outcome. The power of positive suggestion plants a seed which redirects the mind—and through the mind, the body—toward a positive goal. . . .

Dr. Carl Simonton, a radiation oncologist, is another physician who has made the bold leap to the application of affirmative imagery techniques to the active mobilization of the body's defenses. When he was in the U.S. Air Force, Simonton became very interested in certain patients who seemed to survive, and even reverse, the course of cancers that were judged to be medically hopeless. When he noticed that those patients who saw themselves as active and strong "fighters" seemed to survive longer than patients who had images of themselves that portrayed passive and weak "victims," he began to suspect that psychological factors were involved in these "spontaneous remissions." Simonton wondered whether steps could be taken to actively change bad attitudes by changing the way patients saw themselves, and whether such changes could effect the cause of the cancer.[7]

Briefly, the therapy developed by Simonton and his wife, psychologist Stephanie Mathews-Simonton, consisted of two parts. First, the patient was given as much relevant medical information about the disease as he or she was capable of understanding and willing to know. Then, after a series of lessons in relaxation routines, the patients were asked to visualize their own cancer-fighting cells, and to see them in strong, ferocious, disease-killing images—sharks, jet fighters, knights in shining armor with laser lances, and so forth. Then the patients were asked to see the cancer cells as weak entities.

While it is far too early to conclusively judge the efficacy of their system (which was always conducted in conjunction with traditional radiotherapy and chemotherapy), the Simontons' earliest studies appeared to have overall positive results, with many spectacularly successful individual cases. Although the work was highly controversial when it first began, possible physiological mechanisms by which visualization could work to bolster the body's immune system are now being suggested by the infant field of psychoneuroimmunology.

Yes, beliefs can be changed, lives can be altered, deeds

can be accomplished—gradually, or in a sudden stroke—by a procedure so simple that most people do not believe it until they are somehow persuaded to try it.

Yet the athlete instructed to practice pole-vaulting by lying on a couch with eyes shut and cancer patients told to visualize their cancer-fighting cells as victorius, must at first experience some doubt that the method could possibly work—just as people in biofeedback training find it hard at first to believe that they can actually control their own brain waves. There is bound to be some doubt that the simple repetition of statements could help solve one's problems.

But resistance can be overcome. At first thought it seems incredible that we should all know unconsciously how to live, we have been taught the opposite so well. Of course, we do know how to operate this complex business called the human body; animals with their intricate instinctive behaviors seem to know unconsciously how to live their lives.

For instance, many of us in our youth have wondered whether, when the time came, we would be able to master the art of lovemaking. We may have read many sex manuals, or perhaps sought a teacher. But then comes the day when we discover that we already know unconsciously how to make love; we need only follow that inner knowing. Similarly, we already know how to use our deep intuition.

Thus, to reprogram old unconscious beliefs about limitations and potentials, or to program in new ones such as "I can have a breakthrough," we need only to vividly imagine the new beliefs—either by visualizing or verbalizing them. If this is done persistently, over a period of time, the new belief system will begin to replace the old and become an instinctual part of our lives.

Not only can affirmation reprogram beliefs about limitations and potentials, but it can help program in new ideas—such as the affirmation of success—as well.

As we noted in chapter 2, the stronger the signal we send the unconscious—in the form of "intense inner resolve and fixed purpose," "fervent demands," and "direct appeal"—the higher a priority it will assign a problem, making emotion as important as study or thought in preparing the way for personal breakthrough. One definition of affirmation, of course, involves "intense resolve." So that intention is essential—intention and the decision to turn over all problems to the deep intuition, together with the affirmation that this is all we need or want to do. Simply affirm, imagining the full meaning of each statement to the greatest extent possible, a number of times a day, day after day, for six months, the following:

"I *can* know the solution to this problem." Or: "I *can* know the answer to my deepest questions."

Or you can make it as specific as you desire, tailoring the affirmation to your own personal needs—to achieve your own personal breakthrough.

You might say: "I have high regard for myself in every way." Or: "I have warm affection for others and feel myself to be one with them." Or: "I am quietly confident that whatever I set out to do is already achieved." (Remember the statement from the New Testament, "Whatever you pray for, believe that you receive it and you will.") Or: "I am totally healthy and effective in every way." Or: "My deep mind is telling me how to solve all problems."

Far from being the esoteric provenance of those disciplined enough to master complex techniques and methods of thought, breakthrough can often be as easy as this.

ALERT RELAXATION: PREPARING THE CHANNEL

In the Western world today, there is a growing interest in nonpharmacological, self-induced, altered states of consciousness because of their alleged benefits of better mental and physical health and improved ability to deal with tension and stress. During the experience of one of these states, individuals claim to have feelings of increased creativity, of infinity, and of immortality; they have an evangelistic sense of mission, and report that mental and physical suffering vanish. . . . Subjective and objective data exist which support the hypothesis that an integrated central nervous system reaction, the "relaxation response," underlies this altered state of consciousness.

HERBERT BENSON, JOHN F. BEARY, and MARK P. CAROL, "The Relaxation
Response," *Psychiatry*

Western scientists came to an understanding of the power of relaxation as a way of taking the mind "off-line" and a gateway to self-knowledge and self-control, not from the study of comparative religions or the various psychotherapeutic disciplines, but from investigations in the field of medicine. The discovery of this "relaxation response" was based on decades of earlier investigation into its counterpart—the "flight-or-fight response" and its associated stress reaction.

The flight-or-fight response is a holdover from our evolutionary past, when survival depended on the ability of the individual organism to recognize and deal instantly with life-threatening situations. Take the case of our ancestors, back in the days when humans were hardly the fiercest creatures roaming the plains of Africa: if another animal or human approached, our ancestors usually had to make a split-second choice between three alternatives—running away, engaging in combat, or accepting the newcomer. When the danger-scanning part of an organism's brain came across something suspicious in the immediate environment, powerful physiological reactions triggered a state of hyperalertness to prepare the body for either mortal combat or life-saving flight.

The decision about which alternative to take was made on a higher cognitive level, but the body's reaction to that decision took place on a much more instinctive level. The hormones adrenaline and noradrenaline were released into the bloodstream in order to mobilize glucose molecules to supply the energy needed for short, strenuous spurts of activity and to prepare the body for possible injury by increasing the clotting factor of the blood itself to lessen the possibility of a critical hemorrhage.

The flight-or-fight response remains a dominant force in the human species. When we perceive potentially threatening situations today—a business skirmish, the pressure of an exam, severe criticism, and so forth—we very rarely flee or fight, but adrenaline and noradrenaline are still triggered, and the effect can ultimately be harmful. Excesses of the chemicals that help clot blood in the case of injury can also lead to the buildup of fatty material in the arteries, which is a major cause of circulatory diseases, while as blood pressure increases, its tendency to explode a weakened vessel increases dramatically.

In the early part of this century, a medical researcher by

the name of Hans Selye discovered that the flight-or-fight reaction is one of the most severe and frequently encountered sources of stress in modern life. The interesting part of Selye's research is the connection he discovered between mental attitude and physiological reaction. Although our biological response to perceived threats is unconscious, instinctive, and largely beyond our control, the determination that a specific situation is threatening (and thus the trigger for flight-or-fight hormones) is largely a matter of the mind-set and belief system of the person perceiving the situation.

In his classic work, *Stress Without Distress*, Selye explained this situation in terms everyone can understand.[8]

> If you meet a helpless drunk who showers you with insults but is obviously quite unable to do you harm, nothing will happen if you ... go past and ignore him. However, if you ... fight, or even prepare to fight, the result may be tragic. You will discharge adrenaline-type hormones, which increase blood pressure and pulse rate, while your whole nervous system will become alarmed and tense in preparation for combat.
>
> If you happen to be a coronary candidate (because of age, arteriosclerosis, obesity, a high blood-cholesterol level), the result may be a fatal brain hemorrhage or heart attack. In this case, who was the murderer? The drunk didn't even touch you. This is biological suicide! Death is caused by choosing the wrong reaction.

The medical importance of stress is now widely acknowledged, but as Selye and others began their researching, it challenged the boundaries of scientific belief. Because there was no evidence of a physiological mechanism at that time by which states of mind could directly affect the body, it took Selye nearly half a century to amass enough evidence to convince clinicians of the validity of his work. Now, the body of research literature on stress and its attitudinal components is impressively large and rigorous.

More recently, medical and psychological research has turned towards methods people use to replace unhealthy reactions with healthier attitudes. It was in the context of the therapeutic exploration of counter-stress strategies that the role of relaxation first came under scientific scrutiny.

Relaxation response is the designation for a well-defined set of innate, physiological processes that balance the potentially harmful effects of flight-or-fight response. The term was coined and the supporting research was conducted at Harvard Medical School by a team led by Dr. Herbert Benson, a well-known cardiologist and director of the Hypertension Section of Beth Israel Hospital in Boston. Their studies demonstrated the existence of a response involving metabolic, respiratory, and glandular processes that seem not only to counteract the harmful effects of stress but to promote maximal states of health significantly beyond those human beings normally experience.

This response is not only the physiological reverse of flight or fight, but like the flight-or-fight response, the relaxation response produces a state of alertness to certain kinds of phenomenon. It is a state of alertness to the inner world, to the symbols, signs and portents of the unconscious.

Benson's studies, described in the book the *Relaxation Response*, demonstrated that this response could be elicited by psychological means—by using the mind to relax the body. If the potentially harmful effects of the flight-or-fight response are a result of "choosing the wrong reaction," the beneficial effects of the relaxation response comes as a result of choosing the right reaction. Although the research was medical, the means by which people can learn to activate this response turned out to be known to the world's oldest religions:[9] "The basic technique for the elicitation of the relaxation response is extremely simple. Its elements have been known and used for centuries in many cultures throughout the world. Historically, the relaxation response has usually been elicited in a religious context. . . ."

The relaxation method that Benson arrived at consists of four fundamental elements:

1. A quiet environment.
2. A mental device.
3. A passive attitude.
4. A comfortable position.

If the reader experiments with none of the other methods discussed in this book, it is very likely that a great deal can be gained—psychologically, creatively, and in terms of health—by setting aside time to regularly practice these elements.

Obviously, if there are no loud sounds or sudden motions, there is far less likelihood that the flight-or-fight response will be triggered. Benson's first element, quiet and peaceful surroundings, reduces the possibility of encountering activity that might attract the attention of the danger-scanning portion of the brain by selecting an environment where sensory stimulation is significantly lessened.

This external quietude also helps remind one of the internal quietude necessary if one is to hear the still, small voice of the unconscious emerge from beneath the outer layers of consciousness.

Even when one is sitting quietly, the stream of consciousness is hardly quiet. Memories, stray thoughts, internal perceptions, images—what some meditation teachers call "chatter"—arise to distract one from the original purpose of quieting the mind. The brain, by its nature, is restless, constantly active, scanning the environment, both internal and external, for potentially harmful or beneficial perceptions or cognitions.

Benson's second tool, the mental device, is a method of focusing on a specific object to steady and quiet the ongoing chatter of consciousness to help shift the brain off line.

In Eastern religions, this attention-focusing device is often either a mandala (a symmetrical visual design) or a mantra (a special sound or word repeated over and over to clear the mind). In the system developed by Benson and others, called clinical meditation, which was devised for use by hypertension patients for whom relaxation is a medical necessity, a one-syllable sound, like the word one itself, is used to avoid the religious connotations that most traditional mantras possess.

The third element, a passive attitude, is critical, if subtle, for it is self-defeating if a person tries so hard to relax that the effort itself becomes a source of stress. The paradox of forcing oneself to "let it happen" is often the first, frustrating barrier for the novice to overcome. The object is not to force thoughts into a particular mold, but to relax and observe them until they begin to quiet down of themselves.

The fourth element, a comfortable position, obvious though it might sound, is explicitly prescribed by Benson to counter the notion most Westerners have that meditation involves bodily contortions. In Asia, the full-lotus position is comfortable because people are used to sitting that way. In America and Europe, people are used to sitting in chairs. The main idea is to start out as physically comfortable as possible, short of lying down, which could induce sleep.

What is important here is that these scientific studies have confirmed that relaxation is conducive to states of consciousness that are gateways to states usually associated with breakthroughs and creative experiences.

The attitude of several schools of psychologists who have emerged from previous obscurity to present prominence could generally be described as viewing the body as the guardian of the unconscious, with relaxation seen as a means of slipping past the internal censor at the portals of waking consciousness. The work of Wilhelm Reich, Ida Rolf, Moishe Feldenkrais, Alexander Lowen, and others, has revealed a profound relationship between deep physical relaxation and the release of buried or repressed psychic energy of the type that interferes with the breakthrough state. Whereas Freudian and Jungian analysts insist that hidden parts of the psyche can only be released through psychological processes like free association and dreamwork, these "body psychologists," as they came to be called, felt that direct physical relaxation of tension buried deep in the body could serve to facilitate the same process.

The earliest discoveries in this field came about from attempts to relax patients who complained of unusual tension in specific parts of their bodies. Physical massage with conscious relaxation of the area in question resulted in the release of a flood of repressed memories and images. In one case, a laborer whose right arm had seized up so tightly that he could no longer work was taught, over a period of time, to relax the muscles in that arm. At the moment this was achieved the laborer remarked to his analyst that he had suddenly remembered instances in his early life when his parents' mental abuse had made him so angry that he would tense up his right arm to strike them but would instead repress the desire, tightening the muscles of the arm even more fiercely to stifle the impulse. Thereafter, although he was not conscious of doing it, the man tightened those muscles whenever he repressed similar feelings in situations that create anger and other strong emotions, until finally the effect became so pronounced he could no longer work.[10]

Although they differ in their theoretical explanations and their therapeutic approaches, body-oriented psychologists agree that these patterns of muscular tension, or armoring, are a means by which repressed psychic material is locked or frozen into the musculature of the body. In this school, the relaxation methods are the gateway to a kind of emotional growth.

Other psychologists took different but equally valid psychological approaches to relaxing deeply buried tensions. In two of these schools, Autogenic Training and Progressive Relaxation, rigorous research and decades of therapy demonstrated that just as the thought of food can cause physical salivation, images of relaxation can cause muscles to loosen and release their tension.

In the early years of the twentieth century, a student of hypnosis, Dr. J. H. Schultz, developed Autogenic Training, by which the patient learns to move through a series of bodily states that correspond to shifting states of consciousness. If the patient concentrated on making their hands feel warm and their limbs feel heavy, they were on the way to inducing a state of self-hypnosis. It isn't a technique that can be mastered instantly, but neither is it extremely arduous. Those readers who want to test it out should sit down, close their eyes, breathe deeply and relax for a few minutes, then repeat silently: "My hands are warm, my arms are feeling heavy." Many people find it easier to think about warmth and heaviness than to concentrate on something as abstract as "relaxation."[11]

Progressive Relaxation, pioneered in the 1930s by Dr. Edmund Jacobson, was also a means of focusing attention on the skeletal musculature of the body, thereby creating a new communication channel between volition and relaxation states.

Jacobson felt that achieving relaxation during waking hours was a matter of self-education, and like Schultz, he noted the close correlation between what people hold in their mind's eyes and what happens to their bodies.[12]

In one early experiment, Jacobson elegantly demonstrated our innate powers of mind over muscle: He asked his patients, after they were introduced to his technique of deep relaxation, to imagine that one of their fingers was tapping a telegraph key, even though they were actually to keep their finger immobilized. With the relatively primitive biomonitoring equipment available at that time, Jacobson was able to show that the precise muscle groups in the arm that command the imagined finger movement exhibited bursts of activity during the exercise. In the experimental sense, this demonstrated how actions that exist "only in the mind" can have a measurable effect on our bodies.

Jacobson developed a set of exercises designed to illustrate and demonstrate to the practitioner the experiential difference between tension and relaxation. If you tightly clench your fist, for example, then let it return to a state of relaxation, you can create an opportunity to observe and focus on the way your body naturally relaxes itself. By systematically tensing and relaxing muscle groups, moving progressively through your body—starting with your toes, working your way up your legs, midsection, chest, arms, fingers, neck, face, scalp, and so forth—you can achieve a state of deep relaxation in which the conscious is subdued and quieted, and that still, small voice from the unconscious can come through.

READING THE IMAGERY OF NIGHT: TAPPING INTO YOUR DREAM POWER

We spend a third of our lifespans asleep and it seems only natural to wonder what is going on in this state.

But until fairly recently, Western scientists (other than psychoanalysts) seemed unwilling to state or were at least uninterested in what each of us knows privately—that dreams do occur. Only in the 1950s, when Kleitman and Aserinsky, sleep researchers at the University of Chicago, correlated the appearance of rapid eye movements and distinctive brain-wave patterns in subjects with their reports of experiencing dream imagery, did experimental psychologists validate, in their own terms, a connection between our nightly dreaming and actual physiological events.[13]

But physiological research does not address itself to the most pressing question: Are dreams flights of fancy, figments of the imagination, meaningless residue of our waking lives, or are our dream visitors our teachers in disguise? If dream images do indeed represent messages from the unconscious, how do we learn to read them? How do we bring those answers back to our waking lives?

One thing is certain: when we sleep we cease to be conscious (except in a special case called "lucid dreaming," which we will be discussing later in this section). We are in the realms of the unconscious and it can speak to us directly with no interference from exterior distractions, the babble of thought, or the demands of the body. Is that why so many inspirations, illuminations, revelation, ideas, breakthrough and symbols come to us in "our dreams?"

The process of interpreting dreams was one of the pillars of Freudian theory. But where Freud was concerned with the aspects of imagery that showed disguised messages (usually of an unsavory or forbidden nature) that the "dream censor" couldn't allow to become conscious, Jung was more interested in those images that could act as signposts, clues to messages our unconscious was trying to send us in the only real way it could, at the only time it was in full control.

Even though Freudians and Jungians have their own theoretical frameworks for interpreting the meanings of dreams, they both agree that dream symbols are highly personal and that a period of guided self-training is necessary in order to fully interpret the messages of one's dreams. It is not possible to write a dictionary of dream meanings, because every symbol has a unique meaning for the person who dreams it.

First, however, we have to learn to *remember* our dreams. Although everybody experiences several prolonged periods of dreaming every night, most of us don't remember these episodes on awakening. But once we become skilled at recalling dreams, the process of interpretation can begin.

Dreamwork has become an important tool to psychoanalysts precisely because of the highly personal nature of these nocturnal scenarios. While one may or may not trust advice proffered by a book, guru, or therapist, it is hard to deny one's own dream-wisdom once the significance of dreams in conveying messages from the deep unconscious is realized.

Psychological explorers who came after the classic psychoanalysts began to use the dreamwork tools as probes for other kinds of psychic explorations. Gestalt psychologists and the various practitioners of humanistic psychology began to expand on the theme of positive growth initiated by Jung. The older methods used by the Greeks and Tibetans came to the attention of the newer generations of dreamworkers in the latter half of this century. There is now a considerable "dream underground" of nontraditional therapists, psychologists, and interested amateurs who have unearthed old sources and experimented with contemporary applications of dream techniques.

In general, the beginning stages of any of these synthetic or experimental dreamwork systems involve the same five steps:

1. The "I'm listening" stage—a conscious intention to remember dreams, and focus attention on them.

2. Learning to tune into and receive—practice in remembering how to remember dream episodes. Using a dream journal, dream discussion groups, conversations about dreams with those in one's daily life are all tools for learning to tune into and receive dreams and their meanings.

3. Decoding and clarifying—working with personal dream imagery. Try to learn the grammar, syntax, and vocabulary of the source of the image messages. Reading back over old dream episodes, asking questions about them, drawing dream images, sharing them with others, can contribute to understanding the significance of the symbols and portents witnessed.

4. Lucid dreaming—learning to act with the dream ego. This is

the first of the advanced stages. Confronting dream figures from which one would normally flee, or learning to turn falling dreams into flying dreams, are appropriate techniques for this stage.

5. Integrating the messages into daily life—learning to guide oneself. When the language of one's dreams becomes known, and the messages from the unconscious begins to reveal their meaning, the final stage of dreamwork is reached. Or perhaps, the first real step is begun.

Many different dreamwork classes, therapies, groups, tapes, books, and teachers are now available to help guide the dream student through the early stages. The following tips on beginning dreamwork were distilled from three of the best popular sources: Gayle Delaney's *Living Your Dreams*; Patricia Garfield's *Creative Dreaming*; and Ann Faraday's *Dream Power*:

1. Keep your recording equipment (notebook or tape recorder) within reach of your bed.

2. Record the date before you go to sleep.

3. Repeat to yourself, or write in the journal, just before you go to sleep, your intention to remember a dream.

4. Try to ask questions while you are dreaming. ("Why are you chasing me?" is appropriate for a threatening figure. "What does this mean?" is appropriate for a puzzling situation.)

5. Reenter the dream while you are awake. If you can't remember to ask questions during a dream, then try to reconstruct the dream in your mind's eye and ask yourself the same questions when you are awake.

6. Record every thought, phrase, word, image, or emotion you can recall, either in the middle of the night or first thing on awakening.

7. Look over dream notes written at night as soon as you awaken.

Dreamwork is generally a little more difficult than relaxation techniques and can take a little longer to master. If you practice the four aspects of clinical meditation every day, you will find yourself growing quite adept in a matter of weeks, perhaps even within days. Sometimes, dreamwork can take weeks or months before progress becomes discernible. But often, it works on the first night that it is attempted—your dream messengers are eager to get your attention, and they often respond quite rapidly and dramatically to your first attempts at making contact.

Sleep researchers' confirmation that distinctive brain-wave and eye-movement patterns are associated with the verbal reports of dreams provided an objective means of verifying a subjective claim that a certain state of consciousness had taken place. But such monitoring provides no validation for reports of the dreams' contents. By definition, waking a subject to report on a dream removes the subject from the state they are trying to describe.

In 1980 Stephen La Berge began to research lucid dreaming at the Sleep Research Center of the Stanford University School of Medicine. Approaching this exploration experientially as well as experimentally, La Berge taught people to have lucid dreams at will and to communicate to outside observers from within their dreams. These dreamers were then used to carry out rigorously controlled experiments exploring the nature of the dream-state—experiments that were never before deemed possible.

In sleep laboratories, a great many physiological measures can be monitored—respiration, pulse, brain waves, muscle activity, eye movements. La Berge was able to use these physiological measures to "signal" to observers from inside a dream. By using a combination of very faint fist clenches and stereotyped eye movements, La Berge and other subjects were able to send Morse code–like signals while they were still in the dream state. The specific state of consciousness involved with such communication across the sleep barrier is paradoxical, because in a sense, the subject is both awake and asleep at the same time.

Scientific research into dreaming and consciousness, as important as it may be to a general understanding of the human mind, is not the only possible application of lucid dreaming. La Berge considers it to be a very powerful new therapeutic tool. He noted:[14]

In our usual kinds of dreaming, we find ourselves acting in accord with habits, events just happen to us, and we are moved around by impulses beyond our control—this dreaming is a totally passive experience. But in the case where you *know* that you are dreaming, you can act intentionally and actively intervene. That brings within view a remarkable set of possibilities for dream control, one where you *can* determine what happens in your dreams, from indulging your wildest fantasies to fulfilling your highest spiritual aspirations.

For example, many people have nightmares, or anxiety dreams, where some kind of conflict is going on that they have not been able to resolve on the interior level. Once you learn to be aware that you are dreaming, rather than acting in accordance with the habit of avoidance or fear that led to that dream in the first place, and running away from your nightmare's shapes, you could deliberately turn around, face it, and then *transform* what happens to you. And that has meaning even though the setting is a dream.

This "nightmare judo," as he calls it, is an example of a "conscious intentional integration" of some part of the self that is calling for attention, a shadowlike aspect that is in "the unconscious, if you like." This, La Berge says, should be a problem in ourselves that we are not fully conscious of, but which, through lucid dreaming, we are able to bring into our awareness and make part of our consciousness. La Berge relates:

In one dream, I found myself in the middle of a riot in a classroom, and people were throwing furniture and scuffling. A ten-foot-tall ogre had a grip on me, and I was struggling to get away from this monster. That is when I realized I was dreaming. In the middle of this scene I said to myself: "Look what I have created—this monster!"

I realized that it was my creation, that I had responsibility for him, but I still wanted to get away from him. I knew that the solution was to intentionally accept him, and if I simply said, "Okay, you're mine," that would transform him, which I had found to be the case from my past experience. But when I looked at him, I felt repelled and just wanted to get away. I was able to inwardly find love in my heart and spoke words of loving acceptance to my ogre. Then he simply melted into me and the riot vanished. I woke up feeling wonderfully invigorated.

Lucid dreaming is typically a rare occurrence, but La Berge's experiences and research demonstrate that it can be induced by anybody who sincerely wants to awaken to their dreams. The induction procedure he and his colleagues worked out through trial and error is quite simple and can be applied by anyone committed to exploring this aspect of themselves. La Berge's procedure, which he calls MILD (Mnemonic Induction of Lucid Dreams), is as follows:

1. During the morning, I waken spontaneously from a dream.

2. After memorizing the dream, I engage in ten to fifteen minutes of reading or any other activity demanding full wakefulness.

3. Then, while lying in bed and returning to sleep, I say to myself, "Next time I'm dreaming, I want to remember I'm dreaming."

4. I visualize my body lying asleep in bed, with rapid eye movements indicating that I am dreaming. At the same time, I see myself as being in the dream just rehearsed (or in any other, in case none was recalled upon awakening) and realizing that I am in fact dreaming.

5. I repeat steps three and four until I feel my intention is clearly fixed.

When he explains his research to an audience, La Berge often begins by asking questions about how we are sure we are awake. For instance:

Right now, you are holding this book in your hands, moving your gaze across the pages. You are probably sitting, although you might be reclining or standing. One thing is certain—you know that you are awake.

But are you sure that you are awake? Is it possible that you could be dreaming that you are reading this book, in which case you will sooner or later awaken to find yourself in bed?

According to La Berge, our cultural belief system takes for granted that being asleep and being awake are two distinct and opposite states, and that it is not possible to combine them (in other words, we can't dream when we are conscious or be conscious when we are dreaming). It is this belief, he says, that prevents most people from having lucid dreams much of the time.

The analogy between lucid dreaming and the metaphor of enlightenment as a kind of awakening from the waking state were not lost on Dr. La Berge, although his primary concern has been to establish scientific criteria for investigating the phenomena of lucid dreaming. But in an interview with the authors, La Berge pointed out that if a person can learn to awaken to a dream, the possibility exists that it is possible to "awaken while awake."

Dreams such as the one described by La Berge suggest that what the sages say might be true. There might exist a state of consciousness that is to normal waking consciousness what lucid dreaming is to dreaming—*a state in which one consciously wields the power to act with intention in the creation of one's reality.* Having a lucid dream demonstrates how it is possible to see in color when formerly one saw only in black and white, and shows all parts of the psyche how it might feel to awaken to a new, richer, and fuller dimension of consciousness—one way of making a breakthrough.

HIGHER CREATIVITY: THE ULTIMATE BREAKTHROUGH

"The creative process ... is the emergence in action of a novel relational product, growing out of the uniqueness of the individual on the one hand, and the materials, events, people, or circumstnces of his life on the other.... The mainspring of creativity appears to be ... man's tendency to actualize himself, to become his potentialities."

CARL ROGERS, *On Becoming a Person*

Most of us have a tendency to save the creative problem-solving process "for emergency use only." We try to get the answer or solve the problem with the rational analytical part of our mind, and only when that seems to fail do we turn to the creative intuitive side for for help.

But when the choice of which questions to turn over to our idea processor is left to the conscious mind, our unconscious belief systems automatically censor out many critical questions—thus preventing us from gaining the fullest use of our inner capacities.

If this is true, and since there appears to be no known limits to capacities of the deep unconscious: Why not turn all questions over to it? Including such questions as: "What should I do with my life?" Or "How can I become the best me." Or, "What should I do in the next moment?"

Because the breakthrough experience is not limited to geniuses and visionaries, and the utility of consciousness-related tools is not limited to art and invention. Any experience that can solve our deepest problems has the power to change the way we lead our lives as well. "How should I live my life?" has been a fundamental question in every society that has ever existed. The kinds of answers and kinds of authorities people accept them from—the king, the church, and most recently science and society—change from age to age. But one source has remained constant throughout history, tapped by people of every time, to their own and the world's benefit.

If the sages are to be believed, inner teachers, helpers, and guides are available to all of us, ready to respond to our requests for assistance. This knowledge is not new. What is new is both the possibility of and the necessity of that knowledge being made widely available. In Europe during the birth of the industrial age, the invention of the printing press changed literacy from a privilege of the elite to a tool shared by a majority of the population. In the same way our current knowledge allows, and current planetary circumstances demand, that access to the higher spectrum of human potential shall no longer be limited to a few.

The very idea that we all have higher capabilities which are latent but attainable is a revolutionary notion. When groups of people question their beliefs in the legitimacy of their sources of personal guidance, the nature of the group can change drastically—from a feudal to a democratic society, for example.

The last great transformation of public beliefs regarding the proper source of values and guidance occurred nearly a thousand years ago, when the other-worldly perspective of the Middle Ages changed to the pragmatic, secular earth-oriented worldview that produced the Renaissance, the Industrial Revolution, and the world we live in today. The evidence of recent widespread popular Western interest in Eastern contemplative disciplines demonstrates that many people are ready to re-admit the idea of higher human capacities into their images of themselves and others.

In the midst of the ruins of our former value systems, an old message is surfacing, stated in modern form: *Guidance can be found, and the authority is the most trustworthy possible mentor—one's own higher self.* It is in this capacity that the informed use of imagery to mediate a dialogue with the inner self has been used with a high degree of success by some psychotherapists. It is only necessary to construct an image of this inner self we find personally acceptable, one that can serve as a focus and symbol for the dialogue.

Jaffee and Bresler recommend this method as one of the simplest but most effective means of creating a route between the conscious and the unconscious and back is: "One of the dramatic techniques we have used involves what is known as 'the inner adviser.' . . . By creating and acting with an inner adviser, a person learns to gather important information from their subconscious, and is able to feel comfortable and familiar with parts of themselves that had previously been inaccessible to conscious awareness. . . ."

This technique uses mental imagery as a tool for employing the imagination, under the direction of the intellect and the will, to explore unconscious aspects of the personality. The connection between conscious, rational faculties, and deeper, unconscious aspects, is deliberately mainstayed, in order to teach the skill of "shifting gears" between these states. In this way, the split between the different parts of the self can be bridged.

As Jung pointed out, most people, no matter what their

cultural or religious background happens to be, find it easy to ascribe this kind of wisdom to the figure of a *wise elder*. Stuart Miller, an authority on psychosynthesis, describes using this image in initiating an interior dialogue:[15]

> Assume, with many ancient traditions, that you have within you a source of understanding and wisdom that knows who you are, what you have been, and what you can most meaningfully become in the future. This source is in tune with your unfolding purpose. It can help you direct your energies toward achieving increasing integration, toward harmonizing and unifying your life.
>
> Having made this assumption, close your eyes, take a few deep breaths, and imagine that you are seeing the face of a wise old man or woman whose eyes express great love for you. (If you have difficulty visualizing this, first imagine a candle flame, burning steadily and quietly, and then let the face appear at its center.)
>
> Engage this wise old person in dialogue, in whatever way seems best: use the presence and guidance of the sage to help you better understand whatever questions, directions or choices you are dealing with at the moment. Spend as much time as you need in this dialogue, and when you are finished, write down what happened, amplifying and evaluating further whatever insights were gained.

According to Dr. Miller, the theory behind this exercise is that by creating a symbolic or imagistic context, symbols that may be trying to surface from the unconscious can more easily be received, since they do not have to struggle against, or try to take form and become part of, the stream of words normally plunging through our unconsciousness.

Another device for creating a channel for messages from your unconscious was discovered by Joseph E. Shorr, Ph.D., a psychologist who practices a form of psychotherapy called "Psycho-Imagination Therapy." Shorr asked hundreds of his patients to perform a variety of different imagery exercises, which he had found useful as diagnostic and treatment aids in psychotherapy.

One particularly revealing exercise that Shorr found to be was called "The Three Gates." The idea is very simple: Relax yourself, then slowly imagine that you are standing in front of

Opening the Mind's Gate   111

three gates in a row, one behind the other. Take your time seeing yourself opening each one in turn, then report what you see, do, and feel.

After several months of observing the responses of his patients, Shorr concluded, in a report on "Discoveries About the Mind's Ability to Organize and Find Meaning in Imagery," that:[16]

> In about 90% of the persons responding to "The Three Gates" imaginary situation, the first and second gate responses led into the deeper levels of the unconscious of the person, that then seemed to be revealed from what they saw, did and felt as they entered the third gate.
>
> With hundreds of respondents, it now seems clear that a highly reliable view of the person's unconscious can be observed from the patient's responses to the opening of the third gate. This seems to be true in 90% of the respondents. About 5% of the persons reverse this and give the first gate the same prominence that ordinarily appears in the third gate. . . .
>
> There is a very small group of persons that go past the third gate to a fourth gate before revealing heavily unconscious material. Only actual experience with one's own imagery and that of others will yield the clarity I believe exists in the 'Three Gates' imagery.

These exercises—the gates, the wise old man or woman, or any other devices for visualizing dialogue—can stimulate profound discoveries through or about one's inner or higher self.

But all of this seems to take us beyond creativity, however high the spectra, into psychological and philosophical considerations. Values and guidance, although tangentially involving problem solving and creativity (and bringing us paradoxically, again from consciousness to social and cultural issues), are really another order of reality altogether. Or are they?

If we can solve the problem, answer the question, of how to best lead our lives, and we implement that knowledge as we would the result of any other kind of breakthrough, couldn't we in the highest sense, be said to be creating our own lives?

Wouldn't this, in fact, be "higher creativity?"

And wouldn't it be the ultimate breakthrough?

⑤

The Still, Small Voice

Toward a New Science of Religion

> The very beginning, the intrinsic core, the essence, the universal nucleus of every known high religion (unless Confucianism is also called a religion) has been the private, lonely, personal illumination, revelation, or ecstasy of some acutely sensitive prophet or seer. The high religions call themselves revealed religions and each of them tends to rest its validity, its function, and its right to exist on the codification and the communication of this original mystic experience or revelation from the lonely prophet to the mass of human beings in general.
>
> ABRAHAM MASLOW, *Religions, Values, and Peak-Experiences*

TWO COURSES IN MIRACLES

Jane Roberts sat down with her husband to experiment with a newly purchased Ouija board, fell effortlessly into a trance state and accompanied by dramatic changes in voice and facial expression, became one of the twentieth century's most famous channels to "another personality no longer focused in present reality."

Since that initial contact, Jane Roberts and her husband, Robert Butts, have held more than 1000 sessions in which Roberts undergoes definite physiognomic changes and takes on a voice and personality that calls itself Seth.

It is the style of his discussions more than anything else which distinguishes Seth as a personality in his own right.

In the form of taped or transcribed sessions, Seth, when

allowed to occupy Jane's "focused reality," responds to questions, acts as psychic consultant, describes with intensity his metaphysical perceptions of "multiple realities," the "simultaneous nature of time," our own multidimensional selves that are waiting to become included again in the whole, and the continued existence of the personality through time on a very large scale. The description of life Seth relates is far more elaborate and all-encompassing than the popular concept of reincarnation, although related to it.

In all this, Seth demonstrates a great deal of knowledge of fields ranging from history to psychology to technical areas of physics, subjects with which Jane Roberts is personally unfamiliar. The substance of Seth's discourses poses the question of whether what Seth says about his identity is true, or whether Jane Roberts is merely an exceptionally gifted writer as well as being deluded or fraudulent. (A third possibility is that there is a deep source of knowledge which acquires a Seth-like coloration as it bubbles up out of Jane's unconscious.)

From discussions of systems of reality, Seth leads to a central theme in his discourses: the importance of personal, societal, and global belief systems, and the illusions common to all persons and societies who think that their particular belief system indeed represents "reality."

The theme of alternating, changing, and uncovering belief systems is covered in nearly all of the Seth literature published so far. There is talk about how personal beliefs can and do affect the way we perceive and live, as well as how we can affect others around us, individually or in groups, by the core beliefs we hold:[1]

> In your terms, beliefs are accepted initially from your parents, this . . . having to do with mammalian experience. You can perform physical feats that you would consider impossible otherwise—all because you willingly suspend certain beliefs and allow yourself to accept others for the moment. . . . It is somewhat of a psychological trick, in your day and age, to come to the realization that you do in fact form your own experience and your world, simply because the weight of evidence *seems* to be so loaded at the other end, because of your habits of perception.

Sounding like a number of modern medical researchers, Seth comments on the relationship between our psychological states and physical illness:

> They are a byproduct of the learning process, created by you, in themselves quite neutral. . . .
> Illness and suffering are the result of the misdirection of creative energy. They are a part of the creative force, however. They do not come from a different source than, say, health and vitality. Suffering is not good for the soul, unless it teaches you to stop suffering. That is its purpose.

His comments on creativity sound remarkably like recent laboratory findings:

> The creativity of the species is also the result of your particular kind of dream specialization. It amounts to—*amounts to*—a unique state of existence by itself, in which you combine the elements of physical and nonphysical reality. It is almost like a threshold between the two realities, and you learned to hold your physical intent long enough at that threshold so that you have a kind of brief attention span there, and use it to draw from nonphysical reality precisely those creative elements that you need. Period.

Whatever we make of Seth, a "voice from beyond," a sundered fragment of Jane Roberts' personality trying to merge with the whole, or outright lunacy, he leaves us with a last unsettling thought that seems to mock all we hold true:

> *If the universe existed as you have been told it does, then I would not be writing this book.*
> There would be no psychological avenues to connect my world and yours. There would be no extensions of the self that would allow you to travel such a psychological distance to those thresholds of reality that form my mental environment. If the universe were structured as you have been told, the probability of my existence would be zero as far as you are concerned. There would have been no unofficial road for Ruburt [Jane] to follow, to lead him from the official beliefs of his time. He would never have acknowledged the original impulse to speak for me, and my voice would have been unheard in your world.

Jane Roberts was interested in extrasensory perception, and her experiments with a Ouija board led to Seth's emergence. Suppose, however, that you were a trained research psychologist who didn't believe at all in this psychic stuff. One night, relaxing in your home, an inner voice suddenly commands, "This is a course in miracles. Please take notes."

That is precisely what happened to Dr. Helen Schucman one day in the mid-1960s:[2]

> Psychologist, educator, conservative in theory and atheistic in belief, I was working in a prestigious and highly academic setting. And then something happened that triggered a chain of events I could never have predicted. . . . The head of my department . . . unexpectedly announced that he was tired of the angry and aggressive feelings that our attitudes reflected, and concluded that "there must be another way." As if on cue I agreed to help him find it. Apparently this Course is the way. . . .
>
> Three startling months preceded the actual writing, during which time my friends suggested that I write down the highly symbolic dreams and descriptions of the strange images that were coming to me. Although I had grown more accustomed to the unexpected by that time, I was still very surprised when I wrote, "This is a course in miracles. . . ." That was my introduction to the Voice. It made no sound, but seemed to be giving me a kind of rapid inner dictation.

What she did was telephone a colleague and ask him if he thought she was losing her mind. He reassured her that this was probably not the case and suggested that if the voice came back she should take down what it said in shorthand, and he would type it up for her the next day. Together they would decide whether to keep the transcription, hide it, or destroy it. At any rate, her friend didn't see how this could do any harm, since the voice seem determined to make itself heard despite the hearer's skepticism.

That was the beginning of what ultimately became more than 1500 pages of manuscript.

Schucman and her friend and colleague, Dr. William Thetford, were on the staff of Presbyterian Hospital, Columbia University. In that atmosphere of orthodoxy and academic skepticism any public revelation of what they were doing would have met with derision and hostility. And so through the early 1970s Schucman and Thetford, using what came to be called "the Course" in their personal lives, kept the single copy of the manuscript carefully hidden in a locked file drawer.

It remained there until one day early in 1975, when it was disclosed to Judith Skutch, a sort of impresario to parapsychological researchers, whose apartment on Central Park West in New York City had become a main nerve center of the slowly growing activity in modern-day psychic research.

Skutch had been feeling what she described as "a growing emptiness" and feeling of "unfulfillment"—much as Schucman's department head had. Shortly before her encounter with the course, she had a dream in which she was desperately looking for what she called "my map home," which had somehow been lost. These feelings grew so intense that she "did something totally out of character: I asked the universe for help." Apparently coincidentally, within days she was having lunch with Schucman and Thetford to discuss research on more holistic approaches to healing.

In the middle of their luncheon, Skutch turned to Schucman on an impulse and asked her if she had "heard an inner voice." Rather abruptly, Schucman and Thetford suggested that they all leave the cafeteria and go to their office. Arriving there, Thetford locked the door behind them, pulled down the shades, and after briefly relating the story of the genesis of the manuscript, unlocked the file drawer and handed the transcripts to Skutch. According to her account, she read the first paragraph and immediately knew this was the "map home" she had been seeking.

So Schucman and Thetford weren't completely surprised when with Skutch's impulsive remark at lunch they "felt" she was the women to whom the voice had referred. Schucman's inner voice had asserted early in 1975 that "the time has come" and that a woman would appear who would know what to do with the manuscript.

Stranger yet was the way in which Saul Steinberg (who later published the Course) came to read the manuscript. His brother-in-law Paul, decades earlier had been lying on his bed, late in the evening, when he suddenly found himself near the ceiling in the corner of the room, looking down at his body. As he watched, the flesh had fallen off his body and then reassembled, and he heard a voice saying, "This is to teach you that you are not the body. It is important that you understand this, because you have a role to play in bringing to the world the most important spiritual document of your time, twenty years from now."

The incident had long since slipped Paul Steinberg's mind. Then suddenly twenty years later, while discussing a piece of unrelated business with Judy Skutch, he suddenly blurted out, "Are you the lady with the manuscript I'm supposed to see?" And with those words the memory came back to him. She said she didn't know, but went to the bookcase and handed him the black-bound manuscript of *A Course in Miracles* to take home.

What is the content of *A Course in Miracles?* Basically, it is a text and a set of 365 psychospiritual exercises, one for each day of the year. Based largely on the power of affirmation, it provides a way by which some people can find their own "internal teacher," to guide them much in the sense that we have been referring to in the last chapter. But its focus is not individual enlightenment or salvation alone, for because of our inherent interconnectedness, one person is not totally free until all are.

The underlying principle is the same as Seth's central teaching and the findings of modern psychology: Our internal beliefs create what is perceived as reality, and we are imprisoned by the cage of our wrong beliefs.

Since these beliefs are the problem, the basic solution is to replace these unconscious beliefs by different ones, through affirming new beliefs.

The one crucial choice is to accept direction by the part of yourself that knows the way to health, wholeness, and success—the still, small voice within.

Fear will be an obstacle in this process. Fear is an unconscious choice, based on wrong beliefs. You can choose differently. You can learn there is nothing to fear. Fear arises from lack of love, or lack of acceptance of perfect love.

Love is the natural state when the choice for fear, guilt, and grievances is unmade (reprogrammed). Love without specialness is also a central means for removing fear, guilt, and grievances.

Since the publication of the course, scientists, lawyers, foundation heads, businessmen, psychologists, housewives, and others have utilized its exercises and attested to their benefit. Among the results they reported are the elimination of anxiety, fear, depression and guilt from their lives; a feeling of deep connection with the universe; feelings of effortlessness, peace, and love; increased creativity; and an increasing frequency of things "working out," "luck," "synchronicity"— "miracles," if you will.

These two examples of Seth and *A Course in Miracles* are offered, not as proof of the existence of disincarnate entities from other realities, but because of their obvious similarities in certain respects to the earlier examples of creativity and deep intuition. They amplify, by example, the earlier claim and they illustrate once again that the spectrum of human creativity somehow connects the familiar but no less mysterious feats of daily life like the functioning of memory and the use of language, to minor hunches and intuitions, to breakthrough scientific insights artistic inspirations, and to the most profound revelations of the world's spiritual traditions.

REVELATION: MYSTICAL BREAKTHROUGH?

The kind of phenomenon in which Jane Roberts and Helen Schucman found themselves involved with have been given many different names over the centuries, but the term "channeling" has come into use in recent years as a more neutral word for what was once called mediumship and divine inspiration. It implies that one is receiving information, words, or images, often on cosmological, metaphysical, or spiritual subjects, *from* somewhere *via* some sort of conduit. The "somewhere" may claim to be a discarnate entity or a being existing in other dimensions.

Let us presume, for the sake of discussion, that the "somewhere" is the faculty of the human mind we have been calling the unconscious idea processor. The "conduit," then, is at least the communication channel between unconscious and conscious aspects of the mind.

Recent research on the phenomenon of so-called "multiple personalities" suggests that this term may prove to be an extremely useful metaphor that reduces the scientific aversion to the channeling phenomenon. The term "multiple personality" ordinarily refers to persons who appear to shift from one personality to another, often quite different one, this shift being generally outside their conscious control. The alternate personality—or personalities, since there are often a number of these part-time residents—is typically very dissimilar in such characteristics as speech and thought patterns, mood and temperament, etc.; these differences may show up in physiological changes such as: voice, gender, physiognomy, posture and body movement patterns, gender, brain wave patterns, chemical balance in body fluids, and so forth. It is clear that, although personality as a behavior pattern is not something that is easily measured or defined, nevertheless there is some sense in which these alternate personalities "really exist."

The establishment of the reality of alternate personalities may open the door to a scientific dialogue about channeling, a dialogue which has thus far been largely conspicuous by its absence. The term "channeling" is usually used with the connotation of a source having the attributes of a personality but extraordinary—perhaps superhuman—knowledge and wisdom. It is already the case in the literature on multiple personalities that some of these alternates have rather remarkable capabilities. Using the scientifically accepted metaphor of multiple personalities, it is possible to begin to explore the channeling phenomenon in a scientific way without getting hung-up on the usual metaphysical questions. The existence and apparent wisdom of the channeling source can be noted and explored, while leaving open questions about the nature of that source, as whether the alternate personality is "really" a person who once lived on the earth, or a being that exists in some trans-terrestrial space or dimensions or merely a psychological off-shoot of the channeler's psyche. Such questions may never fall within the domain of science other than as alternate hypotheses, and yet the fruits of the channeling phenomenon can come to be appreciated and used to the benefit of humankind—leaving open the issue of the ultimate nature of the channeling source, as scientists in fact leave open the issue of the ultimate nature of consciousness and of "ordinary" human personality.

As with earlier examples in science and the arts, this phenomenon generally takes one of two forms. The term *channeling* itself usually refers to the act or process of receiving information. that comes in the form of words, often as a sort of "inner dictation" or as "automatic writing," or even the production of another "voice" that speaks through the individual's vocal cords and speech apparatus, as with Jane Roberts and Seth. Older terms such as *illumination* and *inspiration* often connote information that comes in the form of images, or as a nonverbal, deeply intuitive understanding, expecially of a spiritual sort. But the definitional boundaries of all such terms are fuzzy and there is definitely overlap.

The state in which all the world's mystical and religious traditions seem to have been formed is certainly related to all these other states. Certainly the experience of revelation that underlies the genesis of all their doctrines, prophecies and sacred writings appear similar in description to what others have said, in wholly different areas, about the breakthrough experience. There is little question, for instance, that channeling and revelation are connected, and revelation might even be said to be channeling which for one reason or another is assumed to be of high quality. After all, nothing endures for centuries unless it has some value or wisdom.

This brings us to the subject of another allied state, mysticism. Is the *Higher Self* or *Kingdom within* mentioned by these scriptural teachers also related to these phenomenon? If so, how does it happen that any faculty or faculties of the human mind could produce such apparently disparate experiences?

If we are to judge from the accounts of extraordinary individuals, it isn't hard to believe that the unconscious mind has capabilities that go far beyond the ordinary range of mental activity. The unusual creative experiences of artists and scientists have been widely held to be valuable, valid, and inspired.

Yet, certain of these experiences have been dismissed as crazy or schizophrenic, especially when these experiences were of a religious rather than an artistic or scientific nature. Indeed, many people to whom such experiences have occurred were unbalanced, in the sense of having lost their ability to differentiate between the testable and the delusional. But clearly, not all such experiences should be classed as mental illness, unless one is to extend that classification to include the founders of Christianity, Judaism, Islam, Buddhism, and the other religions of the world.

Muhammad and Moses and Paul heard the word of their God, and nations believed them. But our mental institutions today hold thousands of people who claim to have heard voices and seen visions. Joan of Arc followed the direction of her voices and marched into history—but our present age has been marked by the kind of individual and mass mayhem that has resulted from the urgings of less benevolent voices. The fates of nations and the lives of billions of people have been changed by the breakthrough experiences that occurred to Moses on Sinai, Jesus in the wilderness, Paul on the Damascus road, Buddha under the Bo tree, and Muhammad on his night journey. To the skeptical, the experiences of these individuals will be seen to be nothing more than historical and psychological anomalies. But we suggest that if only for their effect on history, they are evidence of the significance of these phenomena.

Everyone is aware, although we sometimes minimize it, of the importance of "inspired writings" in the history of civilizations. Most cultures have held certain scriptures to be sacred, and almost all of these scriptures—the Bible, the Koran, the Torah, the Veda—are alleged to be inspired, to be written through, rather than by, the person responsible for them becoming manifest. Most of them were transmitted during an extraordinary state of awareness—a dream, a vision, a theophany—and were widely believed to contain wisdom far beyond the conscious awareness of their transcribers.

These writings, the origins of which are so mysterious have shaped history so profoundly that one can hardly imagine how different the world would have been without them.

Yet modern science has found strangely little to say of this consummately important phenomenon.

It isn't hard to understand why mainstream scientists, despite the very significant role these experiences have played in human history, have found them extremely difficult to deal with. The phenomena, no matter what they are called, pose a particularly thorny problem for the modern scientifically oriented Western thinker. "Occult" explanations that involve communication from "spirit" planes are, to say the least, not completely compatible with current ideas about reality.

But if we accept the importance of the contributions that the unconscious idea processor has made to producing breakthrough insights in the arts and sciences, then we are led to an obvious question: What about the potential of this creative/intuitive mind to contribute breakthrough insights with regard to spiritual, psychological, and metaphysical issues like the nature of reality, the way to inner fulfillment, or the meaning of life? Does the mysterious competence and apparent wisdom of our deep intuition also extend to this realm? Are these kinds of experiences totally unrelated to the ordinary experience of being awakened by the squeaky door, or the less ordinary but comprehensible experience of a scientific or artistic vision or the special states revealed by hypnosis or meditation? Or do even "divine inspirations" belong on the creative continuum? Is there a connection between the breakthrough experiences of artists and scientists, the trance-communications of mediums, the channelers' influx of knowledge, the religious revelations of spiritual figures?

Attitudes and beliefs about the "higher" end of the spectrum can be strangely paradoxical, for the course of history has been profoundly affected by precisely those experiences that most people find hardest to believe. In science and the arts, we have seen how those who were derided by their contemporaries as crackpots or lunatics were often hailed by later generations as geniuses or visionaries. The same seems to be true in the realm of spiritual experience, at least in certain notable instances.

Of course a great deal of what purports to be channeled material does not come from any mysterious source, neither the deep unconscious nor "divine" inspiration from above, outside, or beyond. Instead, the material is the result of out-right fraud, perpetrated for financial or psychological gain, or the result of psychological delusion or illness. However, the same could be said for claims of discoveries and research into the physical sciences during the later part of the last century and the early portion of this one. Even today, among govern-mental and industrial scientists, corporate scientists take one position while consumer-oriented, or private, scientists take the opposite. A fair amount of trash must be sifted through to find the residue of fact.

In a similiar fashion, when all the reports of channeling that can be laid to fraud or delusion are sifted out, what emerges are certain common patterns and beliefs that are remarkably consistent, from culture to culture and age to age. If these beliefs had no practical validity they would have been abandoned long ago. Humanity may be superstitious, but even its superstitions have a core of fact if they survive very long in a significant portion of the population (e.g., walking under a ladder can bring bad luck). Millions of people in every age have attested that their lives became better and their relation-ship with the world improved after they began to follow some of the common beliefs that have emerged from channeling over the years. Our concern is with the residue that cannot be dis-missed as imagination, illness, or fraud.

THE PERSISTENT QUESTION OF INTERPRETATION AND VALIDATION

The question of how we are to determine the difference be-tween insanity and revelation is obviously of critical impor-tance to any understanding of these phenomena. There are really three related questions, all important to our more gen-eral concern with the spectrum of creativity and to the scope of the unconscious mind.

1. How veridical is channeling as a source of spiritual, religious, or metaphysical knowledge?

2. What does it, or can it, tell us about the nature of reality and/or the nature of mind?

3. How can an individual test the validity of his or her own experiences of this sort?

The first question is essentially the question: "Can there be constructed, eventually, a 'science of religion?' " William James thought so. In *Varieties of Religious Experience* he wrote that:

> I do not see why a critical science of religions ... might not eventually command as general a public adhesion as is commanded by a physical science. Even the personally nonreligious (in terms of religious *experience*) might accept its conclusions on trust, much as blind persons now accept the facts of optics. . . . The science of religions would depend for its original material on facts of personal experience. . . . It would forever have to confess, as every science confesses, that the subtlety of nature flies beyond it, and that its formulas are but approximations.

Many writers since James have argued that modern scientific methods can be applied to the subject of mystical or spiritual breakthroughs, including Pere A. G. Poulain, a Catholic scholar, and Ken Wilber, the author of *Eye To Eye*.

Building upon terminology first employed centuries ago by the Christian philosopher-mystic St. Bonaventure, Wilber asserts that there are three ways by which individuals experience some kind of contact with reality. These are: the eye of flesh (the physical senses), the eye of reason (the intellect), and the eye of contemplation (spiritual intuition).[3]

Of these three kinds of knowledge, the first two lead to science of the sort most commonly recognized as such. The measurable world, as explored by the physical senses, is described by empirical science. Mental data, as explored with the intellect, leads to such disciplines as mathematics, logic, and phenomenology. But what about the data of transcendental experience? Does it lead to a science of religion?

Wilber argues that the validity criteria for a science of religion need not be significantly different than those applied to any other branch of science. Just as breakthrough insights in the scientific and mathematical realms must be tested and verified by determining if they prove valid in practice and in comparison with each other and known scientific data, so insights in the spiritual realm must surely be tested.

In *The Graces of Interior Prayer*, Poulain suggests three criteria by which we should test the validity of a spiritual or mystical experience: Does the insight lead to virtuous conduct, to feelings of deep and lasting satisfaction, to a sense of joy, peace, and love, or to actions which seem to produce good results? Does it check with the similar experiences of others, (in other words, with tradition)? This criterion is often misunderstood. It does not mean that tradition is right and unchanging. It does mean that the historical experience should not be ignored. Is it accompanied and followed by a noetic sense of profound truth that persists long after the experience is over?

In the past few years, Western-trained psychologists have begun to combine the methods of scientific observation with the concerns evidenced by more spiritual disciplines, in an attempt to gain new understandings of some of humanity's oldest, most revered, and least understood experiences. *Transpersonal psychology* is the name some of these investigators have used for their new discipline, and channeling is one of the phenomena they have studied.

In correspondence with the authors, Dr. Arthur Hastings of the California Institute of Transpersonal Psychology, who has studied these phenomena in some depth, identified three main categories of content in regard to spiritual and mystical insight: (1) cosmology instructions for founding a religion, (2) demonstrations of humanity's unsuspected potentials, and (3) transformation—of beliefs, self, society.

The first and the oldest category, which has had an effect on history at least the equal of any scientific discovery, includes material which has been interpreted as an accurate cosmology and instructions for founding a religion. The correctness of this interpretation may be questioned, but the impacts of these revelations on history and geography are inarguable.

The second type of content, of which there is an enormous preponderance recorded in nearly all the nineteenth-century accounts of channeling and mediumship, has to do with a series of issues which have loomed with nearly equal import in humanity's consciousness: Is death the end of existence for the human personality, and is there more meaning to human life than just blind chance? The channelings, revelations and breakthroughs in this area relate to such subjects as the existence of the soul, the survival of the personality after death, and claims or demonstrations of paranormal phenomena, extrasensory perception and so forth—all of which seem designed to suggest *that there is far more to human beings and their potential than our belief systems would ever allow us to conceive.*

A third type of content, which, once again while equally old, crops up in more recent examples, particularly those in the last quarter-century, has to do with questions about how humanity can become more than it is. This concerns *transformation*—transformation of beliefs, transformation of self, transformation of society in the same way that the Seth materials and *A Course in Miracles* do.

Although channelers and mystics of every age have always received breakthrough insights pertaining to material in all three of these categories, each seems to have dominated at successive periods in history. The very fact that these transmissions have confined themselves to such an astonishingly limited range of subject matter over tens of thousands of years suggests that something more than sheer randomness or psychological aberration is at work.

Since Wilber and Poulain suggest that material received via channeling be subjected to the same criteria science applies to any other kinds of knowledge, supposition or theory, we might start by surveying what light, if any, science has to shed on the content of these categories. To explore this highly fascinating subject, we will consider these three categories briefly in chronological order.

CHANNELING, COSMOLOGY, QUANTUM PHYSICS, AND YOU

The oldest channeled scriptures, such as the Old Testament of the Judeo-Christian Bible, the ancient Buddhist *canons* and

Hindu *sutras*, the more modern "channeled" writings of Alice Bailey, Madam Blavatsky, Rudolf Steiner, and other occult writers, and even the modern Seth materials and *A Course in Miracles* appear to contain a number of remarkably similar statements about the origin of the universe and the fundamental nature of physical reality.

At the beginning of the twentieth century, each of the assertions would have been dismissed by physicists as sheer superstitious nonsense. Since the advent of basic discoveries in quantum theory, relativity, the uncertainty principle, and development of the "big bang" theory, and the physics of fundamental particles, the world view held by many theoretical physicists, mathematicians and cosmologists has come to bear an equally remarkable resemblance to the world view described and received through many instances of channeling, revelation and mystical insight—as these scientists have noted and discussed at length in their own work.

In particular, these scientists have called attention to several of the following correspondences, one of which relates to creation itself.

One of the more remarkable achievements of twentieth-century science has been the formulation of testable, mathematically quantifiable theories regarding the origin of the universe. At present, the dominant cosmological model is the theory known as the "big-bang theory." When, on the basis of evidence gathered by analyzing the light spectra of objects observed through telescopes, it was discovered that all the galaxies seem to be rushing away from each other, it was hypothesized in the "big bang" theory that all the matter in the known universe must have been packed together into one unimaginably dense "singularity" sometime between 15 and 20 billion years ago. According to this theory, the universe began expanding and continues to expand as the result of a cataclysmic explosion.

Once astrophysicists traced the evolution of the cosmos backward to this big bang, they also conjectured about the possible future fate of the universe. If there is a critical amount of matter in the universe—a supposition that has not yet been ascertained—then it appears that gravity will one day draw the exploded matter back together, in which case it is likely that the incredible gravitational pressure could well trigger yet another cosmic explosion, starting the cycle all over again.

Amazingly enough, the expansion-contraction cycles hypothesized by contemporary cosmologists were prefigured with astonishingly accurate descriptions in the earliest inspired scriptures, bible of the Hindu religion—the Sanskrit Upanishads, which described cosmic cycles known as "the Breath of Brahma." These cycles not only corresponded to "fiery," explosive phases and eventual contractive phases, but were predicted to be on a time scale of hundreds of millions of years—within an order of magnitude of the time scale hypothesized by modern astrophysicists!

One of the other things this kind of channeling repeats endlessly is that time is not what it seems, and that time in the usual physical sense of the word does not even exist. Suprisingly, several scholars of modern mathematics and physics have made similar assertions about the nature of time. Thus, the cyclical theory is probably not literally true, either. And the truth itself, probably stranger than science fiction.

Another statement common to channeled literature is that light is a fundamental and primordial substance.

To find inspired statements regarding the nature of light and its connection to the godhead and the origin of the cosmos, we need only turn to Genesis, in which the primary act of creation began with light. In the Tibetan Book of the Dead, the "clear light of the void" is discussed as the fundamental "substance" of which the universe and mankind are made; the Hindu Bhagavad Gita mentions "the splendor of a thousand suns"; and countless Kabbalistic, Buddhist, shamanist, metaphysical, and occult works dwell on this subject at length.

Einstein's relativity theory and his famous equation $E = mc^2$ linked light to the other two cosmic fundamentals—energy and matter. According to cosmologists, "let there be light" is a scientifically accurate description of the opening moments of the cosmic drama. According to one of the most popular theoretical conjectures among contemporary astrophysicists, in the first unimaginably violent fractions of the first second of the cosmos, before there was matter, the primal substance was light—light far different from any kind we know today, for it was billions of times denser even than any known *matter* that now exists.

Additionally, in channeled writings the material universe is more like a web of interpenetrating vibrations than it is like a collection of solid building blocks, and the term *vibrations* turns up frequently. Throughout history, the esoteric core of religion and mystical groups worldwide have held that the universe is made of a web of vibration.

The analytical view of the universe—the kind of mechanistic, reductionistic thinking that is often called the Cartesian paradigm—likens it to a huge clock consisting of intricately connected yet separate parts. This mechanistic paradigm was shattered by the advent of the quantum worldview, which in some senses views the universe as the same kind of cosmic web of fundamentally interrelated forces first portrayed by Buddhist scriptures and religious revelations.

In *The Tao of Physics*, physicist and mystic Fritjof Capra explains the quantum "worldview" this way:

> The material world, according to contemporary physics, is not a mechanical system made of separate objects, but rather appears as a complex web of relationships. Subatomic particles are not made of any material substance; they have a certain mass, but this mass is a form of energy. Energy is always associated with processes, with activity; it is a measure of activity. Subatomic particles, then, are bundles of energy, or patterns of activity. The notion of separate objects is an idealization which is often very useful but has no fundamental validity. All objects are merely patterns in an inseparable cosmic process, and these patterns are intrinsically dynamic, continually changing into one another, in a continuous dance of energy.

Finally, the view of channeled material is that *consciousness is not distinct from the physical universe; mind, not matter, is primary.*

The primary tenet of the Buddha's revelation was that the solidity of the world as we see it is an illusion—that the creation of the world is the result of our perceptions as much as it is the manifestation of cosmic forces. This, of course, put consciousness in a much more central position than old-fashioned physicists would have ever considered. But in the 1920s, Werner Heisenberg announced his uncertainty principle, stating that it is impossible for science to obtain any truly objective information as to the state and nature of the fundamental particles that make up the universe because the very act of attempting to study them inevitably changes their location, direction, or charge. Thus, the primary constituents of reality, once believed to lie within the provenance of the most objective observations of physical science, were revealed to be inextricably influenced by consciously observing them (which is what the "new Copernican revolution" we have spoken of is about).

Almost inevitably, by attempting to understand the makeup of reality physicists found themselves moving across the dividing line from the realm of the purely physical to the realm of the almost purely metaphysical.

Sir James Jeans, knighted for his achievements in the new physics, sums up the implications of Heisenberg's discovery in a line as unsettling as it is poetic as it is scientific: "The universe begins to look more like a great thought than a great machine." According to Rex Weyler, a contributing editor of *New Age Journal*, in a forthcoming survey of the emergent sense of these congruencies among American scientists, many scientists are coming to agree that reality emerges "from a unified field of consciousness." But an article on quantum theory puts it most simply: "The universe is consciousness."

MYSTICISM: THE INEFFABLE EXPERIENCE

This concept is also contained in almost all the earliest religious revelations and became central to their philosophy. Michael Murphy, one of the founders of the Esalen Institute, which has brought together many of the world's great spiritual teachers and leaders, sums up their common testimony: "The central perception ... is that there is a fundamental reality, godhead, or ground of existence that transcends the ordinary world, yet exists in it." *The Encyclopedia of Mysticism* states it this way: "Mystics believe that there is an Ultimate Being, a dimension of existence beyond that experienced through the senses. This Ultimate Reality is Absolute *Being*. It is often, though not invariably, conceived in personal terms, and called God. It is the source and Ground of all that is." The Upanishads tell us: "The Atman [godhead] is that by which the universe is pervaded."

But the ancient mystics never ask anyone to take this tenet on faith. Central to their teachings is the proposition that a person can, under certain circumstances, attain a higher form of "cosmic consciousness," in which he or she has immediate knowledge of a reality underlying the physical world. *The Encyclopedia of Mysticism* explains it this way: "The mystics claim that the Ultimate can in some sense be known or apprehended. God is not wholly other, not utterly withdrawn. IIe is a God who hides Himself, but he is also a God who reveals himself."

At the core of the esoteric beliefs systems, according to Murphy, is the idea that "the spiritual reality that is the source of all consciousness can be known." This is what Rufus Jones, writing in *The Encyclopedia of Religion and Ethics* called "the type of religion which puts the emphasis on direct and immediate consciousness of the Divine Presence," and this is what St. Thomas Aquinas meant when he spoke of "the knowledge of God through experience."

One is reminded of the practices of the Kabbalists, of whom a modern scholar has written:[4]

> Immersed in prayer and meditation, uttering the divine name with special modulations of the voice and with special gestures, he induced in himself a state of ecstasy in which he believed the soul had shed its material bonds and, unimpeded, returned to its divine source.

There are ten thousand names for this state, phenomenon, condition, or being—even to define it beggars the capacities of language. Almost every one who reads this book will already have a term by which they identify it to themselves when thinking about it—whether they have ever had such an experience, or even believe them to be possible.

In fact, one of the primary characteristics of this experience is that it does not lend itself well to precise verbal expression. The most important teachings, it appears, have not been written, or even oral traditions, but *experiential* traditions. Certain sages have claimed that the highest kind of knowledge cannot be described in traditional language, but can only be apprehended through a kind of experience, a certain state of consciousness.

William James called this quality *ineffability* and defined it this way:[5]

> ... The subject says that it defies expression, that no adequate report of its content can be given in words. It follows from this that its quality must be directly experienced, it cannot be imparted or transferred to others....

The Sufis also insisted that this level of consciousness cannot be satisfactorily described in written or spoken language, but something of its quality can be conveyed through a master teacher or in the form of a direct experience.

Obviously, no one can deny that individuals have reported experiencing such a state with extraordinary frequency and consistency, across diverse cultural barriers and thousands of years, and in the face of considerable public disapproval. But do human beings really possess such a capacity? Certainly if we do, the deep unconscious would in all probability be aware of it and would be trying to communicate such potentially valuable information to our conscious minds.

All we can do here is what we have been doing all along: let those who have had such an experience tell us about it in their own words, and then contrast that with what science has to say—leaving it up to the reader to arrive at his or her own conclusions. In almost every case we or others have surveyed participants describe an awareness of oneness with the universe and all its powers, of intimate relationship with the Earth and all its creatures, of a knowing—a *gnosis*—related to that of the creator (or creative principle).

One issue on which a great deal rests is what we are to make of these feelings. Quite obviously, they could be mere delusions, resulting from any one of a number of quite plausible sources—chemical imbalance, trauma, and so forth. On the other hand, since science tells us that the universe, of which we are a part, is "unitary" in nature, we should not be forced to resort to theories involving hallucination or pathology to account for the numerous examples on record of individuals perceiving it correctly.

But, even granting that the universe is a seamless whole, many people will still find it difficult to credit the possibility that man, with his limited senses, could somehow come to perceive that unity directly and unaided. What is difficult to keep in mind (because the weight of the *experience* of how our senses *allow* us to perceive reality is so compelling) is that normally our senses bring us just such a perception of "unbroken wholeness"—of reality as it is. It is our mind and our perceptual system that preselects from among the "vibratory nodes" in that field to present a picture of reality simplified enough for us to find comprehensible.

As children we are born tabula rasa, perceiving the world without any prior filtering system or conceptual framework. It is in this sense that Claire Myers Owens, writing in *Main Currents in Modern Thought*, says: "The unitary experience of infant and mystic are alike."

We learn to fit ourselves into the world by learning to perceive or not perceive whatever the adults around us are perceiving. We receive no inducement to perceive something that adults don't perceive—indeed, we may receive active discouragement. "The intellect," D. T. Suzuki reminds us, "is primarily intended to have us get on well in the world."

Admirable as this arrangement of the senses may be in helping us cope with some aspects of day-to-day life, it does have certain noticeable drawbacks. Among them, Alan Watts notes, "is the tendency to impose too quickly the conventional structures like time, space, the subject-object dichotomy, and self-other value systems." It is these *left brain* tendencies which come between us and any direct perception of the fundamental unity of the universe as it is.

However, our normal mental conditioning is certainly not an unsurmountable barrier to the direct perception of reality, as the yogis, mystics, and shamans have shown us. Writing in *The Relaxation Response*, Dr. Benson observed that:

> By the twelfth century ... it was realized that this ecstasy could
> be induced in the ordinary man in a relatively short time by
> rhythmic exercises, involving posture, control of breath, coor-
> dinated movements, and oral repetitions.

In fact, this barrier is so easy to overcome or transcend—
and here we are speaking indeed of what many have called
transcendence or even the transcendental experience—that,
according to Abraham Maslow, the father of humanistic psychology, most people report having had a profound sense of
"what has been called 'unitive consciousness' " at some time
in their lives, just as they report experiencing the more general
case of what we have been calling the breakthrough experience.

Modern science has even reduced this "mystic" state to
an explainable phenomenon through laboratory research. "In
neuropsychiatric terms," says Alan Watts, "the state of consciousness is quite easily intelligible."

The major precondition, according to one group of
Harvard researchers, is a "nervous system devoid of mental-
conceptual activity ... in a state of quiescence, alert, awake,
but not active."

When the nervous system is in this condition, according
to Durand Kiefer, reporting on a two-year study in a paper
called "Meditation and Biofeedback," "the mind is simply
still, at last at peace, and consciousness is clear, total, and
ecstatic. As later noted in the Zen Buddhist literature, self,
ego, psyche, personality, mind—all are nonexistent, a normally persistent illusion momentarily dispelled."

Although mystics, in one guise or another, have been telling people how to achieve this state for thousands of years,
science has only officially begun to recognize it since it
became possible to reproduce the experience under laboratory
conditions, via biofeedback, where it could be quantified and
analyzed.

Biofeedback itself is based on a simple principle, one that
sounded incredible to Western scientific circles when it was
first revealed: People can learn to control previously autonom-
ic physiological processes, such as heartbeat or brain-wave

production, by learning to shift attention to those processes., The sensitive electronic equipment which signals changes in these functions is simply a tool for helping us learn to distinguish very minute physiological and psychological states which otherwise escape our attention.

Numerous books and articles have been written popularizing the relationship between certain *rhythms* detected in the electrical activity of the brains of yogis and mystics when they have reached the deepest part of their meditations, and the stimulation of *higher* or *altered* or *mystical* or *unitary* states of consciousness. Through the use of an EEG machine to register the *rhythms* of the brain, it is possible to tell when our brains are producing brainwaves (indicators of states of consciousness) most like those of meditation and by cultivating and deepening them, to reach these states relatively easily and in a much shorter time than the usual meditative methods.

"The more meditation is practiced," explains C. Maxwell Cade, author of *The Awakened Mind: Biofeedback and the Development of Higher States of Awareness*, "the easier it becomes to produce and to maintain alpha rhythm, and the longer continuous alpha rhythm is maintained, the more often the individual experiences states of higher awareness."

But while all this scientific evidence and theory help substantiate the fact that such a condition or state *does* exist, it tells us absolutely nothing about what *effect* the experience has upon the person who undergoes it.

According to the mystics, when one comes to truly know oneself, the pull of the material body and ego personality become greatly decreased and one finds that the deepest motivation is to participate fully, with conscious awareness, in the evolutionary process and the fulfillment of humankind. To put it another way, one becomes aware that what appeared to be driving motivations were mainly illusory ego needs and that the desires of the true Self are one's real needs—this sounds a lot like the phenomenon we have termed "higher creativity."

Thus, one of the tests to be applied to contemporary experiences of channeling is to ask whether or not it or its content seems to lead toward psychological and spiritual growth and transformation.

Dr. Edwin Severinghaus, a psychiatrist who was initially skeptical, became intrigued with what he called "the transformative power" of the channeling experience:[6]

> Since I have had some twenty-four years of experience in clinical psychiatry, I believe I can claim sufficient skills in interviewing to determine the subject's reliability. . . .
> I would say that there is a definite congruence with their strivings for personal and spiritual growth. There is also evident . . . an evolution over time: the individual's growth and consciousness is clearly influenced . . . and conversely the transmissions become "higher," or more profound, or more universal.

Abraham Maslow's studies of his own patients who had "mystical" experiences led him to a similar conclusion:[7]

> This is not as simple a happening as one might imagine from the bare words themselves. To have a clear perception (rather than a purely abstract and verbal philosophical acceptance) that the universe is all of a piece and that one has his place in it— one is a part of it, one belongs in it—can be so profound and shaking an experience that it can change the person's character and his Weltanschauung forever after. In my own experience I have two subjects who, because of such an experience, were totally, immediately, and permanently cured of (in one case) chronic anxiety neurosis and, in the other case, of strong obsessional thoughts of suicide.

THE FURTHER END OF THE SPECTRUM

Now we come to a subject that, had we drawn our definition of creativity more traditionally (that is to say more narrowly) earlier would seem to take us far outside the bounds of creativity. But, we are to look on certain kinds of religious revelation and mystical prophecy as phenomena that may also have been associated with or produced by the unconscious—and if we consider some of the breakthroughs and inspirations the unconscious has produced in physics, psychology, medicine, biology over the years—then we have to conclude that anything this part of ourselves has to say on *any* subject is not only worthy of attention but still well within the creative spectra.

What we are leading into so carefully is the second category of material Dr. Hasting's identified in his study of channeling and revelation. This concerned issues like the possible survival of the personality after death and the question of whether there is any meaning to life.

Admittedly, we enter a realm somewhere in the creative *ultraviolet* or *infrareds* but one which if ever validated might well be more closely related than we normally imagine to the higher ends of the creative spectrum and to the kinds of phenomenon we have been discussing in this book.

But when the ancient esoteric philosophies speak of the "survival spirit outside the body" or afterdeath, and of extrasensory perception, mind over matter, and so forth, we find ourselves dealing with issues where it is much more difficult to come by validation.

Although there has been some scientific research into these areas, the conclusions reached by scientists are by no means as unanimous as they are in regard to the basic findings of physics. However, a number of very distinguished figures, among them astronaut Edgar Mitchell, have come forth to state that they believe that the possible existence of such phenomena have been sufficiently demonstrated to warrant serious study. Their position was not given the warmest of welcomes by the scientific community on the whole. Still, organized research and course work in dozens of universities in countries all over the globe is well under way, and the Parapsychological Association, formed in 1957, was admitted to membership in the American Association for the Advancement of Science in 1969.

But since the early 1960s, there has been increasing public acceptance that such capacities do exist. Police departments on several continents have made frequent use of psychics in the solution of crimes. Archaeologists have employed psychics to assist in the location of buried sites and artifacts. Mining and oil companies have used clairvoyants to locate underground deposits. There has also been active interest in military applications of psychic phenomena on both sides of the

Iron Curtain. In the United States, various military and intelligence agencies have sponsored, supported, or conducted research into the strategic applications of these capacities.

And still the debate, pro and con, goes on. We are not interested here in trying to prove to the skeptical that particular psychic phenomena have been demonstrated to exist. But we, too, want to point out well-designed research which warrants further investigation, and we want to explore the implications of such research.

Most paranormal phenomena now under scientific investigation fall into one of following three classes:

1. *Extrasensory Perception.* Information is apparently obtained through means other than the known sensory channels, in waking consciousness, trance state, or dreams. This includes telepathic (mind-to-mind) communication, clairvoyant perception (remote viewing), precognition ("remembering" an event that hasn't happened yet), and retrocognition ("remembering" a past event that one has no knowledge of in the ordinary sense).

Consider the phenomenon known as "remote viewing." Recent work by Puthoff and Targ at Stanford Research Institute (SRI-International) illustrates the connection between this phenomenon and questions concerning the limits of the knowable. In one form of the experiment, the subject is given two randomly chosen numbers representing a latitude and a longitude. In other words, the two numbers identify a spot somewhere on the surface of the earth. But no one knows where it is, since the numbers were randomly chosen.

The subject is asked to send his or her mind out to the spot corresponding to the two coordinates, "see" what is there, and come back and make a sketch of what was "seen." The sketch is then compared with a photograph made by taking a camera to the spot. A sophisticated scoring system is used to ensure that the comparison amounts to more than a single impressionistic "correct" or "wrong."

2. *Psychokinesis* (PK). The physical environment is affected in some way that is apparently a consequence of some mental state, but without physical linkage between agent and

effect. Examples include teleportation (movement of an object from one location to another); levitation; producing thermal or electromagnetic effects at a distance; "thought photography" (producing an image on unexposed film); extraordinary physiological effects ("instantaneous" or rapid healing; walking on fire).

3. *Survival phenomena.* Events appear to be caused by discarnate personalities. Examples include channeling or mediumistic communications, poltergeists, and apparitions.

If there is anything to this mediumship hypothesis, it is natural to wonder what happens when the researchers themselves die. Do they continue their interest in demonstrating that death is but a transition? Do they do better in transmitting veridical information after death than the untrained?

Several of the leading researchers in this area died around the turn of the century—Edmund Gurney in 1888, Henry Sidgwick in 1900, and Frederic Myers in 1901. A few weeks after Myers' death, Mrs. A. W. Verrall, lecturer in classics at Cambridge and a friend of Myers, began producing automatic writing. Verrall and her husband had been infected by Myers' enthusiasm for physical research, and after his death she felt compelled to undertake the task of seeing if he would attempt communication. It took about three months of effort before she began to write automatic scripts which showed some sort of meaning. They were mostly in Latin and Greek, cryptic and less than coherent, and were signed "Myers."

Some months later, a curious thing happened. Mrs. Piper, in the United States, began making allusions in her trance to some of the material in the Verrall scripts, and these comments also claimed to come from Myers. In another year or so, the Verralls' daughter, Helen, also began to write automatically, and it was found that she was alluding to the same subjects as her mother and Piper before Helen had seen her mother's scripts. After this, their scripts were all sent to the Society for Psychical Research for comparison.

Next on the scene was a sister of Rudyard Kipling, a Mrs. Fleming, living in India. In 1903 she had read Myers' book *Human Personality and Its Survival of Bodily Death*, and this renewed her interest in her own gift for automatic writing. She, too, began to receive scripts signed "Myers," and in one of these she was instructed to send it "to Mrs. Verrall, at 5 Selwyn Gardens, Cambridge." She had heard of Verrall but had never met her, nor did she have any idea where she lived.

The address was indeed correct, as it turned out, but Fleming had the usual skepticism of the educated about these matters and did not follow the instructions. However, she did eventually send the scripts and subsequent ones to the Society of Psychical Research, which acted as a clearinghouse for such information. Here they were dutifully filed away, with no connection made to the Piper and Verrall scripts.

It was almost two years later that the connection was noticed, and by then the scripts themselves seemed to be making the extraordinary claim that Myers, Gurney, and Sidgwick had devised them to demonstrate their continued existence and prove their identities! Before they died, these three pioneers had come to realize the extreme difficulty of attempting to prove identity through messages that were inevitably distorted by their passage through the subconscious desires, photos, belief systems, and feelings of the medium.

According to the scripts, the intention of the authors was to make these fragments appear random and pointless to the individual automatists, in order to avoid giving clues to the train of thought behind them. They would only become meaningful and show evidence of design when pieced together by an independent investigator. Most, though not all, of the fragments could have come from the minds of the writers; a few contained information to which they did not appear to have had previous access.

The investigators at the Society for Psychical Research concluded that the claim made in the scripts appeared to be justified, in that the scripts appeared to show evidence of design by minds more familiar with classical scholarship than the automatic writers—only the Verralls had any classical training at all. In the view of the researchers, the scripts also displayed some of the characteristics of their purported authors and made apt references to their past lives.

In the end, six or seven automatic writers were involved, all producing a series of literary quotations, allusions, references to Greek mythology, and anagrams, which seemed to refer to one another's scripts. Typically the messages made little sense when taken separately, but together they seemed to form a jigsaw puzzle of associations, and the scripts themselves implied that this was the intention. Mrs. Verrall's "Myers" wrote: "Record the bits and when fitted they will make the whole. . . . I will give the words between you; neither alone can read but together they will give the clue he wants."

Over all, more than three thousand documents, stretching out over thirty years, make up the total of these "communications," which finally faded out in 1932.

In *Beyond The Reach of Sense*, Rosalind Heywood writes:

> From the evidence . . . available it is hard for the dispassionate critic to avoid the conclusion that for over thirty years in dozens of cases something was causing a number of automatists, not only to refer to the same topic—one often abstruse—but to make their references complementary, to create what have been called classical jigsaw puzzles.

Needless to say, it is not an easy task to validate such presumed after-death experiences. The annals of channeling include a great many such reports, and there is much commonality among them. Those who believe tend to consider this agreement among channeled sources to be impressive validation; the skeptics have more mundane explanations.

As for the "controls," clinical cases of secondary or multiple personalities suggest that these may be very similar phenomena. In some cases the medium has seemed to reproduce the mannerisms, tricks of speech, habits of thought, and even the facial expressions of the deceased to a remarkable extent. Even so, the "survival" hypothesis could hardly be said to be proven by these channeling experiments.

In another version of remote viewing a second person, referred to as a *beacon*, leaves the laboratory and, at a prearranged time, opens a randomly chosen envelope containing the location and identification of a nearby target (for example, a particular distinctive building, fountain, or airport). The beacon drives to the target and gazes intently at the target at a prearranged time and interval. At the same time, his partner back in the laboratory is requested to sketch whatever image presents itself to his closed eyes. Again the sketch is compared with a photograph of the actual site by a panel of judges.

If the SRI results are accurate, the ability to know what is happening at a place one has never visited is not a rare talent but a trainable skill latent within all of us. This training primarily involves the removal of negative unconscious beliefs that it can't be done. Since demonstrations of such abilities are actively disparaged in our society, the SRI experiments brought the subject into a well-equipped scientific laboratory in the midst of a huge, high-tech research institute, where they were told by reputable scientists that it had already been established that such feats were possible.

In one modification of this experiment, everything remained the same with the exception that the subject in the laboratory was asked to make the sketch half an hour *before* the envelope was randomly chosen (although the subject did not know this modification had been made). In other words, the impression of the target was sketched half an hour before anyone knew what the target would be. This precognitive test worked almost as well as the standard version. After all, once you are willing to speculate about taking the researchers from remote viewing, it is not that hard to leap even further out the spectrum of plausibility to precognitive remote viewing.

Research on psychokinesis has been conducted with the same care for established scientific protocols as the remote viewing work, by equally competent and distinguished researchers, at equally prestigious institutions—with equally startling results. One such experiment was conducted by Robert Jahn, dean of engineering and applied sciences at Princeton University.

Conditioned as we tend to be in this culture to think of "mind" and "matter" as two incompatible polarities, we expect to draw the line at the mind having influence over the physical environment. Of course, we don't think of this "normal" influence as being extraordinary: When we decide to open a door, our hand turns a doorknob. Surely there is nothing miraculous about that.

If you were to gaze at an object on a smooth tabletop with the objective of mentally causing it to move, you would probably become discouraged quite rapidly. You don't expect it to move, and sure enough, it remains stationary. Suppose, Jahn hypothesized, the situation is something like biofeedback, where unconsciously you know how to control muscle tensions, dilate blood vessels, change organ functioning, and so forth, but without the feedback signal you don't know that you know and can't become conscious that you know. What if it is the same with psychokinesis? Could it be that unconsciously you know how to move that object, but without feedback you cannot draw upon the knowledge?

Jahn employed a device called a Fabry-Perot interferometer. Basically, the interferometer consists of two parallel plates. A light beam bounces back and forth between the plates, producing an optical interference pattern that can be displayed on a screen. If the space between the plates is changed by even a fraction of a wavelength of light, the rings in the interference pattern expand or contract noticeably. With that feedback signal to tell subjects how well they are doing, it appears that some of them can move those plates by focusing their mind on an image of the plate moving.

In both the SRI remote-viewing research and the Princeton anomalies research, the findings indicated that the perennial wisdom may be right, we may all know unconsciously how to perform these kinds of extraordinary feats. We simply need to remove the negative belief that inhibits us from doing them. In the end, when the meager evidence available today is closely examined it appears that John Lilly was right when he said that it is not clear that there are any limits to the abilities of the human mind that are not fundamentally *beliefs* about the limits of that mind.

Certainly, there have been many reports through the centuries of just such occurrences. In the New Testament, in the book of Matthew, Jesus advises: "If you have faith as a grain of mustard seed, you will say to this mountain, 'Move hence to another place,' and it will move; and nothing will be impossible to you."

All these results are preliminary and highly controversial, but they do seem to make a beginning at establishing something our unconscious idea processors have been trying to tell us about our inner capacities for generations beyond counting.

Surprisingly enough, this exploration of paranormal phenomena brings us back squarely within the spectrum of creativity. For research on remote viewing suggests that the creative/intuitive mind could be getting information in other ways than from the lifelong learning of the person. Research on telepathic communication suggests that we are all joined at a deep level, thus emphasizing that we should not be too hasty to assume limits to the creative unconscious. Research on psychokinesis indicates a connection between mind and the external environment, which opens up the possibility of some kinds of miracles. In the end, *it is not clear that there are any limits* to the creative/intuitive mind other than those stemming from the individual's belief system.

THE TRANSFORMATIVE WISDOM

According to Hastings, the final category into which most channeling, revelations, and illumination fall consists of both personal and social transformation. Although this seems to have come to dominate twentieth-century channelings, as with Seth and *A Course in Miracles*, it has been a part of the higher wisdom received and taught by all the followers of mystical or revealed wisdom.

Long before modern laboratory researchers began to make a science of potential keys to breakthrough insight and personal transformation like affirmation, relaxation, imagery, or dreamwork, practitioners of the perennial philosophy had already developed each of these into highly effective technologies of their own.

Whatever other inquiries may be undertaken in constructing a "science of religion," some of the most important sources of input are the records of earlier pioneers and explorers, even if those prophetic explorations were couched in languages other than the modern lingua franca of industrial-era society.

Many of the folk medicines of the so-called primitive societies were once dismissed as superstition or witch doctoring, but how many lives have been saved by quinine, digitalis, and other pharmaceuticals that were originally derived from folk medicines that were derided as primitive superstition? Perhaps the same reversal of attitudes will take place in the future, when the theories and methods of the earlier consciousness researchers are more clearly understood by Western science.

There is no dispute that questions about the nature of consciousness and reality were theorized, tested, and applied by ancient—but not unsophisticated—knowledge systems many centuries ago. Sufis, monks, yogis, and prophets, often acting on and guided by the evergrowing body of esoteric teachings, left a formidable body of literature concerning the ways and means of mental health, and the reprogramming (transformation) of the human psyche. Although they were not written in psychological jargon or neurochemical terminology (any more than folk medicine was expressed in pharmaceutical terms), these early observations are astonishingly accurate about areas of psychology which we in the West are only beginning to explore today.

In institutionalized religions, prayer probably originated as a living exercise in affirmation, but degenerated to a ritual of supplication or penance directed toward some external being. Yet those whose devotion leads them to the true meaning beneath the outer form of their religion's prayers come to realize that it is not an external message system, but a dialogue between self and Self, a channel to the wisest of our inner personalities.

In the 1970s, Benson and other psychophysiologists

studying the relaxation response took a closer look at the esoteric literature of the world's great religions and discovered
that very similar techniques could be found hidden within
every one of the major traditions; prescribed postures and
breathing patterns and special modulations of the voice bore a
marked similarity to the clinical meditation techniques arrived
at by Benson and his collegues.

The famed scholar Gershom Scholem noted that the
Jewish mystical system called the Kaballah[8] "represent(s) but a
Judaized version of that ancient spiritual technique which has
found its classical expression in the practices of the Indian
mystics who follow the system known as *Yoga.*"

Yoga, of course, is the form of these ancient teachings
most familiar in the West. It would be perhaps nothing more
than a curious coincidence if only the Kabbalist and yogic systems harbored such exercises, but several Christian traditions,
including the Byzantine church, particularly treasured a
method of prayer used extensively at the monastery of Mount
Athos in Greece. It was called "The Prayer of the Heart" or
"The Prayer of Jesus," and Benson noted that:[9]

> It dates back to the beginning of Christianity. The prayer itself
> was called secret meditation and was transmitted from older to
> younger monks through an initiation rite. Emphasis was placed
> on having a skilled instructor. The method of prayer recom-
> mended by these monks was as follows:
> "Sit down alone and in silence. Lower your head, shut
> your eyes, breathe out gently, and imagine yourself looking into
> your own heart. Carry your mind, i.e., your thoughts, from your
> head to your heart. As you breathe out, say 'Lord Jesus Christ,
> have mercy on me.' Say it moving your lips gently, or simply
> say it in your mind. Try to put all other thoughts aside. Be calm,
> be patient, and repeat the process very frequently."

The chanting systems of the East, based on the oldest of
the Hindu scriptures, the Japanese Zen practice of sitting
meditation, Chinese Taoist yoga, are other methods of eliciting
the relaxation response, as were certain practices of the Sufis:[10]

The basic elements that elicit the relaxation response in certain practices of Christianity and Judaism are also found in Islamic mysticism or Sufism. . . . It is a means of excluding distractions and of drawing nearer to God by the constant repetition of His name, either silently or aloud, and by rhythmic breathing. Music, musical poems, and dance are also employed in their ritual. . . .

The oldest known revealed scriptures also indicate the existence of a very detailed and sophisticated inquiry into the nature of dreams and the proper conduct of the dream self. From the yogic dreamers of Tibet to the dream temples of ancient Greece, it appears that yet another "discovery" of modern science was explored in detail by practitioners of the perennial wisdom.

The Brihadarmyaka-Upanishad, one of the eleven fundamental scriptures of Vedanta philosophy, dating back to about 100 B.C., has particular significance to contemporary students of dream state with regard to questions about the nature of the self within the self that creates all the phenomena we have been discussing in this book:[11]

Ganaka Vaideha said: "Who is that Self"

Yagnavalkya replied: "He who is within the heart, surrounded by the Pranas (senses), the person of light, consisting of knowledge. He, remaining the same, wanders along the two worlds, as if thinking, as if moving. During sleep (in dreams) he transcends this world and all the forms of death. . . .

"And when he falls asleep, then after having taken away with him the material from the whole world, destroying and building it up again, he sleeps (dreams) by his own light. In that state the person is self-illuminated.

"There are no (real) chariots in that state, no horses, no roads. There are no blessings there, no happiness, no joys, but he himself sends forth (creates) blessings, happiness and joys. . . . He is indeed the maker.

"As a large fish moves along the two banks of a river, the right and left, so does that person move along these two states, the state of sleeping and the state of waking.

"And as a falcon, or any other (swift) bird, after he has roamed about here in the air, becomes tired, and folding his wings he is carried to his nest, so does that person hasten to that state where, when asleep, he desires no more desires, and dreams no more dreams. . . .

"But when he fancies that he is, as it were, a god, or that he is, as it were, a king, or 'I am this altogether,' that is his highest world."

Several points worth noting in this passage are only now gaining scientific credence. First, the creator of the illusions of the dream is equated with the creator of the "illusion" of the world—an early statement about the relationship between beliefs and perceptions. Second, it is pointed out that to obtain knowledge, the self moves between two different states. Third, there is a certain kind of dream that the dreamer can create which can be a tool for dispelling illusion. To dream, to awaken to that dream, and to seek the highest world: three thousand years ago, the perennial wisdom was pointing the way.

At about the same time, during the age of the Trojan War, a hero named Aescalapius was written of by Homer as a man who had learned the secret arts of healing from Cheiron, the dreaded ferryman of Hades whom many scholars consider a metaphor for the passage to the unconscious. Half a millenium after the burning of Troy, the dream cult of Aescalapius spread to more than three hundred temples in Greece. Scholars today feel that the dream cults were a grafting of older Egyptian knowledge about "true dreams" onto local fertility cults centered on magical springs, caves, and places of healing.

The parallels between the Greek dream-healing cult and what is now being discovered about the role of suggestion and imagery in healing and dream therapy; lucid dreams are especially noteworthy. The main dream temple at Epidaurus was in continuous operation for nearly a thousand years. The extraordinary longevity of this cult was said to stem from its success in granting special healing dreams. After undergoing purification and meditation rituals, pilgrims to these temples slept in special dormitories, where Aescalapius was said to visit them in dreams, giving them diagnoses and suggesting remedies for their ailments, which they remembered upon awakening.

The Bible has many things to say about the vehicle of dream knowledge, one of the most succinct statements being: "If any man among you is a prophet, I make myself known to him in a vision, I speak to him in a dream." Dream prophecy is prominent in the Old Testament, notably in the cases of Joseph and Daniel.

The phenomenon of lucid dreaming and the use of the dream state as a tool for exploring and reprogramming the unconscious was long a subcategory of esoteric teachings. The Buddhist yogis of Tibet had developed a "yoga of the dream state," in which the development of control over their dreams became a step in a much grander process of soul shaping. And lucid dreaming itself was seen as a direct way in which the student could experience at first hand something similar to what they were really pointing toward—the experience of a far more fundamental awakening; the awakening from the dream or illusion of our belief systems to a far more conscious state.

Imagery and the techniques we have called "dialogue with the unconscious" were practiced in India and elsewhere thousands of years ago. Dr. Stuart Miller has written extensively about this tradition:[12]

> In the Hindu tradition, this higher aspect is sometimes called the Atman. As is well known, Mahatma Gandhi, a practical and most successful political leader, used to talk of the "inner light of universal truth," which he would consult on important matters. . . .
>
> The Bhagavad Gita, the most revered of Indian scriptures, is presented as a dialogue between a young man in crisis, Arjuna, and the great Lord Krishna, a major Indian deity. But interpretations of the Gita going back over 2500 years have described it as an internal dialogue—a dramatic presentation of the dialogue between the aspiring personality and the divine light, or Higher Self, symbolized by Krishna.

Here, again, we find profound, but as yet unexplored, interconnections between the breakthrough state, revelation, and the unitary experience, which deserve far greater attention than they have so far received from the scientific community.

Stepping back to view all the foregoing material in perspective, we see that as far as the content of Hasting's three categories and the findings of modern science go, the two are not as clearly opposed as once might have been the case. In cosmology modern physics no longer dismisses, as an earlier science did, the possibility that channeling might be a valid source of information. Potentiality—likewise. Transformation —the human transformation is substantiated by current psychotherapies, and the social transformation story is coming from other evidence as well.

THE PERENNIAL PHILOSOPHY

This brings up a critical question regarding *content* of channeling and revelation: If we examine the material within each of these categories, does it meet Poulain's second criterion and "check with the experience of others"—as any other scientific theorem or discovery should? Or, will we find it contradictory, mutually exclusive, or random—as many people no doubt imagine we would?

Has the unconscious idea processor produced breakthroughs and insights in these areas that have tended to share common themes across cultures and throughout the ages? One might be tempted to assume that such is not the case, given the great variability and dissension that exists between the outward form of the different religions. And yet, as we shall see, there are certain universal insights that seem to have been passed on and continually rediscovered since before the dawn of history.

We are not the first to claim that this question can be answered in the affirmative. From the esoteric core of the world's spiritual traditions (which, of course, come partly from channeling and partly from mystical experience), we can distill a highest common factor.

Aldous Huxley referred to this "highest common factor" by the term the *Perennial Philosophy,* and wrote of it:[13]

Rudiments of the Perennial Philosophy may be found among the traditionary lore of primitive peoples in every region of the world, and in its fully developed forms it has a place in every one of the higher religions. A version of this Highest Common Factor . . . was first committed to writing more than twenty-five centuries ago.

Of course, this perennial wisdom is not a philosophy, in the strict sense, and even to define its core is not easy, but those who have studied it agree that it does have a distinct, if indefinable, form. Huxley discussed this aspect of the perennial philosophy, too:

> *Philosophia Perennis*—the phrase was coined by Leibniz; but the thing—the metaphysic that recognizes a divine Reality substantial to the world of things and lives and minds; the psychology that finds in the soul something similar to, or even identical with, divine Reality; the ethic that places men's final end in the knowledge of the immanent and transcendent Ground of all being—the thing is immemorial and universal.

Yet, in spite of the fact that this "perennial wisdom" has been written about in every religion of the world and in all the principal languages of Asia and Europe, serious comparison of the essential claims and tenets of the world's diverse spiritual traditions has become a subject of scholarly and scientific interest only within the last half-century or so. For the most part, this neglect was due to two prejudices of the dominant culture: Why bother investigating the other religions of the world if it is already established that Christianity is the one true, revealed religion? And why bother if it is assumed that scientific, empirical, positivistic inquiry has replaced religious inquiry (or "mere superstition") with superior method or if such beliefs and teachings are considered only cultural curios, the primitive misconceptions of a less knowledgeable age? And of interest only to those fascinated with the dead past like historians and archeologists?

When efforts at systematic comparison of religions finally began, two important generalizations became increasingly well documented:

1. These religions typically include various *exoteric*, or public forms, and an *esoteric* hidden version, usually maintained by some inner circle and involving meditative discipline and alteration of consciousness (spiritual exercises).

2. Although the exoteric versions are very different from one another (Hindu rituals differing from Christian; Islamic beliefs differing from Buddhist, and so forth), the esoteric versions appear to possess a number of common core beliefs.

   Perhaps the oldest known variant of the hidden wisdom is shamanism, a pragmatic yet other-worldly system of mind-body exercises, passed on through direct experiential training in tribal societies from Siberia (where it is now thought to have originated) to South America (where it continues to flourish in remote areas and even in the midst of modern cities). Anthropologist Michael Harner, chairman of the anthropology department at the New School for Social Research, estimates that this system is at least 30,000 to 50,000 years old. Portions of the shamanic stream of knowledge passed into the younger traditions of Asia.

   Elements, artifacts, and symbols of the practice of the perennial wisdom can be found in every culture, every religion, and every part of the world. In one form or another, often hidden in parable, metaphor, and myth, its principles and beliefs have been incorporated in the teachings which underlie every faith by which we live.

   While these teachings are older than any historical records, they have rarely prevailed as a dominant element in any very large group for any length of time. Furthermore, paradoxical as it may seem, while the proponents of these principles have often been the guiding wisdom responsible for the spiritual content of their church's religion, they have frequently been the object of persecution from their more conservative brothers.

   The fact that much of the content of channeling tends to point in the direction of the perennial wisdom is the ultimate answer to Poulain's second criticism, namely that insight be tested for congruence with the accumulated experience of inner exploration through the ages. Much of the content of channeling is no doubt accretions and distortions because of signals that have bubbled up to conscious awareness through the individual's unconscious mind. But whatever final interpretation we may give to the sources of these transmissions, the residue of apparently valuable insight, credible because of its consistency, is the reason for the importance attached to this phenomenon throughout history.

What are the teachings of the perennial wisdom and how valid are they? We will summarize them below and the reader can compare them to certain scientific findings that we have described earlier in this chapter and the ones preceding it.

1. The most essential part of the Self is the supraconscious, not ordinarily accessible to conscious awareness.

   Access to the supraconscious may be enhanced by meditative disciplines, life crises, attitudes (e.g., nonattachment), auto-suggestive approaches, ritual, etc.

2. All persons are hypnotized from infancy by the culture in which they grow up. The prime task of adult life is dehypnotization, "enlightenment"—the process of discovering that the perceived world is partial and illusory, with "another reality" behind it.

3. At higher states of consciousness there is awareness of participation in a transpersonal Mind, of the oneness of all.

4. The ego self is threatened by the existence of the real Self and throws up a variety of smokescreens to block awareness of the true Center. In the end, for integration the ego self must become subservient to the real Self.

5. Enlightenment involves all questions and problems being turned over to the supraconscious mind which is identical to the one Mind. Answers will then be best not only for the individual, but for all. There are no limits to the supraconscious mind; experienced limits are only the consequences of beliefs about the limits of the human mind.

   Integration of the personality implies alignment of conscious with supraconscious choice, so that the whole of one's being—subconscious, conscious, and supraconscious—is conflict free and all directed toward the same ends.

THE FINAL CRITERION

As Poulain and Wilbur point out, in addition to the criteria already examined, there is a last criterion by which we should judge the content of channeling, revelation, and illumination in these areas.

This test has more to do with savor and feeling than fact, though its purpose is not to supercede fact but to supplement it. What we are talking about here is what James has called a "noetic sense of truth."

In *Varieties of Religious Experience,* James argued that:

Although so similar to states of feeling, mystical states seem to those who experience them to be also states of knowledge. They are states of insight into depths of truth unplumbed by the discursive intellect. They are illuminations, revelations, full of significance and importance, all inarticulate though they remain; and as a rule they carry with them a curious sense of authority for aftertime.

Curiously, this seems to echo the words of the mathematician Poincaré, who claimed his breakthroughs were always accompanied by a feeling of "perfect certainty." And, indeed, many mystics as well as artists and scientists report experiencing this "noetic" sense of the validity of their deepest illuminations.

In *The Invisible Writing,* his autobiography, Arthur Koestler describes the way in which the two different "orders" of reality (fact and feeling) complement and illuminate one another to produce something which might be called "universal" or "divine" truth:[14]

Certain experiences ... filled me with a direct certainty that a higher order of reality existed, and that it alone invested existence with meaning. ... The narrow world of sensory perception constituted the "first order [of reality]"; this perceptual world was enveloped by the conceptual world which contained phenomena not directly perceivable, such as gravitation, electromagnetic fields, and curved space. This "second order of reality" filled in the gaps and gave meaning to the absurd patchiness of the sensory world. In the same manner, the "third order of reality" enveloped, interpenetrated, and gave meaning to the second. It contained "occult" phenomena which could not be approached or explained either on the sensory or on the conceptual level, and yet occasionally invaded them like spiritual meteors piercing the primitive's vaulted sky. Just as the conceptual order showed up the illusions and distortions of the senses, so the "third order" disclosed that time, space and causality, that isolation, separateness, and spatio-temporal limitations of the self were merely optical illusions on the next higher level.

The concept of fact and feeling as complementary methods for testing the veridicality of mystical insights is to be found, among other places, in the writings of French philosopher Henri Bergson, particularly *The Two Sources of Morality and Religion*.[15] He argues there that two important kinds of knowledge exist, one based on reason and empiricism, and the other, no less important, based on intuition and noetic understanding.

It was in this sense that astronaut Edgar Mitchell described the impact of an experience that occurred in February, 1971, as he was returning to Earth from his Apollo 14 walk on the moon:[16]

When I went to the moon, I was as pragmatic a test pilot, engineer, and scientist as any of my colleagues. . . . Many times my life has depended upon the validity of scientific principles and the reliability of the technology built upon those principles. . . .

But there was another aspect to my experience during Apollo 14, and it contradicted the "pragmatic engineer" attitude. It began with the breathtaking experience of seeing planet Earth floating in the vastness of space.

The first thing that came to mind as I looked at Earth was its incredible beauty. Even the spectacular photographs do not do it justice. It was a majestic sight—a splendid blue and white jewel suspended against a velvet black sky. How peacefully, how harmoniously, how marvelously it seemed to fit into the evolutionary pattern by which the universe is maintained. In a peak experience, the presence of divinity became almost palpable and I *knew* that life in the universe was not just an accident based on random processes. This knowledge came to me directly—noetically. It was not a matter of discursive reasoning or logical abstraction. It was an experiential cognition. It was knowledge gained through private subjective awareness, but it was—and still is—every bit as real as the objective data upon which, say, the navigational program or the communications system were based. Clearly, the universe had meaning and direction. It was not perceptible by the sensory organs, but it was there nevertheless—an unseen dimension behind the visible creation that gives it an intelligent design and that gives life purpose.

But long before men were flying to the moon, or James was helping psychiatry become a scientific discipline, the third-century philosopher Plotinus was familiar with "noetic knowledge" and its central place in the world of thought: "Knowledge has three degrees—opinion, science, illumination. The means or instrument of the first is sense; of the second, dialectic; of the third, intuition. To the last I subordinate reason. It is absolute knowledge founded on the identity of the mind knowing with the object known."

This sounds a great deal like a version of the *unitary* or direct perception of reality the perennial wisdom speaks of so frequently. Which in turn suggests that certain aspects of breakthroughs may originate with or be associated with some kind of direct perception by the deep intuition of the subject involved.

Those influenced by Western outlooks will be suspicious of such a transcendental viewpoint as we have been presenting here. First, because it does not seem to be based in public perceptions as to what is scientifically credible. Second, because attempts to communicate about it often sound dangerously close to superstition or nonsense or both. And third, because its teachings are said to connote some sort of quietistic retreat from the pragmatic problems of the world.

The first objection is gradually being countered by science itself, as it becomes apparent that the rules of scientific evidence can be applied successfully to the study of inner knowledge; and that the findings of science and the reports coming back from these states present nowhere near so clearcut a contrast as had once been assumed. Although, as we have tried to point out through this book, a truly comprehensive "science of religion," breakthrough states, and human consciousness is far from completion, but its foundations are already being built as modern science incorporates both inner and outer empricism.

The second ground for suspicion—poor communicability—is fundamental. Because ordinary perception as experienced is a partial perception (at least in this expanded out-look), the language and metaphors built up from ordinary perception have never incorporated terminology to describe any expanded view of reality. Tools for testing and exploring the experience and then, as will other sciences, developing a better language to describe what we find might be better than attempts to force the experience into our present language or dismissing it because we can't.

As to the third objection, to be sure some versions of the *essential premise* do sound like an escapist retreat from the world. But the major difference between these experiences taken in the wisdom system of the perennial philosophy, and the sheerly narcissistic seeking of inner experience is the fact that *work* is placed at the heart of humane living—not the compulsive old-fashioned work ethic of our fathers, that saw work as a means to pay off the original sin, nor work for economic gain alone, but the joy of creative work "in the service of the Divine Architect" of the world or one's fellow man or a saner healthier way of living.

Ultimately, for the time being at least, no complete answers are available or even possible in the transcendental realm. The explorers of this world might use the same technique for the same period of time, but there is nothing to guarantee that they will all achieve the same depth or even kind of spiritual insight. However, many scientists are now beginning to recognize, as did Edgar Mitchell, that such knowledge cannot be dismissed. But the question of how to regard transcendental data remains the central question to be answered by a future science of the religion.

6

The Quicksilver Stream

Beyond the End of the Spectrum

THE TRACK OF THE PERENNIAL WISDOM

As with all research, every question we answer, or attempt to answer, only seems to raise further questions.

It is not difficult to conceive of breakthrough insights in terms of an unconscious idea processor or to conceive of religious revelations in terms of breakthrough insights—or even to understand why spiritual channelings should concern themselves primarily with the three categories described by Hastings.

What is not so easy to understand is why each category should predominate at successive times in history, instead of being rather evenly distributed, as we might expect.

Various scholars have theorized that the unconscious may be setting its own priorities on where humanity's attention needs to be directed at different stages in our social, psychological, and cultural evolution. It cannot be denied that our conscious minds have unarguably often misled us, selecting superficial and blindly suicidal priorities in the face of facts so obvious that later generations have been at a loss to account for their predecessors' foolhardiness. Certainly it does not strain credulity to suggest that if the unconscious can solve mathematical theorems and determine the individual's deepest needs, that it might be able to do the same for humanity's needs as well.

In which case, then it might be worth examining the track of the perennial wisdom as it winds its way in and out of history in an attempt to determine what effect the collective urgings of humanity's unconscious might have played in the shaping of our destiny and the guidance of our evolution.

We have chosen to focus here on the more recent cultural manifestations that led to the creation of Western civilization—the Judaic, Christian, and Islamic traditions. As we have seen, within each of these traditions an esoteric core has always existed, and hidden teachings have always been passed down directly from master to initiate. Because liberation (from ego illusion, cultural hypnosis, self-limitation, separation from God) is at the core of all these systems, the implications not only for the exoteric, popular religions, but for Western history have been profound. For the kind of liberation that sages talk about is, as we shall see, is inextricably bound up with the kind of liberation that political figures also talk about.

Indeed, one of the most startling conclusions that can be inferred by our examination of the history of these breakthrough states is that the modern political beliefs in the importance of "liberty, equality, and fraternity," which form the base of our most cherished values, are directly related to the same mysterious experiences that many people regard as "superstition" or "insanity" when they are voiced by ordinary individuals rather than prophets.

Therefore, our examination of these unorthodox elements of Western religious thought covers not only what these traditions have to say about human consciousness and creativity, but what the relationship between personal liberation and political liberation is as well.

Again, we do not ask that these claims be taken as proven—only that you consider something as possible that conventional history books have not taught.

THE TRAIL OF THE KABBALAH

To those readers born in the West, the most familiar form of the perennial wisdom is embedded within the Judeo-Christian tradition. Some scholars, comparing data on the positions of the stars as recorded in the principle book of the Kabbalah, the *Sepher Yetzirah* (The Book of Formation), earliest text of mystical Judaism, date its origin at 2000 years before the birth of Christ.

Although most people today would consider Judaic mysticism to be an obscure footnote to history, it was actually one of the two principal roots of the intellectual growth that eventually resulted in the Renaissance. The transmission of key ideas between East and West, Islamic and Christian thought, was accomplished by many of the same people who were deeply involved in building the Kabbalist tradition.

The mystic stream adopted by the Hebrews flowed from even older sources. The mystery schools of Central Asia, Palestine, Babylon, and Egypt were in existence long before and during the formative stages of Judaism, and they were still highly active when and where Christianity was born. But the origins of the perennial philosophy will always be lost in the mists of time because it seems to have been with humanity since long before the dawn of remembered history.

The eminent Jungian scholar Ira Progoff noted that the Jewish mystical tradition contributed to the evolution of Western thought in three ways: by setting the scene within which Christianity came into being; by continuing a dialogue over centuries and across continents with questing individuals and groups within Christendom; and, perhaps most importantly, the Kabbalists contributed an attitude regarding the evolution of consciousness, an attitude that was to significantly affect other mystical traditions and to eventually influence even Freudian theory.

Progoff describes the relationship between Christian and Jewish mystical traditions and their profound impact on Western civilization:[1]

These movements of mystical thought within Christianity proceeded always as the work of outsiders, persons not in conformity with the doctrinal orthodoxies of the established Church. ...

The Jewish mysticism of the early and later Middle Ages was thus able to carry a large part of the burden of individual religious experience and exploration for Western civilization as a whole. Much of what was done by the light of Kaballah ... found its way into Christian thinking and provided added sustenance for the tendency toward mystical feeling that is inherent in Christianity but is fettered by its position of cultural dominance and conformity. Below the surface of society, on the level where free spirits meet, there was thus a lively dialogue taking place during the medieval centuries between those Christians and Jews who were concerned with the ultimate mystery of messiahship, the mystery of how the world can one day be redeemed and how God can become manifest in the life of man.

It would seem to be folly to attempt to condense even a fraction of the many levels of symbol, theory, and practice of that branch of the perennial wisdom that makes up the Jewish mystical tradition known as the Kaballah. It incorporates a complex, detailed, multicultured and multilingual cosmology, theology, and psychology. Metaphysical discourse, mystical passion, and experimental consciousness technologies were combined in texts originally composed in Hebrew, Spanish, Arabic, French, and Italian.

Of particular importance to our investigation of breakthroughs, channeling and spiritual revelation is the phase of Kabbalism, known as the *Merkabah*, or Chariot, epoch, which flourished in Palestine from about the first century B.C. through the tenth century A.D. The origin of this body of thought and practice lies in the Kabbalist's interpretation of the prophet Ezekial's description of the "celestial chariot." Although the language might seem alien to the modern reader, a number of contemporary scholars have pointed out that these passages actually mask metaphors for sophisticated consciousness-altering methodologies.

The specific means by which humans might experience a unitary form of consciousness, the relationship between this experience and the more orthodox beliefs of the faith, and the relationship between individual evolution and cosmic redemption were the chief themes of the Merkabah mystics:[2]

> Initiates in the visionary tradition were known as *Yorde Merkabah* ("those who descend in the chariot") because they would "descend" ever deeper inward to the recesses of their own mind. In the deepest realms of meditation, the etherial Chariot was said to be hidden, ready to raise the disciple through all levels of consciousness until Ezekiel's heavenly image was beheld. . . . The masters of this system charted like expert cartographers the difficult inner terrain to be crossed by those on the

quest. They described what the initiate might be expected to see and feel. . . . Typically, fasting, special breathing exercises, and rhythmic chants were used to help guide the initiate into an altered state of consciousness.

Many important Kabbalists were also among the most important figures in Jewish history. Several were also documented "channels." The case of the famed Kabbalist Joseph Karo, born in Spain in the late fifteenth century, and his *maggids* sound remarkably like those of Jane Roberts and Seth. He and his family settled in Constantinople, now Istanbul, after the great expulsion of Jews from Spain in 1492:[3]

He became renowned as a Talmudic scholar and legal thinker, but eventually found himself drawing close to Kabbalistic circles. Under careful tutelage, Karo experimented with what psychologists today would call altered states of awareness and trance phenomena. After a time, he learned to enter into a mediumistic trance.

In this condition, as described in his lifelong diary and confirmed by independent observers, Karo would lose his ordinary frame of mind and speak in a changed voice. He would then proceed to discourse—sometimes freely, at other times in a strange, halting manner—upon such evocative themes as the higher nature of dreams, the right way to meditate, the nature of the deity, and even life after death and reincarnation. Karo and his contemporaries in Safed (Palestine) referred to this as the *maggid* (a technical term indicating an agent of celestial speech) phenomenon and believed that a spiritual entity was actively communicating through the channel created by the human medium. Scholars today are finding that this fascinating occurrence was actually far from rare in the Jewish tradition. . . .

Characteristically, Karo would retain awareness of what was happening as his voice would alter and its tone and rhythm drastically change. Without any conscious volition on his part, rational speech of an exotic nature would issue from his mouth. Claiming to be the spirit of the *Mishnah* (the Jewish holy book of biblical commentary), this secondary personality or *maggid* would speak on a wide range of esoteric topics—from analyzing the nature of higher consciousness and reincarnation to voicing actual prophecies.

Judaism, after all, has always been a prophetic faith. The

experiences of Moses, Ezekiel, Isaiah, Daniel, and many others, as recorded in the Old Testament, are filled with descriptions of paranormal phenomena—visions, prophetic dreams, and clairvoyance.

The messianic, mystical, and prophetic cults of Palestine in the years preceding the birth of Jesus were deeply involved in exploring these states and in transmitting knowledge of them that was old even then. The experiences of Jesus in the Wilderness and Paul on the Damascus road, as they were described in scriptures, were most certainly paranormal, if not classical cases of channeling or breakthrough phenomenon experiences. Paul even went so far as to admonish: "Make love your aim, and earnestly desire the spiritual gifts, especially that you may prophesy."

It is not surprising, given the setting, that the third great faith to spring from the Middle East was also a prophetic one and that it contains an esoteric core.

CONVERGENT STREAMS

In 610 A.D., a devout camel driver from the Arabian peninsula received a revelation that was to affect the lives of a large segment of the Earth's population, East and West. At the age of forty, during a period of fasting, prayer, and solitary meditation, Muhammad heard a voice calling him and saw a flood of light of "intolerable splendor." An angel in human form displayed a silken cloth covered with written characters. The angel commanded him to read, and although he had been illiterate until that moment, Muhammad read the revelation that was to become the Koran.

During the century after Muhammad's revelation, the horsemen of Islam burst out of desert obscurity to conquer most of the ancient empires of the world, from the ancestral lands of the Hebrews, Persians, Egyptians, Byzantines, and Greeks, to the south of France in the West and the Indus valley in the East. These conquests were cultural and political as well as religious. Within the huge conquered territory were nearly all the ancient centers of learning and traditional schools of mystical or esoteric teachings. Communities of scholars, mystics, and consciousness technologists from Carthage to Central Asia, who had been cut off by the rise and dogmatism of Christianity as a state power and had not had contact with one another for centuries, were suddenly subjects of the same empire.

Like Judaism and Christianity, Islam also has an esoteric core. The spread and extraordinary hidden influence on history of Sufism, thought by its followers to be the true secret teaching concealed within every religion, coincided with the explosion of Islam from the Arabian desert to the farthest reaches of Asia, Africa, and the Pacific.

As Dr. Benson tells us, Sufism developed in reaction to the external rationalization of Islam and made use of intuitive and emotional faculties which are claimed to be dormant until utilized through training under guidance of a teacher.

Idries Shah, a direct descendant of the prophet Muhammad, a Sufi, and a Western-educated scholar of some reknown, has introduced the Sufi tradition to many Western readers. He writes:[4]

> The Sufi is an individual who believes that by practicing alternate detachment and identification with life, he becomes free. He is a mystic because he believes that he can become attuned to the purpose of all life. He is a practical man because he believes that this process must take place within normal society. And he must serve humanity because he is a part of it. . . .
>
> In order to succeed at this endeavor, he must follow the methods which have been devised by earlier masters, methods for slipping through the complex of training which makes most people prisoners of their environment and of the effect of their experiences. The exercises of the Sufis have been developed through the interaction of two things—intuition and the changing aspects of human life. Different methods will suggest themselves intuitively in different societies and at various times. This is not inconsistent, because real intuition is itself always consistent.
>
> The Sufi life can be lived at any time, in any place. It does not require withdrawal from the world, or organized movements, or dogma. It is coterminous with the existence of humanity. It cannot, therefore, accurately be termed an Eastern system. It has profoundly influenced both the East and the very

bases of the Western civilization in which many of us live—the mixture of Christian, Jewish, Moslem, and Near Eastern or Mediterranean heritage commonly called "Western."

Arab mystics began to travel, acting on the esoteric doctrine of unity among the mystical teachings of all faiths—conqueror and conquered alike. Representatives of the ancient schools of esoteric Judaism, Christianity, Hinduism, Buddhism, and Zoroastrianism were invited to participate in what the Sufis called "a confluence of essences."

Because the cultural and linguistic backgrounds of these different doctrines were so different on an exoteric level, the Sufis used metaphors to bridge the apparent doctrinal gaps the way scientists of different countries use mathematics. "Confluence," the idea that the Sufis, although Moslem, were in contact with the essential doctrine of every culture, was expressed in the image of the bee that drinks from many flowers (and thus helps fertilize them), without becoming a flower.

Many classical Sufi commentators noted that the breakup of the old order in Asia was the occasion for a reunion of long-separated spiritual traditions. In their phraseology, the Islamic conquests reunited the "beads of mercury" that had been carefully maintained by the esoteric schools of Egypt, Persia, Palestine, Afghanistan, India, and Greece, and created the "stream of quicksilver" that became known as Sufism.

There was a time when the Jewish, Moslem, and Christian esoteric schools were openly and fruitfully allied—in Spain, southern France, the Middle East, and Italy from the eleventh to fifteenth centuries. Southern France in the thirteenth century, by virtue of being a political borderland, was a place of asylum for many whose religious beliefs made them heretics in the eyes of the church-general. It had been a center of Jewish (and Kabbalist) tradition from at least the tenth century, and was western Europe's southern boundary with the Moslem caliphate for nearly as long. It was also the home of the Albigensian heretics (who dared to claim that humans could evolve to become godlike and were bloodily suppressed by the orthodoxy).

The troubadours, who originated in southern France at

this time, and who most Westerners remember from their schooling as rather romantic, carefree minstrels, brought more than entertainment and gossip as they roamed from town to town. The troubadours were the "media" of their day. In an age where only a few churchmen, Jews, and Moslems were literate—centuries before the printing press was invented—these wandering minstrels had to possess at least rudiments of education to compose their songs. The limited means of education available at that time were either in the hands of the Church, who disapproved of them publicly, or in the hands of free thinkers, who preserved the intellectual and spiritual concepts of far more ancient and more enlightened traditions. These Sufis-in-disguise also carried knowledge between the esoteric bretheren of different nations and religions disguised and encoded in the songs and stories by which they made their living.

When, as a result of the crusades and the Inquisition, that ecumenical period waned, the perennial wisdom went underground again, only to emerge in European life in disguised but nonetheless potent form. Manly Palmer Hall wrote of this cultural encoding and transmission of knowledge:[5]

> The wave of Islam's expansion reached Spain where two streams appear to have joined up. In Seville and Granada there were initiated Jews who carried the Egyptian transmission. They met Arab initiates who carried the Greek transmission. . . .
>
> If it is true that some "beads of mercury" were reunited through Mohammed, two more were reunited in Spain. Out of this confluence grew a very large part of the whole of Western civilization. . . .
>
> The current which flowed from the beads of mercury which were reunited flowed into an immense invisible force field over Europe. . . . It externalized into the common life in a series of culture components which in aggregate constitute a large part of Western Civilization.
>
> A selection of these factors at random would include the Christian pilgrimage . . . the Gothic cathedrals; illumination and embroidery; the Troubadours . . . the Arthurian Quest Theme . . . the Wandering Players, Jester, harlequinades and Mystery Plays . . . Freemasonry and Rosicrucianism; gardening (the Spanish Gardens); playing cards . . . archery; some medi-

cine like immunology (Paracelsus) ... and cybernetics (Raymond Lully).

When Christian military forces reconquered Spain after nearly half a millenium of Moslem rule, many Sufi doctrines went underground. Central to the transmission of these ideas were elaborate systems of linguistic double meanings, spiritually oriented puns, and multileveled "teaching stories" that said one thing on the surface but conveyed something else to those who knew how to read the code. Many of these Sufi ideas entered Judeo-Christian culture in disguise, through troubadours, poets, the writings of mystics and alchemists, and by others dedicated to maintaining and passing on the ancient traditions.

The merging of the two streams was not the end of the story of the perennial wisdom's hidden influence on Western thought, but part of the beginning of the "secret history of inspiration" that continued through the Middle Ages and helped set the stage for the Renaissance, the evolution of empirical science, and the beginnings of the Industrial Revolution.

One revisionist historian, Thomas Goldstein, a professor of medieval history at the City College of New York, points out that before modern historians his colleagues reexamined old assumptions, dogma regarded pre-Renaissance centuries as the "Dark Ages," during which relatively little happened in the way of intellectual growth. In the past decade, however, it has become more widely acknowledged that the commingling of Islamic and Jewish thought preceded and paved the way for the revival of learning.

THE MESSAGE OF THE CATHEDRALS

Between the waning of Islamic influence (and subsequent dissemination of classical and Eastern knowledge to the reawakening West) and the era of Cartesian-Newtonian thought—during that fecund epoch when the Middle Ages began to shoot forth the first buds of the Renaissance—perhaps the most important internal turning point in Western history occurred. The people and institutions of Europe, for the first time in nearly a thousand years, began to direct their attention away from the heavenly realm and think about what the human mind might learn and do here on Earth. The first seeds of a "method" of thought were sown—new to Europeans, perhaps not so new to some of the strangers in their midst.

How did this idea, once prevalent in the Hellenistic world but long forgotten or suppressed in Europe and kept carefully within the ruling elite of the Church, come to be revived among the general population? One theory connects this revival of knowledge with the mysterious architects who oversaw the less-educated laborers on the great building projects of the Gothic period. And through these architects, who seemed to have been concerned with spiritual matters as well as technical concerns, the quicksilver stream may have surfaced once again.

The esoteric spiritual wisdom of Western civilization, far from existing solely in the form of cryptic writings or secret rituals, is still to be found in some very public places—for anyone who knows where and how to look. The sources of spiritual knowledge are not the only treasures to be found under our noses. Despite the chauvinism and misconception that science and the modern worldview are inventions of the sixteenth through twentieth centuries, the origins of science were commingled with signal events in the parallel spiritual history of the late Middle Ages.

Several historians of science, Goldstein foremost among them, trace the development of the Western secular educational system to the School of Chartres, which was established in order to train those craftsmen who worked on the great Gothic cathedral that was built there.

One event that seems to have been a vehicle for the transmission of the older knowledge of the East and the transition to the establishment of a newer, Western knowledge system was the sudden appearance in Europe of a new kind of architecture. Toward the beginning of the twelfth century, the spontaneous event known to historians as "the Gothic crusade" began to change the skyline of Europe, and set the scene for the birth of a secular scientific system:[6]

> During the early phase of the Gothic style, bands of faithful enthusiasts—ordinary layfolk under the guidance of architects

or assisted by craftsmen—could be found trekking from site to site, carting the brick and mortar to build another cathedral in honor of the Holy Virgin or God. Many of the cathedrals of northern France were built by this spontaneous lay movement, the "Gothic crusade." They were built in a great wave of mystic fervor, by young people or grown women and men, who were passing the bricks from hand to hand and chanting hymns to the rhythm of their labor, or intoning the holy songs around their campfires at night.

Nor were professional architects or craftsmen aloof from such impassioned motivations. The truth is, the Gothic cathedral embodies an utterly irrational experiment. The scrupulous know-how that binds the tender filigree of stone with solid physical laws represents a rare union between mystical vision and practical experience. The cathedrals are works of art inspired by visions, not mere buildings, but they are artistic creations in which the technological accomplishment was of the highest degree. Nevertheless, the vision was always the decisive factor.

What new knowledge enabled architects and craftsmen to build structures of previously undreamed-of heights? And what older knowledge inspired them? It takes more than brick, stone, and labor to build a large structure. Knowledge is the invisible mortar of a skyscraper, a cathedral, or a pyramid. In the case of the Gothic crusade and the events that followed, this knowledge was something very new to the secular population at that time, and perhaps not so new to those who were familiar with Kabbalist, Sufist, or the younger Masonic traditions.

Certainly, some mechanism for transmitting architectural knowledge had to exist. The prehistoric and ancient cultures were often disrupted or destroyed by wars, natural disasters, and plagues and religious and ideological persecutions—yet when kings or cardinals wanted palaces or temples built, they always seemed to be able to find knowledgeable builders. Did a vehicle exist for preserving these precious technological secrets through the generations, which protected them somehow from the vagaries and hostilities of the external world? And was the knowledge-transmitting mechanism concerned with matters of consciousness as well as construction?

Even in pagan times, there had been strong, clannish associations of those few people who possessed the knowledge and vision necessary to build temples and other large structures.

In the oldest religions, such as Kabbalism and the Hindu tradition, the characters in a language represented both letters *and* numbers. Thus the same figures could be used to express computations or words or both, according to John Mitchell, author of *The View Over Atlantis*, who claims that certain mystical texts, although obstensibly narrative, contain important spiritual, physiological, and cosmological knowledge encoded numerically in the words. Thus, as with Pythagoreans, in most of the mystical traditions associated with the perennial philosophy, the highest initiates in the spiritual mysteries were also the highest initiates in the technological and architectural mysteries as well.

If one of the most important "beads of mercury" was the Islamic inner tradition, and another was the Jewish esoteric doctrine, yet a third part of the "stream of quicksilver" came along with the first Christian guilds and fraternities of European builders.

As Manly Palmer Hall, one of the foremost scholars of the esoteric movement, writes:[7]

> The direct descent of the essential program of the Esoteric Schools was entrusted to groups already well-conditioned for the work. The guilds, trade unions, and similar protective and benevolent Societies had been internally strengthened by the introduction of a new learning. The advancement of the plan required the enlargement of the boundaries of the philosophic overstate. A World Fraternity was needed, sustained by a deep and broad program of education according to the "method." Such a Fraternity could not immediately include all men, but it could unite the activities of certain kinds of men, regardless of their racial or religious beliefs or the nations in which they dwelt. These were the men of "towardness," those sons of tomorrow, whose symbol was a blazing sun rising over the mountains of the east.
>
> While it is difficult to trace the elements of a pattern never intended to be obvious, the broad shape of the design is

dimly apparent. The Invisible Empire, integrated and ensouled by Bacon and his so-called literary group, was the archetype of those democratic Societies which directly and indirectly precipitated the era of revolution. Thus, the way was cleared for the first great experiments in practical self-government. . . .

Over the centuries, assemblies of these artisan-mystics migrated from project to project to build cities, restore shrines, and construct temples, cathedrals, and palaces. One of their most important guild unions and schools was at Chartres. While their main employer was a Church that was engaged in ruthless wars against heresy throughout the Middle Ages, the unorthodox beliefs of the wandering Freemasons, as they came to call themselves, seem to have been tolerated:[8]

It was considered indelicate to inquire into the secrets of these associations of builders. Apparently they combined religious and philosophical speculations with the more prosaic rules of construction. The normal boundaries of prevailing racial and religious prejudices were relaxed in favor of these skilled bands of craftsmen, who were permitted to live according to their natural instincts and preferences while laboring in various districts and countries. Great edifices, such as the cathedral churches, often required centuries to complete. Thus several generations of artisans were employed on a single project, and the camps or towns which they established contiguous to their work became comparatively permanent communities. Like the gypsies, these bands of wandering craftsmen never mingled with other people. . . .

Thus it came about that the early Church employed pagan artisans or those of doubtful orthodoxy when some elaborate structure was required. So great was the power of these builders' associations and so urgently was their skill required that it was deemed advisable to ignore religious nonconformity. Probably, the issue was never raised, at least publicly, as the artificers assumed an outward appearance of conformity and declined to disclose any of their secret beliefs or convictions. These Fraternities of craftsmen . . . had learned discretion in the school of sad experience.

What were the inner teachings behind the ceremonial trappings of Freemasonry? According to Manly Palmer Hall:[9]

Masonry offers us, in dramatic form and by means of dramatic ceremonial, a philosophy of the spiritual life of man and a diagram of the process of regeneration. . . . From grade to grade the candidate is being led from an old to an entirely new quality of life. He begins his Masonic career as the natural man; he ends it by becoming through its discipline, a regenerated perfected man ... with larger consciousness and faculties, an efficient instrument for use by the Great Architect in His plan of rebuilding the Temple of fallen humanity, and capable of initiating and advancing other men to participation in the same great work.

This—the evolution of man into superman—was always the purpose of the ancient Mysteries, and the real purpose of modern Masonry is not the social and charitable purposes to which so much attention is paid, but the expediting of the spiritual evolution of those who aspire to perfect their own nature and transform it into a more godlike quality. And this is a definite science, a royal art, which it is possible for each of us to put into practice.

While the antiquity and continuity of the Masonic tradition is still a matter of debate, a rough outline of certain ancient colleges and guilds strongly suggests that such a continuity of tradition did exist and that, as in earlier times, spiritual mysteries were the objects of transmission as well as their more well-known secular content.

The guilds and lodges, orders and societies, managed to educate larger and larger cadres of freethinkers to the simple, explosive, then-esoteric notion that humans can evolve through spiritual and secular learning. Their ceremonies and symbols were meant to obscure their true interests from the uninitiated—a vital necessity in a church-dominated environment hostile to any learning and thought that might challenge its dogma—but the rituals and codes were meant to preserve and disseminate knowledge as well as to disguise it: knowledge that would show humanity how to use long forgotten inner potentials for building cathedrals, constructing new sciences, throwing off the shackles of ignorance that bound them or planning and preparing new societies to correct the inequities of the old.

When the cathedrals were finished and an international

core of seekers had experienced higher levels of education and states of consciousness, the uninitiated population was ready for a grander design: Nations were ready to be built.

For one of the most important breakthrough experiences in Western history did not occur to an individual or a small group of cultists, but to the entire population of Europe. The perennial wisdom and the states of consciousness associated with it, through its influence on a small avant-garde, eventually effected a less drastic but far-reaching change of consciousness on a larger scale. Quite simply, the new idea was that the human mind is an instrument capable of being trained.

After all, knowledge is not much use unless there exist a number of people who know that it is possible for them to learn how to use their minds—an idea that seems natural today, but was a dangerous heresy a thousand years ago. The rise of secular, earthbound, human-centered thought, and the subsequent gropings toward a rebirth of knowledge, was the necessary psychological preparation for all that was to follow—the Renaissance, the birth of empirical science, the advent of revolution and democracy, the Industrial Revolution.

Where did science, technology, democracy, and revolution originate? Were these characteristics of the modern world brought into being by the acts of well-known historical figures and the intersection of social forces, as traditional history books insist? Today, sources outside the mainstream of orthodox historical thought suggest that there was a conscious, perhaps quasi-secret effort to bring about the birth of an entirely new way of looking at human nature and the nature of human institutions.

As French historian Fernand Braudel has pointed out, the processes of history seem to work on three levels. The personal stories we read about in history books are the short-term crises that precipitate decisive events. Large-scale economic and social forces are the middle level. But underlying both of these is the long-term cultural evolution that is more a matter of social archaeology than of history.

If the deep intuition, the unconscious idea processor

does indeed slowly feed certain humans with revelations appropriate to their time and place, with the ultimate purpose of evolving toward higher and healthier levels of consciousness, then it is at this level that it manifested itself in Europe over the centuries which we are discussing here.

The projects of the Gothic cathedrals, and the intellectual communities they nurtured, set into motion a less visible chain of events—events that were to lead not only to the foundation of institutionalized science, but to the revolutionary political concepts of liberty, equality, and fraternity that were to overturn the old order, centuries later.

To suggest as we do, that there might be a connection between the perennial wisdom, spiritual revelation, the deep unconscious, and phenomena like the idea of democracy and the founding of America, may seem at first glance outrageous. But we have to ask ourselves this: If Carl Rogers and others are right, then humanity can only achieve its full potential and lead healthy, constructive, creative lives in a condition of "external freedom." But wouldn't the unconscious have realized this all along and been whispering it to us over and over, throughout history, in defiance of all contrary authority, whenever it could break through the chatter and preconceptions of the conscious mind and make itself heard?

And wouldn't the best of men have worked this idea out, anyway, whether as the result of intuition or just good common sense?

THE CENTRAL PROJECTS

At critical points in history, those rare, dedicated few who discovered, remembered, or were taught the way to open the channel to their deep unconscious (to their idea processor) seem to have been intuitively led to spread their knowledge where it might do the most good.

It appears that certain of the Kabbalists and Sufis, alchemists, Gnostics, Freemasons, and Christian mystics collaborated, from time to time, in central projects like the Gothic cathedrals. These projects, although involving visible material artifacts, were actually the vehicles for more abstract social and pyschological aims. The great cathedrals, besides serving as highly visible central projects to attract the best and most adventurous minds of the age, also served to educate the consciousness of the larger population.

Throughout history, people have wondered and studied and theorized about the great Stone Age monuments of Europe, of which Stonehenge is the most well known, but far from the only example. Various religious and astronomical purposes have been proposed, some of which make a great deal of sense. Yet even the usefulness of astronomical observatories or the sacred purposes of such spectacular ceremonial sites don't seem to fully justify the estimated tens of millions of man-hours it took to build these monuments.

Recently, social archaeologist Colin Renfrew, in a *Scientific American* article, proposed that the change from simple tombs to elaborate stone structures coincided with, and were in fact vehicles for, the rise of centralized political control. Central projects, in this sense, are means of focusing the energies of a population during an evolutionary transition to a higher level of culture.

The pyramids were such projects. The great megalithic monuments of Europe and temple complexes of Asia, and other massive architectural ventures were also such projects. Perhaps the most recent central project was the Apollo project that culminated in Neil Armstrong's famous footstep on the moon.

We are just dipping into the hidden task of the perennial wisdom here in an effort to show the relationship between states of consciousness, breakthrough experiences, the events of history, and the continuing evolution of human culture. As one delves deeper into this secret history, turning to those accounts which have not been so much disputed as neglected by historians, it gradually becomes clear that many of the aspects of the modern world, and the most magnificent reminders of ages past, have meanings and significances different than or beyond those we are taught in school.

We all learned something about the troubadours, the quest for the Holy Grail, the centuries-long construction projects that produced the Gothic cathedrals, and the bloody wars against witches and heretics. We are less likely to have been taught about the deeper significance of these romantic, terrible tales of long ago—yet the hidden meanings of these cultural monuments remain intact to this day, ready to be deciphered by those who find the keys. The technology of the Gothic cathedrals, for example, was an important bridge between the older streams of the perennial wisdom and the exoteric history of the West, a "central project" that connected the building of the cathedrals with the building of nations.

By the end of the sixteenth century, a transformation in the scope and purpose of these projects, and their associated guilds had taken place.

The discovery of the New World, the age of exploration, and the beginning of European colonialism suddenly spread the various European cultures throughout the world in the sixteenth century, just as the Islamic armies had spread Moslem culture a thousand years before. The underground streams in European culture prepared for their greatest confluence. A change was occurring in the way people thought—the esoteric ideas about new ways of apprehending reality and new methods for using the mind as an instrument of exploration were beginning to surface and to overtly affect the course of history.

Over the centuries, the heresies of former ages were either absorbed into the mainstream belief system, grew from outlawed cults into established religions, or evolved into non-religious forms. One of the examples of the last category was the community of freethinkers who came to be known as humanists. What had formerly been heretical or esoteric teachings about the possibility of evolving earthly civilization to a higher form, rather than concentrating exclusively on the requirements of the afterlife, became a powerful force for change as they emerged from the pens of the humanists.

The humanist and evolutionary currents in European civilization emerged in slightly altered forms when the Reformation (and the invention of the printing press) broke the Church's monopoly on knowledge. As covert initiation evolved into public education, the secret methods had become universal methods.

Science, or natural philosophy, as it was known, had

been locked into a static form for thousands of years when the reformers came along. While the Greek philosophers of the fifth and sixth centuries B.C., had been avid experimentalists, their later European counterparts had little to do with real-world explorations. Strange as it might seem to us now, the principal occupation of medieval scientists was not experiment but scholarship. "What do experts say?" "what did Aristotle say?" were significant questions; "what does nature say?" "what can we observe?" were not. Then a "new method" came along and changed these priorities.

The publication in 1620 of René Descartes' "Discourse on Method" was a milestone in the dissemination of the "new method for determining truth" that Descartes claimed to have found. (The title of Descartes' landmark work was "Project of a Universal Science Destined to Raise Our Nature to Its Highest Degree of Perfection.")

At the same time in England, a remarkable man by the name of Francis Bacon was saying publicly for the first time that "knowledge is power." It might seem self-evident today, but in 1600, such a statement would have been lost on the vast majority of the population.

The influence of Sir Francis Bacon on Western thought and institutions was formidable. He proposed that science could bring into our realm of knowledge entirely new and powerful truths from the "hidden realm" of nature. Instead of waiting for geniuses like Aristotle to apprehend the nature of the universe and then tell the rest of us about it, the idea was to go to nature herself to find the truth, by performing experiments and drawing conclusions, then testing those conclusions by further experiments.

Bacon proposed that entire populations of scientists be trained in the new method of thought—their observations, theories, and experiments could grow into a body of knowledge far greater than that attainable by any one person.

More than perhaps any other individual in history, Bacon consciously bridged the older esoteric traditions and the newly emerging ideas that were transforming the external institutions of the Western world. Bacon believed that humankind could evolve, individually and socially, by removing the false beliefs that prevent true learning, and by practicing disci-plined thought and observation. He saw that a vast educational structure—truly *public* education—would be required.

In 1627, Bacon published *The New Atluntis, A Work Un-finished*, in which he gave what scholars consider a veiled description of the goals of the esoteric schools and showed how the carefully guarded knowledge could now become pub-lic, through universities rather than mysteries, through scien-tists as well as adepts. For science to transform culture, there had to be thousands of scientists. And for there to be truly competent scientists, there had to be populations of educated people, people who knew what only a few had known—how to use and train their minds. In this way, Bacon was trying to apply to the entire world, for centuries to come, what had been preserved and perfected by elites and undergrounds for mil-lenia.

In accordance with his plan, he summoned the wise men of all nations to form "literary groups" and "invisible col-leges," which grew out of the Masonic lodges and fraternal guilds, and grew, in turn, into the royal societies of England and France, the Virginia Company and other New World colo-nies. "I rang the bell that drew the wits together," Bacon later wrote of these activities.

On the continent of Europe, at the same time that Bacon labored in England, a series of pseudonymous Rosicrucian Manifestos were publicly proclaiming the intentions of an-other, perhaps related, long-secret international fraternity. While most people today who even know about the Rosicru-cian Orders think of them as Christian mystics whose secret teachings were infused with esoteric ideas, the declared goal of this group was nothing less than the reformation of exoteric knowledge systems and the establishment of new human rights:[10]

> The burden of the original (Rosicrucian) proclamations is one of broad reform covering art, science, religion, and politics. The means by which this reform was to be accomplished was through the codification of knowledge....
> There is every indication that the Rosicrucians should be

included among the early Humanists. Certainly they advocated the reformation of society, universal education, and the rights of man.... The Humanists were champions of the cause of equal opportunity through the enlargement of knowledge. The *Fama* of the Rosy Cross definitely aligns the Order with those practical utopians of every age who have labored in the threefold cause of liberty, equality, and fraternity.

The Humanists inherited the unfinished labors of the heretics, who preceded them as champions of human rights.... Once, however, the backbone of ecclesiastical authority had been broken and the power of the Church to destroy utterly all nonconformists had been lost, the heretics emerged as Humanists. The essential doctrine remained the same....

There is little doubt that the anonymous founders of these orders were deeply involved in mystical experience and experimentation with altered states of consciousness, based on hermetic, Kabbalist, and Sufist techniques learned in Spain, North Africa, and the Middle East. But their call for a reformation of knowledge was far broader and more ambitious than their call for religious reform. They also included political and social ideas that were far in advance of their times. As one modern student of Rosicrucian thought has written, in addition to their esoteric teachings, they called for:[11]

The political reformation of States toward a philosophic commonwealth....

The creation among the learned of a permanent organization dedicated to essential progress....

The maintenance of whatever degree of secrecy necessary to protect those dedicated to progress from the persecutions instigated by reactionaries, and from those desiring to enslave men for personal power and profit.

The accomplishment of all reformation without such revolutions as endanger the life and property of the private citizen. The principal instrument of the reformation was to be education. The wise man cannot be enslaved, and the ignorant man cannot be freed.

The end should be the application of all tradition, experience, and knowledge to the perfection of the human state and estate. The Great Work was the perfect adjustment of human purpose with the divine plan, through the understanding of the laws of Nature and the practice of an enlightened code based upon the threefold foundation of philosophy, science, and religion."

Now the "central project" of the humanists and the "reformers" had become nothing less than the creation of a new kind of human in a new kind of society. Through the Freemasons and Rosicrucians, several "new" principles of thought laid down the logical foundation for science. Equally important social principles, centered on the radical concepts of liberty, equality, and fraternity, laid the foundations of the present democratic political systems. The blossoming of Utopian thought and literature, coming at the same time that entire new continents were opening up for colonization, led to the boldest central project ever undertaken—the United States of America.

THE PERENNIAL WISDOM AND AMERICA'S CENTRAL PROJECT

The emergence of nation building as a central project, spearheaded by groups with a close connection to the perennial wisdom, was not necessarily solely a matter of individuals who conspired together to make their visions a reality, although some evidence suggests that such conspiracies did exist.

Unarguably, many—perhaps most—of the people who eventually joined in the collective endeavor had no knowledge or participation in these conspiracies. They became part of the general movement because of an urging for freedom, or the reasonings of their intellect, but uncontrovertibly there was also some sort of collective urge on the part of the whole of European culture at that time toward freedom, reason, and the values that were about to transform, not just individuals or individual nations, but the whole continent. And if that urge came from the source of most urges, the unconscious, that brings us right back to where we started again.

Every American customarily carries a symbolic reminder of the central project rooted in the idea of a reformation of public consciousness, toward which the United States of

America was dedicated nearly two centuries ago, and from which we seem to have strayed in recent years. That reminder is the reproduction, on the back side of the dollar bill, of the Great Seal of the United States.

This curious design was chosen in 1782, although there has been some minor modification since. Considerable opposition was expressed to the proposal in 1935 to place on our currency this "dull emblem of a Masonic fraternity" (as the reverse side—the pyramid and the eye—had been termed by Professor Charles Eliot Norton). That these symbols on the dollar bill should come from the traditions of Freemasonry is puzzling if one imagines they were originally chosen by a simple citizenry of farmers, shopkeepers, and country gentlemen.

But on further investigation we discover that both Benjamin Franklin and George Washington were active and high-ranking Freemasons, and of the fifty-six signers of the Declaration of Independence, approximately fifty were Masons. All but five of the fifty-five members of the Constitutional Convention were Masons.

Offshoots of the secret Masonic societies of Europe had transplanted to the New World with the founding fathers 150 years before the Revolutionary War with the arrival of such organizations as the Virginia Company (of which Francis Bacon was a founding member), whose membership included many inheritors of the perennial wisdom like the Rosicrucians and the Masons.

There were also many Masons among those from other nations who supported the American Revolution, including Lafayette, Kosciuzko, Baron de Kalb, and Count Pulaski.

Against this background let us examine the symbolism of the great seal, bearing in mind that it is the essence of any powerful symbol that it says many things to many different levels of the mind, so that any single explanation of its meaning is necessarily a dilution and a distortion.

Dominating the obverse is the bird that is now an eagle, but in earlier versions was the phoenix, ancient symbol of human aspiration toward universal good, of being twice-born or reborn through enlightenment, and higher awareness. The olive branch and the arrows in the bird's claws announce that the new order covets peace but intends to protect itself from those who would destroy it. The banner the eagle holds reads *e pluribus unum*, or unity from many, referring to the nation made up of states and pointing to a higher unity as well. The "glory" over the bird's head traditionally symbolizes the cosmic vision.

The phrase *novus ordo seclorum* on the reverse, "a new order of the ages is born," declares that this event is not just the formation of another guild, lodge, or nation, but of a new order for the world. The project is launched with confidence because *annuit coeptis*, "He (God) looks with favor upon our undertaking."

The most conspicuously Masonic symbol occupies the central portion of the reverse—the unfinished pyramid capped by a radiant triangle enclosing the all-seeing eye. Whatever other meanings this ancient symbol may have (for example, the significance attached to numbers of levels and of stones; the resemblance to the Great Pyramid of Giza, shrine tomb of Hermes, the personification of universal wisdom, and even of the "initiative" experience itself, it clearly proclaims that the works of men—both the individual's inner development and his external works—are incomplete unless they incorporate divine insight.

The central project of the United States was to be, in a way that was unique in history, an exploration and actualization of what human beings can be—despite what the rest of the world "knew" about limitations. At least part of the "American Dream" involved the implicit commitment to this exploration.

And so, once again, we find that our explorations of consciousness, creativity and the breakthrough state have led us directly into the heart of the political and social realm.

In the next chapter we will examine this relationship more closely, and consider the implications it holds for humanity's present and future development.

The Harvest

A New Copernican Revolution

THE CRISIS OF MEANING IN MODERN SOCIETY

At the most fundamental level, the basic problem of modern society is a crisis of meaning. It underlies the dilemma of those for whom society has no meaningful roles—the unemployed and underemployed—as well as the global problems of security, development, and environment.

As a result of the seeming reduction of the workings of our physical and mental universes to a mechanistic model of clockwork and blind chance, experiences such as creative inspiration, illumination, and the unitary experience became disassociated from the religious significance (and moral codes) traditionally associated with them. The great philosophies and religions that stemmed from such experiences, and that in the past profoundly influenced the course of human history, were weakened; and serious exploration of the creative, unconscious processes was discouraged.

One of mankind's most powerful needs is for life to have meaning, to make sense. Severe psychological and physical pathology can follow from failure to sense such meanings in one's life or from the loss or disarrangement of belief systems that help give it, or seem to give it, meaning. Under such circumstances, suicide can be a statement that death is more meaningful than life.

In traditional societies the social matrix simultaneously instructs in meaning and provides the context for meaningful experience. (The musical *Fiddler on the Roof* portrays in a powerful and entertaining fashion the breakup of just such a traditional matrix.) In contrast, the behaviors that the institutions of our urbanized, high-technology, mass-consumption society focus people toward are less and less congruent with the ways individuals can find meaning in their lives.

In the absence of consensus on deeper meanings, the decisions made by such a society, which affect future generations around the world—whether the decisions of governments or of transnational corporations—are made on the disastrous basis of narrowly defined short-term economic or political gains.

Our emerging new understanding of the human mind promises to contribute to a fundamental corrective to this process. The resurgence of interest in meditative disciplines and religious philosophies evinced by the broader society, and interest in research on consciousness spreading through the scientific community reinstates questions of ultimate values and meanings to their central place in human existence. As Nobel laureate neuroscientist Roger Sperry wrote in 1981:[1]

Social values depend ... on whether consciousness is believed to be mortal, immortal, reincarnate, or cosmic ... localized and brain-bound or essentially universal.... Recent conceptual developments in the mind-brain sciences rejecting reductionism and materialistic determinism on the one side, and dualisms on the other, clear the way for a rational approach to the theory and prescription of values and to a natural fusion of science and religion.

No scientist of comparable stature had previously made such a claim, and it would be naive to imagine that Sperry's colleagues are in full agreement. Nevertheless, there exists in the 1980s a field of consciousness research that did not exist even twenty years earlier, and there is a corresponding shift in cultural beliefs that can be clearly demonstrated—although admittedly, until very recently the signs were more apparent in New Age magazine advertisements for "consciousness expanding" courses than they were in the results of survey research. But the application of many of these principles in "peak performance" and managerial "problem-solving" or "creativity seminars" demonstrates that they are beginning to penetrate deeply at last.

The practical significance of this shift in basic premises is probably much greater than is immediately apparent. Modern industrial society, like every other society in history, rests on some set of largely tacit basic assumptions about *who we are, what kind of universe we are in, and what is ultimately important to us.* The scientific materialism which so confidently held forth the answers to these questions a couple of generations ago is a dying orthodoxy. Its basic premises are being challenged by new findings in physics and psychology that call for a broader understanding of human experience—outer and inner. This new view includes increased faith in reason guided by deep intuition.

In other words, a respiritualization of society is beginning to take place—at once more experiential and noninstitutionalized, and less dogmatic, sacerdotal, and sectarian than most of the historic religions. With this change comes a fundamental shift in prevailing values, and in individual and societal priorities.

It is difficult to estimate how very much it could mean in terms of world understanding and the potential for sustained global peace if we came to agree, around the world, on the common basic nature of human strivings and ultimate goals. Just as agreement on the meaning of information in the physical and biological sciences provided the necessary base of knowledge for the development of modern technology, so agreement on matters of fundamental meanings and values could provide a foundation for a truly workable "science of religion" and a global society—one that honors both the universal strivings of humankind and the diverse ecology of cultures which express, each with its own emphases, the underlying unity of life.

It is not an exaggeration to speak of the shift taking place in the premises underlying Western industrial society, that in both cases the impact on society is fundamentally that of a re-perception of the world. In the case of the Copernican revolution, the necessary evidence for the perception of a universe in which the Earth revolves around the Sun had been available all along; what in the end amounted to a complete change in philosophical conception of the universe was in essence a new way of perceiving pattern and meaning in data that were themselves not new.

In the "new Copernican revolution," much of the experimental data and reported experiences that support the emerging perception of a "hidden mind" with a "gold mine" of untapped potentialities has also been around for a long time—some of it for thousands of years. The shift of perception which allows people to see this as a large-scale social phenomenon occurred only very recently in the West. It amounts to drawing new meanings and patterns out of evidence that has always been interpreted in other ways.

In the entire history of science, it is hard to find a discovery of comparable consequence to the discovery of the power of unconscious beliefs as a gateway—or an obstacle—to the hidden mind, and its untapped potentialities. With considerable justification, we could speak of the widespread adoption of this discovery by science and society as a "second Copernican revolution."

Would we be able to recognize a new Copernican revolution if one were actually in progress? One can imagine how difficult it would have been in the early seventeenth century to make a case that from the concepts of Copernicus and the observations of Galileo would emerge a conceptual revolution that would eventually shake Western society to its roots. We can almost hear the rebuttal: that these new ideas about the planets might be of great interest to astronomers, theologians, and philosophers, but they could hardly be expected to make much impact on the practical world of everyday experience. And yet, as we all know, they did in time affect every institution in society.

Our explorations in this book are but the crudest attempts to map the boundaries of a new image of the breakthrough potentials of the human mind, an image of the interior universe, that is beginning to bring about fundamental changes in modern society in the same way that Copernicus' new image of the superior universe did. But the current change is of much vaster scope and will take place in a much shorter interval than the change from a geocentric to a heliocentric view of the universe.

We begin to grasp the fundamental nature of this second Copernican revolution if we recall that practically all of Western science is by now predicated on a cosmology that starts with a lifeless material universe (originating in some sort of Big Bang billions of years ago), which in time produces living matter that evolves, through random mutations and natural selection, to higher and higher forms, culminating eventually in the creation of consciousness in human beings. In the alternative picture of evolution that is beginning to emerge from quantum physics we find that rather than consciousness evolving from the universe, the universe evolved from consciousness, and that consciousness seems to have "pulled" the evolutionary process in certain preferred directions, first in the direction of mind becoming aware of itself and then in the direction of becoming aware of its potentials. The implications of such a "consciousness-produces-reality" conceptualization are so profound and far-reaching, not only for physics, but metaphysics, that one can easily imagine all institutions of society being profoundly affected.

INTIMATIONS OF TRANSFORMATION

Every human culture has at its core some image of the nature of humankind, of the sort of universe we inhabit, and of our relationship to that universe. This image tends to be tacit, to be so subtly interwoven into the customs and institutions that it is osmotically absorbed by every person who grows up in that culture. It seems unnecessary to teach it explicitly, and it is unthinkable to question it seriously.

As we noted earlier, French historian Fernand Braudel has argued that the usual interpretation of events as stemming from other, prior events, is a very deceptive form of history. Cause-effect relationships are implied from very partial and superficial descriptions of society. Meanwhile, at deeper levels of the society, gradual institutional changes, and even more glacial movements of climatic, geographical, demographic, and cultural variables, are going on, which shape the events and even the institutions. To focus on the events (as most history books have) is to misinterpret the present and misjudge the future.

At this deepest level of basic premises and images, change takes place very slowly, over centuries. Yet this cumulative change may build up until some major transformation takes place with what seems like explosive suddeness. Profound changes in the social structure tend to be the consequence of such prior shifts in the psychic structure, the outer manifestations of deeper occurrences in the consciousness of the population. We have already noted, for example, the changes in the focus of consciousness that preceded the Renaissance and Industrial Revolution.

In one of the earliest of the modern spate of "transformation" books, *The Transformations of Man*, social critic Lewis Mumford observed that there have only been four or five periods of change in the entire history of Western civilization fundamental enough to justify the use of the term "transformation." As Mumford observed:[2] "Every transformation of man ... has rested on a new metaphysical and ideological base; or rather, upon deeper stirrings and intuitions whose rationalized expression takes the form of a new picture of the cosmos and the nature of man."

Thus, when agricultural civilization emerged, when the world's great religions were founded, when the Roman Empire fell, when the Middle Ages came to an end, and when the Industrial Revolution took place, there were not only the kind of major changes in social roles and institutions that are recorded prominently in historical documents—there were also fundamental changes in the consciousness of entire populations.

Another scholar who identified a pattern in the changing courses of civilization was British historian Arnold Toynbee, who introduced the once-startling idea that, like human beings, all great societies tend to go through stages of growth, maturity, and decline. Specifically he wrote about the apparent present decline of Western civilization. What seems to have been less widely appreciated is that this was not necessarily meant to be a "doom and gloom" prediction. To the contrary, Toynbee foresaw the possibility of a "transfiguration" of industrial society to one which would display more of a balance between utilitarian and spiritual values. More than half a century ago, Pitirim Sorokin, founder of the department of Sociology at Harvard University forecast that industrial society, with its emphasis on "sensate" values (materialistic, rational, empirical, utilitarian, positivist, hedonistic) would decline, becoming increasingly disillusioned with its materialistic goals. Like Toynbee, he felt that this decline might be simply an early phase of a transformation to an "integral culture characterized by a balance between the material and the spiritual, the rational and the intuitive." Sorokin put no precise time calibration on his forecast, but his descriptions fit well with the cultural changes we have seen in the past two decades.

A similar view was presented recently in Alvin Toffler's *The Third Wave*. Despite controversy over some of Toffler's specific forecasts, the basic metaphor of the wave is a particularly fruitful way of looking at history, and one which complements the ideas of Mumford and others.

Toffler's "First Wave" was *agricultural civilization*. It started somewhere in the Middle East six to eight thousand years ago and spread around the globe, eventually transforming all societies on the globe, with the exception of a few remote pockets of hunter-gatherer tribal societies.

The Second Wave, *industrial civilization*, began to emerge less than eight centuries ago in Western Europe. The secularization of values and education of the general population that took place after the Middle Ages also transformed the societies in its path. Those agrarian and nomadic societies which resisted were exterminated or pushed into backwaters.

Toffler claims that a third wave of revisioning and revaluing has become evident over the past couple of decades. This wave, too, will transform society as it crests—much more rapidly than the previous industrialization wave. Already, as he notes, "in our personal lives and in our political acts, whether we know or not, most of us in the rich countries are essentially either Second Wave people committed to maintaining the dying order, Third Wave people constructing a radically different tomorrow, or a confused, self-canceling mixture of the two."

The chief characteristics of this third-wave civilization, according to Toffler, are that it "brings with it new family styles; changed ways of working, loving, and living; a new economy; new political conflicts; and beyond this, an altered consciousness as well."

THE "GREAT ASCENT"—TO WHAT?

We can hardly understand the possibility of a transformation in the near future without paying particular attention to the greatest transformation of the recent past.

Economic historian Robert Heilbroner, in a book titled *The Great Ascent,* wrote that the historically unique process which began in Western Europe at the end of the Middle Ages was a great evolutionary ascent from the limitations and weaknesses of traditional society around the world. Traditional society at its best was characterized by a richness of life, durable fabric of meaning, magnificent cultural accomplishments, and a remarkable capacity for self-renewal.

Nevertheless, the weaknesses of traditional society were such that in most cases, as the opportunity for modernization presented itself, the people of traditional societies almost always have been quite willing to leave them behind (albeit with nostalgic regret in some cases). These weaknesses included a tendency for the benefits of the social structure to be concentrated on a small, privileged minority who maintained their position by a combination of caste organization and tradition, monopoly on knowledge (sacred as well as technical), and military power. The larger part of such societies was illiterate, unlearned, and intimidated, saddled with brute toil, living at the bare margin of subsistence.

The "great ascent" that changed the old order began in Western Europe in the wake of the cathedral building, with the gradual shifting of the bases for society's guiding values from the traditional religious, other-worldly base to a more pragmatic, utilitarian, earthly life-oriented base. It culminated, according to Heilbroner, in the industrial societies of Europe, North America, and Japan; the path was destined to eventually be followed, more or less by all of humankind.

Although Heilbroner's view became far gloomier as he grew older, a number of writings—notably Mumford in *The Transformations of Man*, George Leonard in *The Transformation*, and Marilyn Ferguson in *The Aquarian Conspiracy*—took up and embroidered his original ideas forecasting a period of transformation to a New Age, and confidently seeing the requisite social force now coming into being or waiting in embryo. Mumford concludes his book:[3]

> So we stand on the brink of a new age: the age of an open world and of a self capable of playing its part in that larger sphere. An age of renewal, when work and leisure and learning and love will unite to produce a fresh form for every stage of life, and a higher trajectory for life as a whole.... In carrying man's self-transformation to this further stage, world culture may bring about a fresh release of spiritual energy that will unveil new potentialities, no more visible in the human self today than radium was in the physical world a century ago, though always present.... For who can set bounds to man's emergence or to his power of surpassing his provisional achievements? So far we have found no limits to the imagination, nor yet to the sources on which it may draw. Every goal man reaches provides a new starting point, and the sum of all man's days is just a beginning.

It was perhaps more fashionable to be so optimistic a quarter of a century ago, when Mumford wrote, than it is today. Nonetheless, the stark contrast between his hopefulness and Heilbroner's later despair poses key questions: Which one is the more realistic view? Which is the less deceived perspective? Most importantly, which is the more wholesome belief?

A LONG-TERM EVOLUTIONARY TREND

Any student of the rise and fall of cultures cannot fail to be impressed by the role played in this historical succession by the image of the future. The rise and fall of images precedes or accompanies the rise and fall of cultures. As long as a society's image is positive and flourishing, the flower of culture is in full bloom. Once the image begins to decay and lose its vitality, however, the culture does not long survive.

FRED POLAK, *The Image of the Future*

Few questions are more important to all of us than the question of how we should interpret the present condition of our society. Our future is shaped by our collective action, and that action is guided by our image of our capabilities and our interpretation of the present. If we see our situation to be a decline from a Golden Age, and believe humans to be passive objects at the mercy of overwhelming historical forces, we tend to respond to events in one way; if we anticipate the dawn of a New Age, and believe humans to be special creatures who possess an unbounded capacity to shape events, then we respond in another way. Because of the question's importance to our actions, we need to explore fully the key characteristics of the "Great Ascent."

It is tempting to define our progress by four crowning accomplishments of the past two or three centuries—the understanding of ourselves and the universe provided by modern science, the power given to us by the development of technology, the vitality (until recently) exhibited by private enterprise, and the fairness (usually) attained by representative democracy. But such a view risks being too parochial and even today, our assessment of these accomplishments is changing. We need to look to characteristics that are somewhat more basic and less ephemeral, that reach back even further than the Renaissance, even perhaps beyond what we conventionally regard as the scope of Western civilization.

Seen in this perspective, four components of the long-term socioevolutionary trend of human progress stand out as underlying the four crowning achievements already mentioned.

Long-term trend of increasing:	Has brought modern:
Awareness	Science
Mastery	Technology
Liberation	Private enterprise
Democratization	Democratic government

Increasing Awareness

From the elementary awareness of the amoeba through the vastly increased awareness of vertebrates to the uniquely self-aware consciousness of the human, the evolutionary path has been characterized by a trend toward higher and higher levels of *increasing awareness*. The same is true of social evolution—from the near-submergence in the collective unconscious of the earliest human societies, through varying degrees of awareness of the self and of the total environment, to the most highly informed and self-aware individuals we know.

The inner secret of every mystery cult, the esoteric core of every religion, has always been based on the experience of *becoming aware of our higher potential*, the interior perception that empowers the notion that we can become more than we are. The long-term trend of increasing awareness has two aspects: self-awareness increasing among ever-larger groups of people and our growing scientific comprehension of the world.

The first aspect, increasing the awareness of populations, has been fostered in society through literature and the arts, philosophy, spiritual disciplines, and more recently, by an assortment of psychotherapies, growth workshops, and the like. The second aspect has motivated the open inquiry of science and the free search for guiding beliefs and values. A great cultural machine for creating knowledge (collective awareness of the universe) was set into motion with the emergence of the idea that human beings have the capacity to *know*, and thus can qualify as scientists and citizens. The technology of printing later provided a medium by which the group awareness could attain scientific achievements and build republican governments.

Increasing Mastery

We have deliberately chosen the word *mastery*, with its double connotation of *power* to control life and the *wisdom* to use it appropriately.

Mastery may be thought of as biological in its origins, in

the sense of the evolutionary struggle and the competition between species and individuals for limited resources. The use
of simple tools and the invention of language changed the vehicle of mastery from biological selection to cultural development. With the evolution of our own species, and the relatively recent invention of that social engine we call *culture*,
mastery grew beyond the slow, inevitable, unconscious sift-
ings of gene patterns. The first humans were distinguished
from competing species primarily by their ability to *alter* the
environment, rather than depending on the ability to *adapt*.

The unique abilities of human beings to devise, use, and
continually improve tools and technologies lead to our increasing mastery of the environment. However, the reach for
mastery has also been embodied in the various religious,
philosophical, and ethical systems by which societies have
guided behvior. In its earliest manifestations, technological
mastery was joined to awareness through the sacred prototech-
nologies of shamanism and metalworking. Those who knew
the secrets of healing, and of smelting iron and bronze, kept
their secrets hidden, for they knew that mastery may endanger
as well as empower those who seek it.

The "Baconian spirit" is the phrase that historians use to
indicate the relatively recent attitude that the goal of science
should be to dominate and control nature through knowledge
and technology. This attitude eventually led to excesses in the
way scientific knowledge has been applied to the manipula-
tion of the environment.

But the Baconian spirit was a tremendously liberating
force when it first emerged. Technology has generally helped
to improve the lot of previously miserable populations. The
humanists of Bacon's time sought well-being here and now,
material comfort, learning for civic life, buildings for human
use. Technological mastery made such dreams possible.

Unfortunately, as technological capability increased, the
wisdom aspect of mastery—in the sense of the master in spiritual traditions—weakened. This was due to the progressive replacement of more transcendentally based values of the
utilitarian, materialistic values as the pendulum swing that
had begun six or eight centuries ago with the weakening of

traditional religious values, went toward the opposite extreme of institutionalized positivism in the post-WW II period. Technology acquired a semi-autonomous momentum, and the guiding force of wisdom was supplanted by considerations of economic gain and military advantage.

Increasing Liberation

There can be little doubt that much of humankind enjoys a freedom that is qualitatively different from that of animals, or that modern men and women are in many senses more free than our ancestors. The goal of liberation is exemplified in modern society in the political ideal of personal liberty within a lawful order, the economic ideal of private enterprise, and the cultural ideal of individuation, self-mastery, and freedom through knowledge.

The humanists, reformers, and early empirical scientists introduced another idea which seems so obvious now that it is scarcely commented upon, but which was a radical notion when it was introduced—the ability to think and act for oneself, to produce works of art, formulate scientific theories, and guide the destiny of others. When man became the ruler of nature, a heightened awareness of self was both a prerequisite and a consequence. From the Renaissance, women of aristocratic families were also given greater opportunities; opinion opposing slavery—an age-old and nearly universal human institution—began to develop. Economic individualism, the forerunner to capitalism, dates from the sixteenth century.

As they developed historically, three important trends helped and triggered one another—increasing liberation of individuals from the tyranny of the state, increasing liberation of populations from the tyranny of ignorance, and increasing liberation of the entire culture from the taboo against independent exploration of the depths of the human mind.

Increasing Democratization

This fourth component of the long-term evolutionary trend has two aspects—*equality* and *participation*. It is somewhat less long-term than the three preceding tendencies, in that the demand for equality and participation became strong only with

the liberal/humanitarian thrust of the Enlightenment, around
the eighteenth century. It finds expression in modern societies
in the social ideals of free education and public dissemination
of scientific knowledge, in the economic ideal of equal opportunity, and in the political ideals of equality before the law,
guaranteed human and civil rights, and participatory democracy.

Some of the causes and manifestations of this trend were
the rise of written law (with the Magna Carta, even kings
became subject to law), evenhanded administration of justice,
and trial by jury. The conflicts and balances between judicial,
executive, and legislative branches of government emerged
and evolved in royal societies and academies for the reformation of science and government before their embodiment in the
United States Constitution. The first forms of representative
government appeared in England and France, secretly at first,
long before the democratic revolutions in those countries and
the American colonies. The democratization of Western societies is far from completed; the most recent manifestations have
been the struggles to extend the trend to the abolition of racial
and sexual discrimination.

These four components of the evolutionary trend are particularly prominent in Western tradition, although they are
present to some extent in all human history. The extraordinary
vitality of the West since the Renaissance can be expressed in
terms of these four elements. Particularly in the United States,
the core faith was imparted to every child in every schoolroom
in the land.

Up to a quarter century or so ago, oppressed peoples
around the globe felt hope because these trends and principles
were fostered in America. It is difficult for younger members
of society to imagine with what lack of cynicism or doubt
these ideals were held in their grandparents' day. Even
through the 1950s the faith remained strong.

But then something began to go wrong. Looking back, one
can discern warning signals as early as World War I and the
Depression. After World War II, one could begin to see, along
with the fantastic economic successes of the United States and

the other democratic countries, growing signs of trouble. These signs became obvious by the late 1960s, and distressing by the 1980s.

RECENT DECADES IN THIS LIGHT

It hardly seems necessary to recite again the familiar litany of symptoms: racism, widespread injustice, oppression, even slavery—despite the centuries-old struggle for individual freedom and human rights—compounded by inflation, high interest rates, high energy prices, growing debt, precariousness of the world financial system, spreading unemployment, shortages of fuel and water, maldevelopment in much of the world, famine, a seemingly apocalyptic arms race, worldwide environmental deterioration, excessive population densities, and so forth.

Severe as these problems are, they seem to be but symptoms of a more fundamental illness. The puzzle of diagnosis is a critical one: What is the underlying malady? What therapeutic measures could possibly remedy such grave crises?

As we well know, the Marxists have taken a try at answering these questions. So have the transformationalists of various ideological hues. To many Americans, such diagnoses invite the image of having somehow to radically change direction, to veer off onto a new and untried road. That image tends to create anxiety and breed conflict. An alternative picture may be more helpful in promoting cooperative action.

One way to describe illness is in terms of a departure from wellness. Thus one way to look at the present predicament of Western society is in terms of departure from a "healthy" evolutionary trend. Awareness begat modern science; mastery engendered the fantastic achievements of contemporary technology; liberation led to the vitality of free enterprise; and democratization brought about representative government and the political enfranchisement of entire populations. The gains, by the early part of this century, in all four dimensions, were most impressive. However, upon reflection we begin to see how far the industrial world has departed from its "healthy" long-term evolutionary trend, especially since World War II.

The "successes" of the long-term evolutionary trend became the source of the global dilemmas we now face. This came about through subtle shifts whose significance was unnoticed by all but a very few observers.

Perhaps most fundamental was the erosion, by the dominant position of mechanistic science, of the belief-system bases for Judeo-Christian values (and, for that matter, any system of humane and spiritual values). Values became relativistic and arbitrary; measures of technological advance and economic indicators gained a powerful influence in guiding public and private sector decisions. But these pseudovalues fail to take into account the deepest motivations and highest aspirations of human beings; similarly, they tend to neglect considerations of the well-being of all the earth's creatures, and of all the earth's present and future population. Economic and technical values do not automatically—perhaps not usually—lead to good social decisions.

Thus the thrust toward awareness tended to become reduced to utilitarian science in the service of technology. Mastery then became manipulative technology guided by the fiction of humankind "controlling" nature and solving environmental and social problems with a "technological fix." Basic research, the search for deeper understanding of ourselves and the environment around us, came to be supported only if it pointed fairly directly to technologies that would contribute either to financial gain or to the might of the nation's military establishment.

The remarkable technological advances that increased the productivity of labor and relieved humans of much onerous and stultifying toil—presumably so they would have more time to be human—by a twisted logic became transmuted into one of industrial society's most perplexing problems. There are not enough meaningful social roles to go around—that is, there are not enough jobs. A fantastic technological success story turned into chronic unemployment and underemployment.

People seek work in vain; they perform work that challenges only the smallest fraction of their capabilities. In less modern societies, technological forces push peasants out of the villages, off the land into urban slums, where they are most likely to be unemployed or underemployed. When guided primarily by economic and technical pseudovalues, economic development tends to produce marginal people—people who aren't needed by their society and are kept as pets at best, or thrown on the discard heap at worst.

Because of the rise of absentee ownership of corporations, large private enterprise after World War II tended to become primarily responsive to signals of financial return, and the corporate world became increasingly dominated by the short-term financial bottom line as opposed to the long-term view possessed by individual owners. In the absence of a strong commitment to overarching social and ethical values, the corporate incentive structure tended to move toward irresponsibility in the face of societal issues, however humane and noble might be the private values of corporate executives.

Thus the vaunted free-enterprise system evolved toward a, virtually autonomous military-industrial-financial complex, pursuing its own goals and institutionally insensitive to citizen concerns about the quality of their lives, the continued well-being of the planet, and the fate of future generations. While this development brought gains in quality of life for a minority of the world's population, it is certainly not clear what will be the future of a world increasingly dominated by system goals of financial gain, economic growth, and technological and military power.

The limitations of representative democracy under these conditions became sufficiently apparent as to lead to demands for a more participative form. When legislative reforms seemed slow and ineffective, or when government appeared to be captured by a powerful interest group, there was recourse to direct challenges to the legitimacy of prevailing institutions and institutional behaviors—as with the recent civil rights and antiwar movements.

Internationally, the number of functioning democratic governments has been falling steadily. In the Third World, the liberated colonies found that political liberation does not automatically bestow economic and psychological liberation. The colonial legacy had created many problems where the new national boundaries failed to coincide with natural cultural boundaries, resulting in serious internal strife. The impacts of external forces brought other problems, such as the dependence for foreign exchange on markets for their raw material—markets over which they had little control. Other problems arose from such factors as population increase and deforestation. All of these put democratic governments under unmanageable pressures.

Overall, it could be said that the global dilemmas which are now so evident and troublesome are largely a product of the *successes* of Western industrial society—which in the end proves to lead, because of biases inherent in its central paradigm, to a serious departure from the long-term evolutionary trends.

In thinking of post-World War II developments as a departure from a "healthy" evolutionary development, the conventional wisdom is essentially reversed. Rather than seeing the postwar period as a representation of "normal growth," we see it instead as an aberration, a falling away from a long-term trend. These recent decades have been characterized by value confusion and lack of an image of a viable future. But the long-term evolutionary goals are still ingrained and *still capable of inspiring as they once did*. A future that involves their fulfillment would seem to be more attractive and less threatening than either the mindless consumption and growth urged on us by the conventional economic ethic, or a touted "transformation" to a New Age that appears not to have its roots in history, and which does not responsibly take into account the fears and dangers associated with abrupt systemic change.

THE PLAUSIBLE DREAM

A useful interpretation results when we examine the long-term evolutionary trend in light of what has been said earlier about the spectrum of creativity, breakthroughs, and the perennial wisdom. Let us for the moment set aside questions of how to get from here to there, and attempt to clarify the image of the kind of society toward which the evolutionary trend would head, assuming the influence of the perennial wisdom were to be in the ascendancy.

Awareness

Of the two aspects of awareness—awareness of the external environment and self-awareness—modern society has specialized in the former to the detriment of the latter. Even though the scientific quest for understanding of the physical world has been distorted by its recent utilitarian emphasis, its successes are awesome. The leap in scientific knowledge since the mid-nineteenth century has no parallel in history.

As we have seen, there has appeared in the past two decades a tendency to balance the awareness of the world around us with a growing emphasis on the world of inner experience. That new awareness includes the sense that the individual is by no means as separate as we ordinarily take ourselves to be, that under certain conditions we may become directly and intuitively aware of our oneness with others and with the universe and of a lack of limits to the potentialities of that oneness.

The sciences of the inner perception have long stated that ordinary men and women go through life in a kind of hypnotic sleep. This is the "cultural hypnosis" that results from becoming successfully programmed by society to perceive the universe around us, in the same way the rest of the culture does. "In the ordinary state man is hypnotized and this hypnotic state is continually maintained and strengthened in him. . . 'To awaken' for man means to be 'dehypnotized,'" wrote P. D. Ouspensky, half a century ago, in his book *In Search of the Miraculous.*

If a person begins to become "dehypnotized," or "enlightened" to a state of increased inner awareness, he or she becomes conscious that certain decisions which formerly might have seemed to be dictated by logic, were actually reflections of choices made on the higher level of the self that we have been associating with the unconscious and the idea processor, that experiences and relationships necessary for personal growth were selected and sought by that part of self and were by no means as accidental or coincidental as they seemed at the time they occurred.

Such a person becomes aware that there is no desire in life as strong as the desire, which previously had been outside conscious awareness and obscured by the clamorous demands of the ego-self, to identify with and follow the guidance of this higher self. Such a person becomes aware that human potential is apparently limitless, and that in some sense, it appears that all knowledge and power is ultimately accessible to the mind looking within itself, and that all limitations are ultimately the consequence of limiting beliefs.

Mastery

The word *mastery* was deliberately chosen to have the connotation of the master in spiritual tradition. It connotes mastery over the external world, but also mastery over the inner forces; it means being in control of one's personal destiny but at the same time realizing oneness with the all. At the level of society, this kind of mastery likewise implies a guiding wisdom to mediate the awesome economic, technological, and military power of industrial societies.

Thus the future direction of the mastery component of the evolutionary trend is neither the continuously accelerating growth of manipulative technology, as predicted by the "technological optimists," nor on the other hand is it the repudiation of technology that sometimes seems to be urged by the doomsayer element of the New Age movement. Rather, the direction is implied by the roots of the word *technology*—technologos—"craft guided by wisdom." This indicates a corrective to the current tendency to let the development and application of technology be guided by short-term bottom-line economic considerations that ignore consequences to future generations and to the broader concerns of humanity.

Liberation

The ultimate goal of the liberation trend is political, economic, and psychological and cultural freedom for every individual human being. It is embodied in the political ideal of personal liberty within a lawful order and the economic ideal of private enterprise guided by an overarching set of communal and ethical values.

Our earlier discussions of unconscious beliefs and choices remind us that liberation is a much more subtle matter than simply achieving freedom from externally imposed constraints. To be free implies "I can do as I choose"—but what does that mean in the light of the fragmented nature of the unregenerate "I"? If I am "free" to follow a self-destructive urge, or to indulge in a compulsive habit, am I really free? If I am free to follow a goal of which I am consciously aware, but unconsciously want something else, am I really free?

Theologian Henry Nelson Wieman defines it thus: "Freedom is . . . the ability to will with the whole self." Psychotherapist Esther Harding observes that: "Only when he voluntarily chooses that which he inexorably must do, has man any free will at all." Poet Robert Penn Warren states: "The recognition of necessity is the beginning of freedom." And author Alan Watts writes that: "True freedom . . . lies in the clear knowledge that the will of the Self is principally one with the will of the ultimate Reality, and thus with its infinite freedom." An ancient folk saying puts it even more concisely: "That man is free who is conscious of being the author of the law he obeys."

Liberation at the personal level is thus clearly linked to awareness. Historian and social critic Theodore Roszak has written of the way in which the spreading awareness of the human potentiality is manifesting itself in the political sense of a "right to personhood." This is the right to consider one's self-discovery and inner liberation to be the central task in life, and furthermore, *the right to be supported in this by all the institutions of society.*

The "right to personhood" is implicit in the various liberation movements of the past two decades, as the right to be whoever one happens to be—be it male or female; white, black, yellow, or brown; Christian, Jew, or Moslem; gay or straight; handicapped, intellectual, athletic, and so forth. It has been caricatured as "the new narcissism" and deplored as the self-centeredness of the "me-generation"; and, to be sure, there is some superficial similarity between selfishness and selfhood-ness. Roszak compares the "right to personhood" with the right to democratic government two or three centuries ago.

One can imagine, in the England of Bacon's time, similar out-
rage and objections were expressed over the idea that peasants
might be educated to participate in their government.

The majority of the world's population lives in the areas
variously termed "the Third World" or "the developing countries." The Third World has been a sleeping giant—a giant
now awakening. Demands for liberation from colonial status
have been followed by pressure to be freed from "economic
colonialism" and there is a faint but rapidly growing realization that in the end liberation must include both psychological
and cultural liberation.

Awareness is increasing that wholesome cultural development builds on indigenous roots; it does not come from dis-
carding one's native origins in favor of an alien, presumably
superior, culture. And at the core of most indigenous cultural
roots are the secrets of the perennial wisdom.

Thus, just as the "right to personhood" movement points
toward an honoring of diversity in lifestyles and personal
characteristics without disapprobation, there appears to be a
parallel "right to culturehood." The ultimate homogenization
of global culture, as the world becomes more thoroughly industrialized and interlinked appears less and less likely; the
emerging thrust of liberation is toward an ecology of diverse
cultures and decentralized societies.

Democratization

However great an advance representative democracy may have
been two centuries ago, it is but a step in a long evolutionary
path. We need only think of the globe as a whole, and the
relative inability of many of the Third World peoples to control their own destiny, to recognize how far the democratization trend has yet to go. Some form of economic democracy
seems to be in the wind—not necessarily the industrial democracy recently popular in northern Europe. Beyond representative democracy would appear to be a kind of noncoercive participatory democracy where a high degree of commitment to a
cooperative ecological ethic, such as the new revolution in
consciousness research seems to be largely about, makes unnecessary a ponderous governmental structure.

PEACE ON EARTH—THE IMPOSSIBLE DREAM BECOMES POSSIBLE

We approach the end of our story. We have seen that the hidden mind holds treasures that can infinitely enrich the life of the individual and provide major breakthroughs in science, the arts, and daily living. We have seen how neglect of this side of human experience contributed to a value confusion that amounts to a crisis in civilization—a crisis in meaning. We have seen that guiding signals are present in some long-term trends that seem to be almost instinctively inherent in human evolution. And yet we have not really confronted the basis for many people's despair. Is there a way to get from our present dilemmas to a world that could be humane and sustainable—a way in which each of us could identify a contributive role for ourselves?

We will be bold and answer in the affirmative. In the remaining pages we want to outline how the emerging knowledge of our hidden mind and breakthrough capacities directly applies to resolving the perplexing web of global dilemmas humanity now faces—including the dilemma posed by nuclear weapons.

Let us first form an image of the goal. Imagine a world commonwealth in which war has no legitimacy anywhere, in which every planetary citizen has a reasonable chance to create through his or her own efforts a decent life for self and family, in which men and women live in harmony with the Earth and its creatures, cooperating to create and maintain a wholesome environment for all, in which there is an ecology of different cultures, the diversity of which is appreciated and supported, as well as a deep and shared sense of meaning in life itself—meaning that does not have to be sought in mindless acquisition and consumption. This goal of "peace on Earth, goodwill to all," is both practical and possible in the foreseeable future. Indeed, we are not sure one can imagine any other practical goal in a nuclear age.

We will summarize the argument for the practicability of this vision in the ten key findings that emerged from our explorations of the mind and spirit. These ten understandings are more general inferences than conclusions and tend to be supported by a wide assortment of research findings. Taken together, these propositions have profound implications for the feasibility of sustained global peace and continued human evolution.

1. *Each of us holds beliefs unconsciously as well as consciously, and our behavior is shaped far more by these unconscious beliefs than by the beliefs of which we are consciously aware.*

This conclusion regarding the hidden mind is basic to the field of dynamic psychology, and yet business, politics, education, and social interchange are carried on as though this proposition were not important or not true.

When individuals have gone through major change, whether by virtue of formal therapy or weekend workshops or spontaneous life experience, the process has typically involved one fundamental discovery: When the seemingly overwhelming life problems that have brought one to a point of basic life crisis are viewed from another perspective, *not only do they appear solvable, but one finds their origins in the unconscious beliefs and finds that all the resources necessary for their satisfactory resolution were present all along.* The basic problem was one of psychological resistance to that discovery—to changing one's unconscious beliefs.

We suggest that an analogous statement can be made for problems at the societal and global level.

2. *Most of these unconscious beliefs are formed early in life and are strongly influenced by the culture in which one grows up.*

At the same time that we recognize the general truth of the above statement, we are personally reluctant to recognize that we might have a very parochial view of the world. We perceive the world as our culture has suggested to us we should perceive it. We take as self-evident that industrial society's dominant beliefs and values are "natural" for people to espouse, that the motivations and goals individuals manifest in it are "normal," and that Western science gives the "best" picture of reality. We would find it extremely difficult, and it does not usually occur to us as particularly desirable, to enter into the cultural hypnosis of someone outside industrial culture and perceive reality as that person does. We implicitly assume that the planet eventually will be populated with an industrial or hyperindustrial monoculture.

The typical American would find it difficult to realize that the implicit goal of United States society, of ever-increasing consumption of goods, services, energy, and information, and the idea that economic considerations should be a major determining factor in social decisions that will affect future generations and peoples around the globe, might be viewed by someone from a different culture as totally insane, in the same way we might perceive *their* values and activities to be "totally insane." As might equally they might find the concept that high-technology armaments are the products of a "growth industry," not to mention the idea of a "national security" program based on weapons and policies that have made us feel less secure than at any time in our history, to be less than wholly logical.

3. *Among these unconscious beliefs are some which contribute to conditions of nonpeace—to inner states of fear, distrust, and hostility.*

One can imagine the influence of an unconscious belief that "people with skins of a different color than mine are alien and dangerous," or that "this is a world in which we are inevitably in competition for scarce resources." However free of them we may feel, it is unlikely (if not impossible) that we would grow up without deep and subtle religious, racial, political, economic, sex-related, and national prejudices.

Even more important—though less obvious—are the collectively held premises that underlie the structure of the present world system. It is those tacit understandings that ultimately are the source of the global arms race, patterns of environmental degradation, the world food distribution system with its shocking disparities, and the other aspects of the world macroproblem. However unaware we may be any hostile or negative feelings, however much we may feel love and compassion for all of humankind, to whatever extent we "buy in" to and lend support to the collective belief systems of Western civilization's current world view, each of us shares complicity in the world's state of nonpeace, insecurity, and alienation from our own nature.

4. *We typically exhibit strong psychological resistance to recognizing evidence or experience that challenges the adequacy of our hidden belief system.*

In psychotherapy, there are abundant examples of resistance to changing even such obviously disadvantageous or self-destructive beliefs as "compulsive cigarette smoking won't endanger my health, in spite of the medical evidence," or "I should be thoroughly competent and achieving in all respects, and if I fall short of that goal I will inevitably feel inadequacy and self-condemnation." This puzzling resistance may be linked to an unconscious fear of revealing repugnant aspects of the hidden mind.

However, even when there would seem to be no possibility of uncovering strong negative response, reexamination of deeply held beliefs will typically encounter resistance. As we noted earlier, we all fear discovering "the godlike in ourselves," for it implies an unacknowledged responsibility.

5. *Despite this resistance, unconscious beliefs can be changed; the powers of suggestion, affirmation, and imagery to alter unconsciously held beliefs are far greater than is ordinarily acknowledged.*

Beliefs that contribute to inner states of fear, distrust, and hostility can be replaced with beliefs that increase the ability to love, trust, share, and cooperate—if the person so desires and is willing to undertake a serious discipline. (We are not talking about direct attempts to reprogram some *other* person's unconscious beliefs through operant conditioning or other techniques. Some utopians urge such attempts, but these proposals run a serious risk of the means subverting the ends. Here, the individual chooses when and how to change.)

It is also possible to alter those unconscious beliefs that contribute indirectly to conditions of nonpeace and insecurity on the planet and the kinds of economic and political institutions that grow out of them. Changing unconscious beliefs by affirmation and imagery has been discussed earlier. Affirmation is powerful in comparison with, for example, conventional educational approaches to changing beliefs, because it bypasses the deep psychological resistance we all have toward changes in the unconscious belief system.

6. *Choices are made unconsciously as well as consciously; through deeper understanding of this fact, the quality of choice-making can be improved.*

We are fragmented, and prone to inner conflict unless these fragments—"autonomous complexes," Jung called them—can be induced to align. This can only be accomplished if the conscious choice is put in the service of the deepest part of the mind, as suggested by the core insights of the perennial wisdom. There is strong resistance to making this fundamental shift, which amounts to an abdication of the ego-mind. Nonetheless, this step is recommended by the mystical practitioners of all the major spiritual traditions and most psychotherapies.

7. *Unconscious "knowing" (as distinguished from unconscious beliefs) is both a far more pervasive aspect of experience than is ordinarily taken into account and also a vastly underutilized resource.*

This proposition is what this whole book has been about. Call it "the breakthrough experience," "channeling," or "contacting the deep intuition"—the knowledge needed to solve any problem is, by the testimony of uncounted explorers who have gone before us, available. And yet we find this proposition to be so unbelievable that we will typically yield to it only inch by inch. "Whatever you ask in prayer, believe that you receive it, and you will" (Mark 11:24). This idea totally contradicts the world view on which our scientific society is based. Which means either that it is wrong, or. . . .

8. *Collectively held unconscious beliefs are the most fundamental cause of the dilemmas that beset the world today.*

Those of the most consequence in determining whether we can achieve a state of planetary peace and a sustainable global society are the unconscious premises in the most powerful nations—the two superpowers and the other large industrialized countries. These unconscious beliefs are particularly obdurate because of the way they are embedded in, and perpetuated by, social, economic, and political institutions. Cultural resistance to reassessing these unconscious beliefs—to discovering the hidden origins of the problems and the nature of their ultimate solutions—is, as in the psychotherapy analogy, the real problem.

9. *Strong resistance is experienced to changing these collective unconscious beliefs, even when the beliefs are obviously disadvantageous to both individuals and the group.*
Anthropologist Ruth Benedict gave a pertinent example many years ago in her *Patterns of Culture:*[4]

> (There are) those regions where organized resort to mutual slaughter never occurs between social groups. . . . It is impossible for certain peoples to conceive of the possibility of a state of war. . . . I myself tried to talk of warfare to the Mission Indians of California, but it was impossible. They did not have the basis in their own culture upon which the idea could exist, and their attempts to reason it out reduced the great wars to which we are able to dedicate ourselves with moral fervor to the level of alley brawls. They did not have a cultural pattern that distinguished between them. . . .
>   War in our civilization is as good an example as one can take of the destructive lengths to which the development of a culturally selected trait may go. If we justify war, it is because people always justify the traits of which they find themselves possessed, not because war will bear any objective examination of its merits.

Singling out beliefs that are partially unconscious as candidates for change is bound to raise strong societal resistance. Societies in the past have dealt rather harshly with those who have done so and branded them "heretics" or worse. The current form of resistance may range from bold counterclaims and rationalizations, to accusations of conspiring with the enemy, being "Communist" or "antiscientific" and so forth. Consider just a few examples of partially conscious beliefs that one could infer from social and institutional behaviors:

Humanity's destiny is to "control nature" (for example, to breed plants and animals that are economically profitable and to relegate to extinction those species that "don't have any use").

The road to social progress lies in continuous expansion of the gross output (a belief which not only contributes to global resource depletion and environmental problems, but also to the dubious conclusion that the global arms race is "good for the economy").

Economic rationality (for example, the financial "bottom line") is a suitable guide for social decisions (for example, the standard economic practice of discounting the future, which formalizes neglect of the impact of present decisions on future generations).

Scientific and technological approaches are the best hope for solving social problems (as exemplified in attempts to deal with such problems through scientifically designed behavior modification).

10. *Nevertheless, these collective beliefs can be changed. Thus the achievement of global peace and a sustainable planetary society is feasible: it requires mainly a change in collective unconscious beliefs.*

This argument is in danger of sounding simplistic. If achieving peace on Earth were as easy as that, why have we not done it long ago? There are two reasons.

One reason is that we never took seriously the proposition that war and starvation are intolerable. There always seemed to be winners in war. But after a nuclear war there will be no winners. Our interdependence and interconnectedness are making it clear that when there is mass poverty and starvation, the whole of the planet is ill. Only now do we have a growing group of people around the world who know that chronic mass starvation cannot humanely be allowed to continue, and that it is intolerable to pass it on as a legacy generation after generation, in the ever-present threat of nuclear holocaust. These are people who know that deterrence was at best a stopgap whose time has passed, and that *Star Wars*-style defenses against nuclear weapons are a dangerous and expensive myth.

The other reason is that we have knowledge not available before about the consequences of unconscious beliefs, how they can be changed, and the kinds of rsources that can thus be unleashed. *Human nature does not have to be changed to eliminate war on the planet for all time. It is human unconscious programming that has to be changed, which is totally feasible.*

What would be the motivation for people to undertake this self-programming? The answer is: Because it leads to personal breakthroughs, to feeling more self-fulfillment, to an exhilarating life, and to a viable global future. This is not theoretical or speculative. Survey research and a vast assortment of less formal indicators make it clear that there is a growing network of individuals who have already started.[5] Others join because of what they hear and observe. This spreading network extends into the socialist and Third World countries as well as the affluent capitalist nations.

It is sobering to recognize the amount of self-limitation that takes place simply because of the widespread belief that global peace is "realistically" impossible. Imagine the effect of reversing that negative affiramation, and regularly affirming: "Global peace is possible, and nothing less is tolerable."

WHAT CAN I DO?

"What can I do to help achieve this goal of sustainable global peace?" To everyone who grasps the reality of this potentiality, this is the question that automatically comes to mind.

Some would argue that working toward agreement on disarmament is the central task; others dismiss that as impractical. Some say we have to have a "fairness revolution" and a "new international economic order"; others find that hard to take that seriously. Some claim we need mechanisms for non-violent conflict resolution—but that was what the United Nations was to be for! Some say if we could just learn to love one another and speak peace around the globe, we would have peace; others dismiss that as simplistic. Some speak up for political action; others for meditation and inner peace. Many sound confused, or despairing.

We believe that there are four kinds of things an individual can do—and they must *all* be done to make a balanced contribution. These are:

1. *Say "no" to the insanity of tolerating an intolerable condition.*

Say no to the prospect that our children and our children's children must grow up in fear that the world will destroy itself before they can have a chance to live their lives. Say no to the continued legitimacy and glorification of war as an instrument of national policy—for any nation.

The nineteenth-century Prussian strategist von Clausewitz defined war as "an extension of state policy by other means." To move from this rational argument for war to a complete deligitimizing of war would be one of the most profound shifts in the history of humankind. Yet it can come about when the people of the world change their minds and demand it. It must happen, because the alternative is the suicide of civilization.

The really fundamental changes in the history of societies—such as the fall of Roman empire or decline of the Middle Ages—have come about not through the arbitrary decisions of a few leaders, but because vast numbers of people changed their minds a little bit. People give the legitimacy to all social institutions, no matter how powerful those institutions may seem to be. On occasion, people remember that they also have the power to withdraw legitimacy.

In the past, legitimacy has been withdrawn from slavery, cruel and unusual punishment, torture, dueling, subjugation and mutilation of women, and female infanticide. The legitimacy can be removed from war when people's consciousness changes, and their will to act—particularly women's—is awakened. The characteristics of a few female world leaders notwithstanding, the feminine consciousness tends to be life-revering and nurturing, and war has always been almost entirely a man's game.

Since World War II, war is no longer a contest between trained armies; it is the decimation of civilian populations. Its legitimacy must be removed; there is no other way.

2. Say "yes" to the evolutionary transformation that alone can bring to the world sustained peace and common security.

Affirm the positive image of a world in which war as a deliberate policy instrument is unthinkable; in which the knowledge of how to create nuclear weapons, devastate cities, poison entire populations, desolate the environment, is not feared because it would not be misapplied.

Recognize, understand the implications of, and affirm the proposition that war can be outlawed only through a total change in the beliefs that separate nation from nation, persons from nature, and each of us from our own deeper selves. No technical solution will suffice to remove the peril of nuclear weapons—no nuclear freeze, no multilateral arms limitation agreements, no particle-beam technologies to shoot down enemy missiles. Affirm that this total change in the global mindset can be accomplished. The change will spread mainly person to person, and every individual's efforts count.

Recognize the power of the images we hold. Holding a negative image—dwelling on the fear that a nuclear exchange might come about or on anger toward our leaders who continue to escalate the numbers of missiles—contributes very directly to bringing about that which is feared or hated. Being against war is not at all the same thing as affirming peace. Holding a positive image, vividly imagining a desired state, contributes to that state coming about—in ways that might seem quite mysterious if the beliefs we hold about the capabilities of the human mind are limited.

We are not talking about a simplistic "power of positive thinking." To hold and affirm a positive image of a world that works for almost everyone in which there is harmony between peoples and between people and the Earth, in which the scourge of war is banished forever is not simplistic. Because of the interconnectedness of all minds, affirming a positive vision may be about the most sophisticated action any one of us can take.

It is true, however, that it may be simplistic to believe that if we just all love one another and speak peace, peace will come into the world. It may be simplistic because powerful unconscious forces make our love ambivalent, and our peace tinged with hidden conflict. Collectively held unconscious beliefs shape the world's institutions and are at the root of institutionalized oppression and inequity. "Peace" will always be no more than a temporary truce if there exist widespread perceptions of basic injustices, needs unmet, and wrongs unrighted. But if one affirms the positive image regularly and persistently, eventually this will modify the unconscious beliefs, thereby changing the perception of the world—and even the world itself.

3. *Do your inner work. Discover that it is possible to shift to a more positive perception of the world, one that is no less realistic than the previous perception and far more likely to lead to a constructive response or a breakthrough idea.*

The inner work consists of at least three aspects: (1) discovering the potentialities of the "deep intuition" as guide and resource; (2) changing the inner beliefs that bring about individual nonpeace and limited capacities; and (3) changing the inner beliefs that, collectively held, shape national and global institutions that perpetuate conditions of nonpeace in the world.

We have, elsewhere in this book, dealt with the means for the first two aspects. We need to say here something more about the third.

The idea that collectively held beliefs create world conditions for nonpeace is much less widely appreciated than is the relationship between individual beliefs and personal problems. In fact, on first reading the above statement may seem not only wrong but nonsensical. We are used to seeking explanations of the state of global nonpeace in the ambitions and frustrations of leaders of countries; in the flaws of past treaties; in competition for Lebensraum, natural resources, and foreign markets; and in religious and economic ideological conflicts.

No doubt these explanations are partially accurate. But underlying them, as a more fundamental breeding ground of nonpeace, are the unconscious beliefs that subtly create barriers,
separations, tensions, and collisions.

It should be anticipated that strong resistance and antipa-
thy may develop toward the challengers of tacit, collectively
held beliefs. Recall the Church fathers who refused to look
through Galileo's telescope because the moons he claimed
were traveling around Jupiter couldn't possibly be there! Recall the pronouncement of the influential Lavoisier committee,
appointed by the French Academy in 1792 to investigate objects supposedly flying in from outer space, that there could be
no such things as meteorites because "there are no stones in
the sky to fall." Recall how reports of operations performed
using hypnotic suggestion as an anesthetic were denied publication in medical journals of three continents because there
was no "mechanism" to explain the absence of pain, patients
must have been "pretending" not to feel pain as legs were am-
putated and abdominal surgery was performed! We are in a
similar position when we seek to unveil ill-serving collective
beliefs for these changes will not be readily accepted.

This inner work is unsettling at first—both the work involved with self-image and the uncovering of pathogenic collective beliefs. Yet as it progresses, it becomes exhilarating and
joyous. As the negative, separating beliefs are brought to light,
there is a strengthening of the positive vision of a world that
could be, and an increasing surefootedness with which one
undertakes actions to help bring it about.

4. *Do your outer work*. It is important to be involved with
some work in the world. It will keep the inner work from becoming too introspective, and the outer work will be increasingly effective as it is informed by progress in the inner work.

Each one of us has his or her own unique outer role to be
discovered and played. It may be a significant public role, or it
may be a small quiet one. It may be the role of social activism,
or of patient healing, of lecturing to great crowds, or of parent-
ing at home. Whatever it is, it is important to do it as well as
possible—with both the nature of the role itself and the way it

is carried out being progressively informed by ongoing inner work.

It is critically important to have an adequately comprehensive picture of the interconnected aspects of global nonpeace. Global nonpeace includes at least the following:

The ever-present threat of triggering a nuclear exchange, with massive loss of life and mass creation of human desolation.

Persistent "local" wars with "conventional" weapons leaving a steady wake of human misery.

A global arms race involving expenditures of over a billion dollars a day, with some of the poorer countries spending more on military preparation than on health care, education, and human welfare combined.

Widespread poverty, with accompanying disease, malnutrition, and starvation, and with strains on the natural environment that include overgrazing, deforestation, soil erosion, and surface water pollution.

Environmental degradation and resource exploitation stemming from the economic activities of the industrialized countries.

Increasing tensions between the industrialized, mass-consuming northern hemisphere and the poverty-stricken southern hemisphere.

It is also important to keep in mind these broader dimensions of nonpeace, because many of them are much longer-lived than the U.S.–U.S.S.R. enmity. Sixty years ago it was the Germans who were inhuman monsters (as we were then taught to perceive them); forty years ago the Japanese were subhuman devils (it is embarrassing to recall). Now it is the Russians who are the personification of evil, but in historical terms that perception is also likely to be a relatively transient one.

Our enemy is not the Russians, but a mind-set. Behind all the components of global nonpeace are the tacitly held premises, conscious and unconscious, that shape the institutions and the policies and the "laws" of economics, and yes, even the sciences and technologies. And each one of us has complicity in the nonpeace to the extent that we uncritically buy into the premises of the prevailing belief system.

Doing one's outer work is important—not only because the work itself, on any aspect of the nonpeace, contributes to a more workable society, but also because the outer work is sensitizing. It keeps the inner work from becoming sterile. It preserves one from indifference.

A PARTING THOUGHT

In one sense, modern weaponry with its fantastic destructive power is the penultimate achievement of the industrial era. No other product of the industrial paradigm so clearly demonstrates its awesome technological power on the one hand, and on the other its anomic indifference to the human consequences of the products it generates. The nuclear warhead, symbol par excellence of man's "conquest" of the secrets of the atom, now holds all hostage. Yet it may ultimately be our salvation, in somewhat the same way that a near brush with death, or an emotional breakdown, may turn out to be the trigger that results in a life being redirected.

Global nonpeace has many faces besides the nuclear threat, and these have needed attention for some time. There are serious flaws in our present materialist, competitive, achievement-oriented Western industrial paradigm that have long called for a reperception of reality, for a better vision of the planetary future. Because the nuclear impasse presents us with a situation which is so obviously insane, it may also furnish the incentive to break through our own resistances and reperceive our own destiny.

Two scientific achievements of the past half-century stand out as not only profoundly affecting history, but as being in an important relationship to one another. One is the unleashing of the power of the atom; the other is major progress toward the unfettering of the human mind. The first, leading to the development of nuclear weapons, almost demands the second, advances in the understanding of human consciousness.

For the fantastic destructive power of modern weaponry, posing as it does a direct threat to the survival of civilization, calls for a far more thorough understanding of deeper human motivations and aspirations, values and perceptions, perversities and potentialities, than any previous society has ever achieved.

There is a magnificent truth about ourselves which can be discovered. Something about it can be shared, under appropriate circumstances; it cannot be "demonstrated" in the way one would demonstrate a mathematical theorem or a law of physics. Nonetheless, when an individual makes the discovery, it can change a life. When a growing network of people share the discovery, it can change history.

This book has been about that discovery—about the breakthrough to our own creative potentials that has been, is, and will be possible for all of us. Much of the book has been about the significance of this discovery to the individual; the last portion has been about the crucial role in offering hope for the Earth. Ultimately, our concerns as individuals are meaningless without an equal concern for our human family.

It is a peculiar fact of life for those of us alive today, of all the generations since our ancestors descended from the trees and began to shape rocks into tools, that without a near-future breakthrough into a true realization of our familyhood, there will be no future generations. Let us envision utopia, and thus bring it into existence. There is no reasonable alternative.

Appendix

Using the Imagination to Free the Person

Here we present a set of more advanced affirmations, to convey a feeling for higher creativity not as an abstract idea, but as an experience. We present the exercise as it has been presented many times to seminars of business and government executives. You may not elect to actually try it, but imagining what it would feel like to thoroughly believe these five simple statements will achieve the purpose we have in mind.

The exercise is this. Simply affirm, a number of times a day, day after day, for six months, the following statements, imagining the full meaning of each statement to the fullest extent possible:

I am not separate.

I can trust.

I can know.

I am responsible.

I am single-minded.

I AM NOT SEPARATE

Two persons who have lived much of their lives together often find that the same thoughts appear in both minds more or less simultaneously. Sharing great beauty, two people may have the feeling of minds merging. More than is commonly recognized, people have experiences in which it seems that an emotionally involving experience for one (such as a death) may be "picked up" by another some distance away.

In numerous ways in everyday life, we get hints of what has also been fairly well demonstrated in some laboratory research, such as the "remote viewing" experiments at SRI mentioned earlier—that at some deep unconscious level our minds interconnect. What is in my mind is not separate from what is in yours. Any human misery anywhere on the planet affects me in the deepest part of my mind, whether or not I am consciously aware of the details.

This can be carried further: I am joined with the other creatures of the earth and with the creative mind behind the physical universe. If this is too much to believe, don't strain. Simply affirm however much of it you can believe relatively easily. *I am not separate.*

I CAN TRUST

I can trust my own mind. Strangely enough, because of the way we have been taught by our culture, we tend to believe the opposite. Although my mind may have many levels, or be split into many fragments, and although in some of these I may have secreted unsavory judgments about myself, unpleasant memories, unsatisfied urges, and other miscellany, nonetheless I can trust that a part of that mind is watching over me (as it keeps me breathing when I am asleep). I can trust that my own deep intuition knows what is ultimately good for me.

As science grew to be the most powerful institution in our culture, we were encouraged to trust the experts rather than to place any trust in our own intuitions. At the same time that students learned to recite "To thine own self be true" and "Know thyself," the subtle subliminal message was: "Don't trust anything fully unless it has been scientized and technologized, and especially don't trust your own unconscious mind."

A well-known psychotherapist puts the inability to trust at the heart of our problems:

> The neurotic's problem at bottom is . . . an inability to *affirm* . . .
> The neurotic cannot affirm himself—and therefore he is at war
> with himself . . . He cannot affirm his situation among his fel-

low men—and so he regards them with suspicion and hostility. And finally, the neurotic cannot affirm life as a whole; he cannot affirm the universe ... Inability to affirm is merely another term for inability to *trust*.

ROLLO MAY, *The Art of Counseling*

If you can't trust your deepest self, what in this world can you trust? Yet our resistance to knowing this fact is strong:

Not only do we hang on to our psychopathology, but also we tend to evade personal growth because this, too, can bring another kind of fear, of awe, of feelings of weakness and inadequacy. And so we find another kind of resistance, a denying of our best side, of our talents, of our finest impulses, of our highest potentialities, of our creativeness ... It is precisely the god-like in ourselves that we are ambivalent about, fascinated by and fearful of, motivated to and defensive against.

ABRAHAM MASLOW, *Toward a Psychology of Being*

In the end we discover that the one thing we can trust is our own deep intuition. As Krishnamurti put it: "Intelligence highly awakened is intuition, which is the only true guide in life."

I can trust others.

Since at a deep level we are all joined, trusting others is more akin to trusting ourselves than it might at first appear. At this point, however, resistance shows itself once more. "Surely it isn't wise or safe to trust the untrustworthy—the thief, the mugger, the rapist, the murderer, the other nuclear-armed superpower!" The truth of the foregoing statement is self-evident. The degree to which it is *not* true is less evident, but more important. Don't press the point with yourself; just start with people with whom you are in daily contact. Don't oppose the resistance; let it quiet down by itself. And imagine yourself trusting others, with your reservations dropping off at their own pace.

I can trust the universe.

Again the resistance. "You can't possibly mean that the environment isn't dangerous! Or mean that I can trust the universe to provide me with food and shelter and my other physical needs." Ignore all these arguments, for the purposes of this experiment, and imagine that the universe is totally benign and friendly. Let the resistance subside of itself, for you give it no power. *I can trust.*

I CAN KNOW

The ego mind appears to know only what it has consciously learned. Unconsciously, I know far more. Biofeedback research discloses that unconsciously I know how to control various aspects of my body's functions that consciously I don't seem to be able to do. Research on various psychic phenomena seems to suggest that I know, unconsciously, how to produce those phenomena even though consciously I may insist that they can't happen. I seem to know how to give myself wise messages through dreams, symbols, insights—messages from the unconscious to the conscious mind. In creative problem-solving, my unconscious mind often proves to be much more effective than my conscious analytical mind.

Ultimately, the deep creative/intuitive mind knows how to solve problems and answer questions. It knows what I (the deeper "I") *really* wants—even though my conscious desires may seem to be quite in contradiction to that.

> Truth is within ourselves; it takes no rise
> From outward things, whate'er you may believe.
> There is an inmost centre in us all,
> Where truth abides in fullness; and around,
> Wall upon wall, the gross flesh hems it in,
> This perfect, clear perception—which is truth.
>
> A baffling and perverting carnal mesh
> Binds it, and makes all error: and to *know,*
> Rather consists in opening out a way
> Whence the imprisoned splendour may escape,
> Than in effecting entry for a light
> Supposed to be without.
>
> ROBERT BROWNING, *Paracelsus,*

It is both a curious and a useful characteristic of the un-conscious mind that it responds to what is imagined as though it were real. Thus, whereas conscious beliefs are changed by learning the evidence that supports a new belief, the unconscious beliefs can be changed by imagining the new beliefs to be true, and ultimately acting as if they were true. We can use what we know about how we know to change what we "know."

I affirm that the deep creative/intuitive mind knows how to answer all my questions. (Don't worry if you don't believe that yet.) It knows what I—the integrated I—really want, even though my conscious desires may seem to pull in quite another direction. It knows what is at the heart of the universe. *I can know.*

I AM RESPONSIBLE

I am responsible for my perceptions and for my feelings about what I perceive. For a while, I may tell myself (and others) that my perceptions and feelings are caused by what happens "out there," that they are "conditioned" by "society." Indeed, there is much to support that view. But as I explore more and more deeply into my own mind, I discover it to be more and more true that *I am cause.* I am the cause of everything I perceive, since my unconscious beliefs shape my perceptions and I choose those beliefs. I am the cause of everything I feel, and of everything that happens to me.

Experience the arguments created by your resistance. "If someone assaults me, it's absurd to claim that I caused it! Think of the starving people in the world—it's obscene to assert that it's their fault!" Again, the truth of this assertion is less evident than its falsity. Experience the arguments against affirming your responsibility, and quietly let them subside. Imagine the statement to be true. *I am cause.*

Some ancient sages, the voices of several channeled "entities," and some perfectly orthodox modern thinkers have compared our experience of "objective reality" with dreaming. When you dream, it seems "real" while you are in the dream state. You may observe cause-effect relationships in the dream, yet upon awakening you find that these were illusory; the dreamer is really the cause of the dream. If our minds are all linked, is it possible that "objective reality" is like a dream dreamed by that collective mind? There appear to be cause-effect relationships that are studied scientifically, yet from time to time there are experiences, psychic phenomena and synchronicities, that defy explanation in that way. The causality of common sense and of scientific explanation is illusory; the real creative cause is the collective mind of the dreamer.

Are there no limits to the truth of "I am cause?"

I AM SINGLE-MINDED

I have one mind. I am of but one mind. All the parts of my mind, conscious and unconscious, are aligned in one intention, to follow the will of the deepest Center. *I have no other desire.* I have no other needs, no other goals, no other plan for my life, no ambitions. My trust that all real needs will be provided for makes it unnecessary to control my life in any other way. I have no other desire than to know and follow the will of the deepest part of myself.

> I have a body, but I am not my body. I have emotions and thoughts, but I am not my emotions; I am not my beliefs. I have desires, but I am not my desires. I recognize and affirm that I am a Center of pure self-consciousness. I am a Center of Will, capable of mastering, directing and using all the psychological processes and my physical body.
>
> (Adapted from R. Assagioli's *Psychosynthesis.*)

Don't worry if you can only believe these five statements in a partial or limited way. Just accept them as far as you can comfortably, and affirm that. Believe them to be true, and experience in your imagination that they *are* true. Be persistent. A number of times a day, with your full attention. Day after day for six months.

Long ago, it was the insight of the man known as the Buddha that suffering comes from wrong beliefs. Think how differently we would lead our lives if we came to believe that all our problems, individual and global, are the result of our beliefs. And beliefs can be changed, as easily as we believe they can.

I am not separate.

I can trust.

I can know.

I am responsible.

I am single-minded.

Notes

Chapter One

1. John C. Gowan, "Creative Inspiration in Composers," *The Journal of Creative Behavior*, vol. 11, no. 4, (1977).
2. Sigmund Freud, *A General Introduction to Psychoanalysis*, (New York: Doubleday, 1943).
3. F. W. H. Myers, *Human Personality and Its Survival of Bodily Death* (1903).
4. Niels Bohr, *Atomic Physics and the Description of Nature* (Cambridge, University Press, 1934).
5. John C. Gowan, "Some Thoughts on the Development of Creativity," *The Journal of Creative Behavior*, vol. 11, no. 2.
6. Carl Rogers, *On Becoming a Person* (Boston: Houghton Mifflin, 1961).

Chapter Two

1. John C. Gowan, "Incubation, Imagery and Creativity," *Journal of Mental Imagery*, vol. 2 (1978).
2. Kenneth Atchity, "To Sleep, Perchance to Program," *The Los Angeles Times* (23 June 1984).
3. G. N. M. Tyrrell, *The Personality of Man* (London, 1946) p. 35.
4. Arthur Abell, *Talks with the Great Composers* (Garmisch-Partenkirchen, Germany: G. E. Schroeder-Verlag, 1964).
5. Abell, *Talks with the Great Composers*.
6. P. 26 Christopher Evans, *Landscapes of the Night* (New York: Viking, 1984).
7. Henri Poincare, "Mathematical Creation," *The Foundations of Science*, tr. G. B. Halstead (Science Press, 1924).
8. Halstead, *The Foundations of Science*.
9. Halstead, *The Foundations of Science*.
10. B. M. Kedrov, "On the Question of Scientific Creativity," *Voprosy Psikologii*, vol. 3, (1957): 91–113.

11. W. B. Kaempffert, *A Popular History of American Invention*, vol. II, (Scribner's, 1924).

12. Walter Ducloux, "Das Rheingold," *San Francisco Opera Magazine* (October, 1977).

13. P. E. Vernon, Ed, *Creativity: Selected Readings* (Penguin).

14. Rudyard Kipling, *Something of Myself* (New York: Doubleday).

15. Tyrrell, *The Personality of Man.*

16. James K. Webb, *Lectures on Stylistics* (Reed College, 1968).

17. S. Longfellow, *Life of H. W. Longfellow*, vol. I (1886), p. 339.

18. Ralph Wood, Ed., *The World of Dreams*, (New York: Random House, 1947), pp. 859–860.

19. L. Talamonti, *Forbidden Universe* (Stein and Day, 1975).

20. Talamonti, *Forbidden Universe.*

21. H. Ellis, *The World of Dreams* (Boston: Houghton Mifflin, 1911), pp. 276–77.

22. Robert Louis Stevenson, "A Chapter on Dreams," *The Works of Robert Louis Stevenson* (London: Chatto and Windus, 1912) vol. 16.

23. H. Shapero, "The Musical Mind," *The Creative Process, A Symposium*, B. Ghiselin, Ed. (University of California 1952), pp. 42–43.

24. Oho Loewi, "An Autobiographical Sketch," *Perspectives in Biology and Medicine* (Autumn 1960).

25. A. Koestler, *The Act of Creation*, (New York: Macmillan, 1964).

26. Koestler, *The Act of Creation.*

27. James Newman, "Srinavas Ramanujan," *Scientific American*, 178 (1948): 54–57.

28. Newman, "Srinavas Ramanujan."

29. Newman, "Srinavas Ramanujan."

30. Tyrrell, *The Personality of Man.*

31. Tyrrell, *The Personality of Man.*

32. J. Lane, *Life and Letters of Peter Ilich Tchaikovsky* (1906), pp. 274–312.

33. Abell, *Talks with the Great Composers.*

34. Abell, *Talks with the Great Composers.*

35. Abell, *Talks with the Great Composers.*

36. Abell, *Talks with the Great Composers.*

37. Abell, *Talks with the Great Composers.*

38. Abell, *Talks with the Great Composers.*

39. Tyrrell, *The Personality of Man.*

40. J. Hadamard, *The Psychology of Invention in the Mathematical Field* (Princeton, 1949), p. 15.

41. Joseph Campbell, *The Hero with a Thousand Faces*, (Princeton, 1949), p. 40.

42. Abell, *Talks with the Great Composers.*

43. J. H. Douglas, "The Genius of Everyman," *Science News* (23 April 1977): 268–285.

44. Roger N. Shepard, "The Mental Image," *American Psychologist*, vol. 33, no. 2, (February 1978).

45. Albert Rothenberg, *The Emerging Goddess: The Creative Process in Art, Science, and Other Fields* (Chicago: University of Chicago Press, 1979).

46. Elmer Green, Alyce Green, and E. Walters, "Voluntary Control of Internal States: Psychological and Physiological," *Journal of Transpersonal Psychology*, vol II., no. 1 (1970): 9–10.

47. Green, Green, Walters, "Voluntary Control of Internal States: Psychological and Physiological," pp. 16–17.

48. Nikola Telsa, "My Inventions," *Electrical Experimenter* (1919).

49. Tesla, "My Inventions."

50. Tesla, "My Inventions."

51. Tesla, "My Inventions."

Chapter Three

1. Abraham Maslow, *Toward a Psychology of Being*, (Van Strand, 1962).

Chapter Four

1. Jacob Bronowski, "The Mind as an Instrument for Understanding," *The Origins of Knowledge and Imagination* (Yale, 1978).

2. Shepard, "The Mental Image."

3. Martha Crampton, "Answers from the Unconscious," *Synthesis*, vol. 1, no. 2 (1975): 140–141.

4. Maxwell Maltz, *Psychocybernetics*, (Prentice-Hall, 1960).

5. Tim Galwey, *The Inner Game of Tennis*, (Random House, 1970).

6. Dennis T. Jaffe and David E. Bresler, "Guided Imagery: Healing Through the Mind's Eye," *Proceedings of the First Annual Conference of the American Association for the Study of Mental Imagery*, J. Shorr, et. al., eds. (Plenum, 1980), pp. 260–261.

7. O. C. and S. Simonton, *Getting Well Again*, (Los Angeles: Tarcher, 1982).

8. Hans Selye, *Stress Without Distress* (Lippincott, 1974).

9. Herbert Benson, "Your Innate Asset for Combating Stress," *Harvard Business Review* (July-August 1974).

10. Ida Rolf, *Rolfing: The Integration of Human Structures* (New York: Harper & Row, 1977).

11. J. H. Schultz and W. Luthe, *Autogenic Training: A Psychophysiological Approach to Psychotherapy* (Grune & Stratton, 1959).

12. Edmund Jacobson, *Progressive Relaxation* (Chicago: University of Chicago Press, 1958).

13. E. Aserinsky and N. Kleitman, "Regularly Occurring Periods of Eye Motility and Concomitant Phenomena During Sleep," 118 *Science* (1953): 273–274.

14. Stephen La Berge, "Awake in Your Sleep," (forthcoming, Tarcher, 1984).

15. Stuart Miller, "Dialogue with the Higher Self," *Synthesis*, vol. 1, no. 2 (1975).

16. Joseph Shorr, "Discoveries About the Mind's Ability to Organize and Find Meaning in Imagery," *Imagery: Its Many Dimensions and Applications*, J. Shorr, G. Sobel, P. Robin, J. Connella, eds. (Plenum, 1982).

Chapter Five

1. Jane Roberts, *The Nature of Personal Reality*, (Englewood Cliffs, N.J.: Prentice-Hall, 1974), p. 324.

2. Jane Roberts, *Seth Speaks* (Bantam, 1972), p. 341.

3. Ken Wilber, "The Problem of Proof," *ReVision*, vol. 5, no. 1 (Spring 1982): 80–100.

4. B. Bokser, *The World of the Cabbalah* (Philosophical Library, 1954), p. 9.

5. William James, *Varieties of Religious Experience*, (Longmanns-Green, 1902).

6. Personal correspondence with the authors.

7. James, *Varieties of Religious Experience*.

8. Gershom Scholem, *Major Trends in Jewish Mysticism*, (Schocken, 1967).

9. H. Benson and M. Klipper, *The Relaxation Response* (Morrow, 1975), pp. 121–122.

10. Benson and Klipper, *The Relaxation Response*, pp. 130–131.

11. R. Woods, *The World of Dreams, an Anthology*, (New York: Random House, 1947).

12. Stuart Miller, "Dialogue with the Higher Self," *Synthesis*, vol. 1, no. 2 (1975).

13. Aldous Huxley, *The Perennial Philosophy*, (Harper & Row, 1945).

14. Arthur Koestler, *Invisible Writing*.

15. Huxley, *Perennial Philosophy*.

16. Edgar Mitchell, "From Outer Space to Inner Space... ," ed. J. White (Putnam's, 1976).

Chapter Six

1. "The Transformations of Jewish Mysticism," *International Journal of Parapsychology* (Autumn 1960): 86–87.

2. E. Hoffman, *The Way of Splendor* (Shambhala, 1981).

3. Hoffman, *The Way of Splendor*.

4. Idries Shah, *The Sufis* (New York: Doubleday, 1971), pp. 28–29.

5. Manly Palmer Hall, *The Adepts in the Western Esoteric Tradition*, Philosophical Research Society, 1950.

6. M. Sworder, trans, *Fulcanelli: Master Alchemist—Le Mystere des Cathedrales*, Fulcanelli, Suffolk, Great Britain, Neville Spearman Limited, 1971, p. 26.

7. Thomas Goldstein, *Dawn of Modern Science*, (Boston: Houghton Mifflin, 1980), pp. 159–160.

8. W. Wilmshurst, *The Meaning of Masonry*, (Crown, 1980), pp. 27, 46–47.

9. Manly Palmer Hall, *Masonic Orders of Fraternity* (Philosophical Research Society, 1950).

10. M. Hall, *Orders of Universal Reformation* (Philosophical Research Society, 1949), pp. 6,7,10,11.

11. M. Hall, *Orders of Universal Reformation*, pp. 11–13.

Chapter Seven

1. R. W. Sperry, *Annual Review of Neuro Science*, "Changing Priorities." 1981, pp. 1–15.

2. L. Mumford, *The Transformation of Man* (Harper & Brothers, 1956).

3. Mumford, *The Transformation of Man*.

4. Benedict, *Patterns of Culture* (Houghton Mifflin, 1934).

5. A. Mitchell, *The Nine Life Styles of North America*, 1983.

Index

The Institute of Noetic Sciences

... towards a new world ...

There are no unnatural or supernatural phenomena, only very
large gaps in our knowledge of what is natural ... We should strive to
fill those gaps of ignorance.

Edgar D. Mitchell
Founder

The Institute of Noetic Sciences was founded in 1973 by
Edgar D. Mitchell, Apollo 14 astronaut, to engage in research,
dialogue and communication on issues concerning the human
mind and consciousness, and their role in the continuing evolution of humankind.

Major programs include:

The Inner Mechanism of the Healing Response: The creation of
a scientific understanding of the mind/body relationship has
been a fundamental goal of the Institute since its inception.
While early work focused on evidence of the **existence** of such
links, the Institute is now sponsoring research to learn more
about the actual **mechanisms** of healing, including physiological, psychological and spiritual dimensions.

Hope for the Earth: Recognizing the power of beliefs and values
—individual as well as collective—the Institute is creating and
disseminating a believable vision of global peace, in its most
fundamental sense. This project is developing scenarios of
plausible paths to peace, drawing on findings from consciousness research, and on studies and insights of the many groups
and individuals concerned about the future of planet earth.

The Institute's pioneering research, communication and networking activities are financed almost completely by donations from members and other sources of private support. A nonprofit organization, the Institute is open to general membership.

Members of the Institute are eligible for privileges which include:

Receipt of the Institute *Newsletter*, which features original articles, research reports, book reviews and news items on consciousness research and its implications;

Receipt of the more technical publication Investigations, which features in-depth reports on promising topics in consciousness research;

Participation in the Institute Publications Service, which assists members in identifying and acquiring important books, papers and other publications. The *Book List and Publications Bulletin* is updated and expanded semi-annually;

Advance information on Institute books, lectures and other events sponsored by the Institute;

Information on the Noetic Sciences Travel Program, for unique tours to places of special interest to Institute members.

By expanding its activities and membership the Institute seeks to foster a global society that can be made more peaceful, humane and fulfilling, through the understanding of the universals of human experience.

For more information on the Institute and membership write:

The Institute of Noetic Sciences
475 Gate Five Road, Suite 300
Sausalito, California 94965
(415-331-5650)